Transcendentalism
and the
Cultivation
of the Soul

TRANSCENDENTALISM AND THE CULTIVATION OF THE SOUL

◄○►

Barry M. Andrews

University of Massachusetts Press
AMHERST AND BOSTON

Copyright © 2017 by University of Massachusetts Press
All rights reserved
Printed in the United States of America

ISBN 978-1-62534-293-5 (paper); 292-8 (hardcover)

Designed by Sally Nichols
Set in Adobe Garamond Pro
Printed and bound by Maple Press, Inc.

Library of Congress Cataloging-in-Publication Data

Names: Andrews, Barry Maxwell, author.
Title: Transcendentalism and the cultivation of the soul / Barry M. Andrews.
Description: First [edition]. | Amherst : University of Massachusetts Press,
2017. | Includes bibliographical references and index.
Identifiers: LCCN 2017036483| ISBN 9781625342935 (pbk.) | ISBN 9781625342928
(hardcover)
Subjects: LCSH: Transcendentalism (New England) | Social movements. |
Spiritual life. | Spirituality.
Classification: LCC B905 .A77 2017 | DDC 141/.30973—dc23
LC record available at https://lccn.loc.gov/2017036483

British Library Cataloguing-in-Publication Data
A catalogue record for this book is available from the British Library.

To Rudy Gilbert,
minister and mentor,
who first set me on the path.

CONTENTS

Introduction 1 ⊕

1. "The Soul of the Age" 7

2. The Transcendentalist Crisis of Faith 18

3. Transcendentalist Spirituality 28

4. The Art of Life 40

5. Three Prerequisites of the Spiritual Life 50

6. Solitude, Contemplation, Sauntering, and Simple Living 63

7. Reading, Conversation, and Journal Writing 80

8. Religious Cosmopolitanism 91

9. Self-Culture and Social Change 100

10. Abolition and Women's Rights 109

11. Education, Environmentalism, and Sustainability 120

12. Church Reform and the Free Religious Association 132

13. The Legacy of Transcendentalism 142

Notes 149

Further Reading 165

Index 171

Transcendentalism
and the
Cultivation
of the Soul

INTRODUCTION

> There are probably words addressed to our condition exactly, which, if we could really hear and understand, would be more salutary than the morning or the spring to our lives, and possibly put a new aspect on the face of things for us. These same questions that disturb and puzzle and confound us have in their turn occurred to all the wise men; not one has been omitted; and each has answered them, according to his ability, by his words and his life.
>
> —Henry David Thoreau, *Walden*

common humanity n concerns

Even though I now live in the Pacific Northwest, I still try to visit Walden Pond at least once a year. And when I do, I make a point of hiking to the site of Henry David Thoreau's cabin there. On one occasion, a few years ago, I saw a middle-aged man sitting quietly on the cairn, a pile of stones near where the cabin once stood. I asked him what brought him to this spot. He said *Walden* changed his life. He had spent over twenty years in prison for various offenses, he told me, including theft and drug possession. One of his teachers in prison taught a class on literature, including Thoreau's *Walden*. The teacher brought the class on an outing to visit Walden Pond. The book and that visit changed his life. Believing, as Thoreau wrote, "there is more day to dawn," he straightened out his life. Now he was clean, he was married, and he had a good job. He had come back to the pond to reflect on his life and the new course it had taken.

I have been reading, reflecting on, speaking, and writing about the Transcendentalists for most of my career as a minister. I'm often asked what fires my passion, and the words from the epigraph above come most readily to mind. What Thoreau is saying, in his nineteenth-century way, is that humans have always struggled with life's fundamental questions: Why do we live and die? What are we here for? How should we live? If we seek out the wise thinkers of the past, we are sure to find answers that will inspire us to live more healthfully and joyfully today. That is how I have experienced the words and lives of the Transcendentalists.

Transcendentalism is often viewed as a literary movement that flourished in the early nineteenth century, ending in the 1850s or so. The major figures of the movement—Ralph Waldo Emerson, Henry David Thoreau, and Margaret Fuller—have been well examined in biographies, histories, and literary criticism, and their works are often assigned reading in high schools and colleges. They are usually grouped with other nineteenth-century authors such as Nathaniel Hawthorne, Herman Melville, and Edgar Allen Poe, though they wrote few works of fiction. Most of their writings were originally lectures or sermons addressing spiritual topics and issues of the day. Their words were meant to enlighten broad and diverse audiences—to help people achieve what they called self-culture, or the cultivation of the soul.

I believe Transcendentalism is more accurately described as a religious movement. It emerged from New England Unitarianism in reaction to Christian theology of the time. The Transcendentalists thought of their lectures and essays as a kind of modern-day scripture, not as accepted truths but as a record of each writer's spiritual experience. They believed, as Emerson did, that what is true for us in our most elevated moments might also be universally true. "To believe your own thought, to believe that what is true for you in your private heart is true for all men,—that is genius," Emerson boldly stated.[2] Their writing is a form of wisdom literature, similar to that of Lao-tzu, Rumi, Marcus Aurelius, and other philosophers and religious figures who wrote about their own experiences in their own times.

Although the Transcendentalists offer scholars much to study, everyday readers have even more to gain, I believe, by mining their words and lives for answers to the perennial questions of human existence. I see them as living voices whose writing is addressed as much today as it was in their time to spiritual seekers and religious radicals like themselves—"restless souls," as historian of religion Leigh Eric Schmidt describes them. The Transcendentalists were in fact the forerunners of what Schmidt calls the

Spiritual Left in America.[3] Their thought has widely influenced American culture. Thoreau's essay on "Civil Disobedience" guided the actions of Gandhi, Martin Luther King, Jr., and continues to inspire many of today's social activists. His reverence for and observations of nature helped give rise to the environmental movement and continue to inspire efforts to combat climate change and species extinction. Emerson's insistence in his "Divinity School Address" that religious truth is grounded in personal experience influenced the thinking of William James and succeeding generations of spiritual seekers. Margaret Fuller's book *Woman in the Nineteenth Century* sparked a feminist movement that continues to have a profound impact on American society.

Almost all the Transcendentalists were Unitarians, and many of them were ministers at some point in their lives. Yet even in contemporary Unitarian Universalist churches there is little awareness of the extent to which they influenced the historical development of Unitarian worship and theology. Historian David Robinson observes: "Like a pauper who searches for the next meal, never knowing of the relatives whose will would make him rich, American Unitarians lament their vague religious identity, standing upon the richest theological legacy of any American denomination. Possessed of a deep and sustaining history of spiritual achievement and philosophical speculation, religious liberals have been, ironically, dispossessed of that heritage."[4]

This could be said of religious liberals in general, including many who do not consider themselves religious in the conventional sense of the term. Today many Americans are experiencing a hunger for an inner life of greater richness and depth, abandoning the exclusive claims and moral correctness of conservative Christianity in search of new sources of inspiration. Many have found wisdom in other, seemingly more spiritual traditions such as Buddhism, Vedanta, Sufism, goddess religion, and paganism.[5] The Transcendentalists were actually the first generation of Americans to look for spiritual inspiration in faith traditions outside their own, clearing the path for future seekers, as Schmidt shows in his book *Restless Souls: The Making of American Spirituality.* Today's restless souls, I believe, will discover hidden treasures in Transcendentalism, a uniquely and authentically American form of spirituality.

"We live in a transition period," Emerson noted. "The stern old faiths have all pulverized. 'T is a whole population of gentlemen and ladies out in

search of religions." In his view, this spiritual hunger could no longer be satisfied by adhering to church doctrine and discipline, but only by embracing
a wider spirituality. "God builds his temple in the heart on the ruins of
churches and religions."[6] Although the Transcendentalists introduced the
distinction between religion and spirituality, their quarrel was not with
"churches and religions" per se, but with the theological and social con-
servatism of Christian churches of their day, Unitarian churches included.
Some traded their pulpits for a podium on the lecture circuit. Others
remained in the ministry, reforming worship and congregational life. The
remedy for a decaying church, Emerson famously declared in his "Divinity
School Address," "is first, soul, and second, soul, and evermore, soul."[7]

The soul and its cultivation were the primary preoccupations of the
Transcendentalists in everything they said and did, from the pursuit of self-
reliance to social reform. "Self-culture" was the defining characteristic of
the age, a term widely used to refer to education and self-improvement. It
took on special meaning for the Transcendentalists. They believed, as Emerson put it, that "every man should be open to ecstasy or a divine illumination, and his daily walk elevated by intercourse with the spiritual world."[8]
They experienced such ecstasies themselves and considered them to be the
spiritual high-water marks of their lives. They sought ways of cultivating
such experiences and incorporating insights gained through them into the
texture of their everyday lives. Self-culture, as they understood it, was a
form of spiritual practice intended to accomplish these aims.[9] Moreover,
the work of self-culture did not end with the individual. The self in question was not the isolated, individual ego, but rather the human soul in its
relation to the Universal Mind, or, as Emerson termed it, the "Over-soul."

Their notion of self-culture thus links mysticism and social action. The
belief that human beings are interconnected with one another and with all
of nature "led its adherents into the world more often than away from it,"
insists Emerson biographer Robert D. Richardson. The Transcendentalists
were not radical individualists aloof from politics and society, as is sometimes alleged, but rather were more activist than many of their Unitarian
and Trinitarian opponents. They found that "the ethical consequences of
transcendental idealism impelled them into social, political, educational,
and religious reform," according to Richardson.[10] They fervently believed
that individual transformation necessarily resulted in social change and that
reform was ineffective without it.

The Transcendentalists were the first to admit that they were not a unified party. In the words of James Freeman Clarke, one of the movement's original members, they called themselves "the club of the like-minded; I suppose because no two of us thought alike."[11] They pursued a wide variety of avenues and interests. Collectively, though, they adhered to a set of common spiritual principles. Their spirituality was very much in this world, characterized by a reverence for nature, an organic worldview, a sense of the miraculous in everyday life, an optimism about human potential, a search for what is universal in religion and human experience, a strong moral conscience, and an encouragement of the individual in her or his own religious quest. Their practices for achieving self-culture—some formal, others informal—all aimed to transform both self and society. Starting as a religious revolt, Transcendentalism soon became a broad-based reform movement as members of the group sought to realize the ethical implications of their philosophical idealism. Because they believed the religious impulse was innate and universal, they looked for common elements in the world's spiritual traditions, embracing an unprecedented religious cosmopolitanism.

No one seems to know who coined the term, but the Transcendentalists took their name from the occasional meetings of a group of young ministers and intellectuals—Unitarians mostly—who gathered to discuss the state of the churches and society at large. The so-called Transcendental Club met nearly thirty times over a four-year period, beginning in 1836. Upwards of fifty men and women attended some or most of these meetings. Some of them pursued literary careers, others practiced ministry. Most were engaged in a variety of reforms, some more ardently than others. While recognizing such differences, I have chosen to deal with the movement as a whole rather than dividing it up into various groupings. I have tried to include as many of the Transcendentalists as possible in this book, but, inevitably, a few of them will appear much more often than the rest. Emerson, Thoreau, and Fuller figure most prominently in any treatment of the movement, primarily by virtue of their published writings, including, in more recent years, their journals and letters. But others played important roles as well. As time went on, the movement attracted new and younger members, too. Some of their names are more familiar to us than others.

Many excellent scholars have studied and written about Transcendentalism and the Transcendentalists. Most of them focus on a rather limited period of the movement's literary productivity and subsequent influence. While I draw heavily on these resources, I write primarily as someone whose personal and professional life has been greatly enriched by the teachings of the Transcendentalists. I believe they are not relics of the past but prophetic voices with a spiritual message that speaks clearly to us today. I've been encouraged by the enthusiasm of those who have attended my classes over the years and the guidance of two fine scholars, David Robinson and Bob Richardson, who believe as I do that the Transcendentalists have much to teach us today about the vitality of liberal religion and the life of the spirit.

I am grateful for opportunities I have had to pursue this project, as writer-in-residence at the Thoreau Institute and Merrill Fellow at the Harvard Divinity School. I also wish to thank Jeffrey Cramer and the late Brad Dean of the Thoreau Institute, Gloria Korsman of the Andover-Harvard Theological Library, and my many friends and fellow Thoreauvians in the Thoreau Society. Kimberly French has provided valuable editorial assistance. Alice Stanton, Mary Dougherty, Sally Nichols, and the staff at the University of Massachusetts Press patiently midwifed my manuscript into print. My wife, Linda, continues to give me incredible feedback and support. While I take responsibility for any errors I have made, every author knows that writing is a collaborative effort.

1

"THE SOUL OF THE AGE"

On Christmas Day 1832 young Ralph Waldo Emerson set sail for Europe. He was seeking respite from grief and also clarity about his career. His wife of barely seventeen months had died the previous year, and he had recently resigned as pastor of Boston's Second Church. He toured Italy, France, and Great Britain. He was looking forward to visiting three authors in particular, William Wordsworth, Samuel Taylor Coleridge, and Thomas Carlyle. The poetry of Wordsworth and Coleridge was well known to American audiences. Less familiar was the younger Carlyle, whose essays Emerson had only recently begun to read.

It was perhaps impossible for Wordsworth and Coleridge to measure up to their reputations. By the time Emerson met them they were old men who had become conservative in their views. His meeting with Coleridge "was rather a spectacle than a conversation," he concluded, "of no use beyond the satisfaction of my curiosity." Visiting Wordsworth in England at his home in the Lake District, Emerson came away with the impression that the poet "paid for his rare elevation by general tameness and conformity." His experience with Carlyle, much more his contemporary, was quite different. He hired a private carriage from Dumfries in Scotland to take him sixteen miles to Carlyle's house out in the middle of nowhere. He spent a memorable night with the writer and his wife, Jane. "We went out to walk over long hills," Emerson wrote. "There we sat down and talked of the immortality of the soul."[1]

Despite his unfavorable impressions of Coleridge and Wordsworth in person, Emerson read their works with increasing interest and appreciation following his return to America the next autumn. Carlyle, too, continued to influence Emerson and his circle of friends and fellow intellectuals, a number of whom sought out the Scottish author on their own travels to Britain later on. What was it that drew them to these writers? They were literary lions whose writings had heralded *new views* of nature, society, and the life of the spirit. In a broader sense, they were representative of the Romantic movement as a whole—in continental Europe, Britain, and America, if we include the Transcendentalists.

Romanticism was much more than a passing phase in literature, music, and the fine arts; it was revolutionary—"a crack in nature," as Emerson put it.[2] It was a reaction against many aspects of life prevalent at that time, and to some extent, even today: political tyranny, Enlightenment rationalism, materialism, the Industrial Revolution, skepticism, conventionality, religious formalism, and the despoiling of nature. It took different forms in different countries, but young poets, artists, musicians, philosophers, theologians, critics, and naturalists of the late eighteenth and early nineteenth centuries were everywhere caught up in the spirit of it. Though he found it difficult to define, Isaiah Berlin, a noted historian of ideas, was of no doubt about its significance: "The importance of romanticism is that it is the largest recent movement to transform the lives and the thought of the Western world. It seems to me to be the greatest single shift in the consciousness of the West that has occurred, and all the other shifts which have occurred in the course of the nineteenth and twentieth centuries appear to me in comparison less important, and at any rate deeply influenced by it."[3]

Boston, Cambridge, and Concord, Massachusetts, were at the center of Romantic intellectual activity in America. Looking back some years later, Frederic Henry Hedge, one of the leaders of the budding Transcendentalist movement, recalled that he and others were conferring on the unsatisfactory state of current opinion in theology and philosophy. The writings of Coleridge and Carlyle had, as he put it, "created a ferment in the minds of some of the young clergy of that day." There was, he said, "a promise in the air of a new era of intellectual life."[4] (Hedge's own article on Coleridge and German philosophy in an 1833 issue of the *Christian Examiner* had done a lot to stimulate this interest.) In Edward Everett Hale's account of the period, their literature formed the countercultural curriculum at the Harvard Divinity School in the 1820s and 1830s, giving rise to "a certain enthusiastic expectation" that "quickened the lives of all young people in New England who had been trained in the freer schools of religion."[5]

Hedge, Emerson, James Freeman Clarke, Theodore Parker, and a number of others were the nucleus of a group of young Unitarian ministers and intellectuals who began meeting in 1836 to discuss the "new views" of religion, culture, and society that were coming out of Europe. These new ideas had huge implications for the kind of theology the Unitarians had been trained in and which these radicals now found terribly wanting. The Transcendentalists, as they came to be called, were spiritual seekers looking for new sources of inspiration and insight in a milieu that was becoming, in their view, increasingly materialistic, dehumanizing, and alienating, and in which more traditional and normative approaches to theology and religious life seemed outmoded and insufficient. Emerson characterized the situation—in language familiar to anyone who came of age in the 1960s and '70s—as a schism between "the party of the Past and the party of the Future; the Establishment and the Movement," materialism and spirituality, old ways of thinking and new.[6]

As early as 1827 Emerson listed in his journal several "peculiarities" of the Romantic period. One was that "it is said to be the age of the first person singular." Another he termed "the reform of the Reformation." A third he referred to as "Transcendentalism. Metaphysics and ethics look inwards."[7] What did he mean? The first characteristic was an emphasis on subjectivity, which had widespread implications both for literature and theology. In an essay on "Modern Literature" in the *Dial* magazine, Emerson observed, "The poetry and speculation of the age are marked by a certain philosophic turn which discriminates them from the works of earlier times. . . . And this is called *subjectiveness,* as the eye is withdrawn from the object and fixed on the subject or mind." Furthermore, "another element of the modern poetry akin to this subjective tendency, is the Feeling of the Infinite" that "has deeply colored the poetry of the period."[8]

In his 1839 lecture series on "The Present Age," Emerson elaborated on his phrase "the first person singular," making the connection between subjectiveness and the "Feeling of the Infinite" somewhat clearer. "In the eye of the philosopher," he announced, "the individual has ceased to be regarded as a part and come to be regarded as a whole. He is the world. The individual learns his deep access to the Universal Mind, is inspired by the sentiment of a deep and total union with Nature."[9] What he had in mind were sentiments such as those Wordsworth described in "Tintern Abbey":

> . . . a sense sublime
> Of something far more deeply interfused,
> Whose dwelling is the light of setting suns,
> And the round ocean, and the living air,
> And in the blue sky, and in the mind of man,
> A motion and a spirit, that impels
> All thinking things, all objects of all thought,
> And rolls through all things.[10]

The emphasis on subjectivity is not the same as exalting the ego or individual personality, however. For Emerson and the Transcendentalists, as for Wordsworth, the turning of consciousness inward reflects a progressive awareness of a Universal Self "deeply interfused" throughout all of nature, including human nature. The individual self is a manifestation of the Universal Mind or Soul, and it is through this unique but limited self that we have access to the Universal Soul in experiences characterized by a "Feeling of the Infinite." Far from implying egotism, the emphasis on subjectiveness attests to the need to transcend individuality in order to achieve a "deep and total union with Nature."

What Emerson meant by the second peculiarity, "a reform of the Reformation," is the progressive secularization of religion, a process well under way during the Romantic period. For the Romantics and particularly the Transcendentalists, philosophical skepticism, historical criticism of the Bible, and comparative studies of religion had undermined the traditional grounds of religious belief in the scriptures and the teachings of the Christian church. Each of these developments called into question the exclusive and supernatural claims of Christianity. The Romantics, including the Transcendentalists, were on the whole deeply spiritual, even if they were not conventionally religious. The Transcendentalists in particular were abandoning faith in historical Christianity.

In what amounted to a radical shift in the religious consciousness of the West two things happened simultaneously. In spite of the name "Transcendentalism," God came to be viewed as a force or power *immanent* in nature, including human nature, and not as a supernatural being entirely separate from it. At the same time nature took the place of the Bible as the source of revelation. The Transcendentalists believed that all of creation was a manifestation of the divine. In his book-length essay *Nature,* an early manifesto of the Transcendentalist movement, Emerson asserted that "the noblest ministry of nature is to stand as an apparition of God. It is the organ through which the universal spirit speaks to the individual, and strives to lead back the individual to it."[11]

This idea can be traced to Carlyle's coinage of the phrase "natural supernaturalism" in *Sartor Resartus,* a book avidly read by Emerson and his Transcendentalist friends. "The Mythus of the Christian Religion looks not in the eighteenth century as it did in the eighth," Carlyle insisted. Those who wish to salvage it must seek "to embody the divine spirit of that religion in a new Mythus, in a new vehicle and vesture, that our Souls, otherwise too like perishing, may live."[12] The phrase was indicative of "the general tendency," according to M. H. Abrams, "to naturalize the supernatural and humanize the divine."[13] For the Romantics and Transcendentalists such as Emerson, who were moving away from traditional Christianity, the term expressed the revelations of nature in familiar religious language and symbolism, including biblical imagery.

For example, in the "Prospectus" for *The Recluse*—a favorite poem among Emerson and his friends—Wordsworth wrote:

> Paradise and groves
> Elysian, Fortunate Fields—like those of old
> Sought in the Atlantic Main, why should they be
> A history only of departed things,
> Or a mere fiction of what never was?
> For the discerning intellect of Man,
> When wedded to this goodly universe
> In love and holy passion, shall find these
> A simple produce of the common day.[14]

Here Wordsworth employs tropes from classical mythology and the Bible to suggest that an earthly paradise might be ours here and now, in the "simple produce of the common day," through a union with nature. Emerson uses similar imagery in *Nature.* "The reason why the world lacks unity, and lies broken in heaps," he wrote, "is because man is disunited with himself." The unification of the world proceeds from the unification of the self, but in actuality "the marriage is not celebrated." If united within ourselves and in union with nature, we would find that "the invariable mark of wisdom is to see the miraculous in the common."[15] Thus the term *"natural supernaturalism"* implies a this-worldly as opposed to an other-worldly form of spirituality. The mundane world of the common and everyday is celebrated over the supernatural realm of God and heaven; and the notion of an eternal now, in the present moment, is substituted for that of eternity at some future point in time.

What did Emerson mean by the third of his peculiarities of the modern age, "Transcendentalism. Metaphysics and ethics look inwards"? Romanticism was a reaction, in large part, to the "sensual" philosophy of John Locke and the skepticism of David Hume, to which it led. Locke argued that knowledge comes to us solely by way of the senses, and Hume went so far as to suggest that empirical knowledge offers no convincing basis for religious belief. Rejecting Locke's epistemology, Coleridge asserted instead that there are two ways of knowing, which he termed the "Understanding" and the "Reason." Understanding, or empirical knowledge, is analytical in nature—weighing, measuring, and quantifying experience. Reason, on the other hand, is a way of knowing that is holistic and intuitive. It is a revelation of the Universal Mind. The emphasis on intuition is what Emerson meant by "metaphysics and ethics look inward."

It would be difficult to exaggerate the significance of Coleridge's contribution to the Transcendentalists. According to historian Perry Miller, the American publication in 1829 of Coleridge's *Aids to Reflection* "was of the greatest single importance in the formation of their minds."[16] In her journal, Margaret Fuller, an editor of the *Dial* magazine, expressed a "conviction that the benefits conferred by [him] on this and future generations are as yet incalculable," and added that "to the unprepared he is nothing, to the prepared, everything."[17] In his *Autobiography,* Clarke recalled, "I became a great reader of Coleridge, and was quite ready to accept his distinction between the reason and the understanding judging by sense. . . . It enabled me to distinguish between the truth as seen by reason, and its statement as formulated by the understanding. . . . I could see that those who had the same spiritual experience, and who beheld the same truth, might differ in their statements concerning it, and that while truth was unchanging and eternal, theology might alter and improve from age to age." It was through Coleridge that Clarke discovered he was "a born Transcendentalist."[18]

Coleridge drew the distinction between Reason and Understanding from his reading of the German philosopher Immanuel Kant. In doing so, he broadened Kant's use of the term "transcendental" beyond its original meaning to suggest that through Reason we might have knowledge of spiritual realities that transcends knowledge gained from the world of sense experience. In thus elevating Reason above Understanding, Coleridge and his American followers sought to rescue faith from the rocky shoals of skepticism.

For Emerson, Coleridge's ideas were key to what he termed his "First Philosophy." He devoted a section of his journal in 1835 to describing its essential principles. The ideas of Reason, he observed, "astonish the Understanding and seem to it gleams of a world in which we do not live." Following Coleridge, Emerson considered Reason to be the superior principle. "Its attributes are Eternity and Intuition," he asserted. "We belong to it, not it to us." On the other hand, "the Understanding is the executive faculty, the hand of the mind. It mediates between the soul and inert matter. It works in time and space, and therefore successively. It divides, compares, reasons, invents. It lives from the Reason, yet disobeys it. It commands the material world, yet often for the pleasure of the sense."[19]

And this is a serious problem as Emerson saw it. In the materialistic worldview of empirical philosophy, the Understanding has gotten the upper hand, to the neglect and disadvantage of the Reason. In living "for the pleasure of the sense," as he put it, we pursue a superficial existence, a one-dimensional life in which appearances count for everything. "We walk about in a sleep," Emerson continued. "A few moments in the year or in our lifetime we truly live; we are at the top of our being; we are pervaded, yea, dissolved by the Mind: but we fall back again presently."[20] The practical-minded, those in whom the Understanding predominates, are not awake. The question is, How to arouse the mind from the lethargy of inaction, the superficiality of our habitual existence?

To a remarkable degree Coleridge anticipated the findings of modern neuroscience indicating that the human mind is divided between left and right hemispheres of the brain, each with distinctive ways of apprehending the world. The left hemisphere of the brain is analytic and linear. It is the center of the ego and discursive reasoning. By contrast the right brain is intuitive, holistic, and atemporal. This is the locus of the soul and feelings of the infinite. In Emerson's felicitous phrasing, the left side of the brain sees "the world piece by piece, as the sun, the moon, the animal, the tree," whereas the right side of the brain comprehends "the soul"; namely, "the whole, of which these are the shining parts."[21] Scientific studies also show that the left hemisphere normally predominates but that under certain conditions the right hemisphere can be activated to a significant degree.[22]

Emerson and the Transcendentalists were drawn to Coleridge's philosophy and Wordsworth's poetry because—like Coleridge and Wordsworth themselves—they recognized the inherent wisdom of the right brain's mode of consciousness. Hence, the Transcendentalists did not merely adopt Romantic notions; rather, they saw in them a more accurate depiction of the way the mind works than the empirical epistemology of Locke. The same can be said of other influences on their thinking, including Greek philosophy and Eastern religions. Their experience resonated with the spiritual teachings of mystical traditions ancient and modern, East and West. As Emerson stated in his address "The Transcendentalist": "The first thing we have to say respecting what are called new views here in New England, at the present time is, that they are not new, but the very oldest of thoughts cast into the mould of these new times. . . . What is properly called Transcendentalism among us, is Idealism; Idealism as it appears in 1842."[23]

Idealism, in their usage, referred to the holistic mode of consciousness characteristic of right-brain cognition. In elevating idealism above materialism, the Transcendentalists were not anti-intellectual nor were they denying the importance of left-brain knowledge and thinking. For them the realm of the Understanding was subordinate to that of the Reason, not divorced from it. The affairs of daily life, including social and political life, should be guided by spiritual and moral considerations, not solely by material or instrumental ones. Unfortunately, as Emerson indicated in his journal entry on the First Philosophy, it is the Understanding, the discursive reasoning of the left brain, that is our default mode for encountering the world. The revelations of the Reason—wisdom associated with the right hemisphere of the mind—come to us only intermittently and largely unannounced. So seldom is their occurrence and so at odds are they with our empirical experience, we are tempted to discount their validity.

Yet these subjective, transcendent moments constitute spiritual reality for us. As Wordsworth writes in his famous "Ode,"

> Those shadowy recollections,
> Which, be they what they may,
> Are yet the fountain light of all our day,
> Are yet a master light of all our seeing;
> Uphold us, cherish us, and make
> Our noisy years seem moments in the being
> Of the eternal silence: truths that wake
> To perish never. . . .

"Shadowy" though they may be, such recollections constitute a spiritual high-water mark for us and are a reminder that even "in a season of calm weather, / Though inland far we be, / Our souls have sight of that immortal sea / Which brought us hither."[24] It was Wordsworth's uncanny ability to express such thoughts—confirmed in their own experience—that drew the Transcendentalists to his poetry. And they embraced it as response to the troubling skepticism engendered by Hume and by the Enlightenment assault on the underpinnings of religious belief. In his study *The Romantic Foundations of the American Renaissance*, Leon Chai argues that in the face of such attacks "it was necessary to find the source of religion within consciousness itself, as the one undeniable Cartesian datum: to create out of the epiphanic experience of consciousness a sense of the sublime and the infinite, a new content of religious awareness."[25]

Emerson shared Wordsworth's validation of this religious awareness. The lines "the fountain light of all our day" and "a master light of all our seeing" are sprinkled throughout his essays and journals. He too recognized that, though rare and fleeting, such experiences are nonetheless both the source and substance of spiritual truth for us. He often quoted these lines from Wordsworth's *The Excursion* as well:

> . . . to converse with heaven—
> This is not easy:—to relinquish all
> We have, or hope, of happiness and joy,
> And stand in freedom loosened from this world,
> I deem not arduous; but needs confess
> That 't is a thing impossible to frame
> Conceptions equal to the soul's desires;
> And the most difficult of tasks to keep
> Heights which the soul is competent to gain.[26]

Emerson found, as Wordsworth did, that "to converse with heaven" was not easy, and he struggled as all poets and mystics do "to frame conceptions equal to the soul's desires." He also knew how difficult it was "to keep heights which the soul is competent to gain."

Wordsworth's poetry often speaks of the loss of spiritual elevation, as the "wild ecstasies" of youth mature with age into sober pleasures in the mansion of memory. Nothing it seems "can bring back the hour of splendor in the grass," of "the primal sympathy" we once felt with nature, now recollected "in years that bring the philosophic mind."[27] Emerson too became more "philosophic" in later years, but even to the end of his life he pondered the ebb and flow of mystic moods and whether they were to any degree within control. "We cannot carry on the inspiration, and make it consecutive," he concluded in one of his final lectures. "But in the experience of meditative men, there is a certain agreement as to the conditions favorable to this reception."[28]

It is on this point that Transcendentalist spirituality ceased to be strictly speculative. For if, as the Romantics asserted, religious truth is grounded in consciousness and revealed in moments of extraordinary awareness then how, if at all, can these revelations be summoned and sustained? What is their value for the individual and for society as a whole? As Emerson had noted in his journal, "A few moments in the year or in our lifetime we truly live; we are at the top of our being; we are pervaded, yea, dissolved by the Mind: but we fall back again presently." In contemplating the essential principles of his philosophy he was led on to ponder one of the perennial quandaries of the spiritual life:

> We stand on the edge of all that is great yet are restrained in inactivity and unacquaintance with our powers. . . . We are always on the brink of an ocean into which we do not yet swim. . . . We are in the precincts, never admitted. There is much preparation—great ado of machinery, plans of life, travelling, studies, profession, solitude, often with little fruit. But suddenly in any place, in the street, in the chamber, will the heaven open, and the regions of wisdom be uncovered, as if to show how thin the veil, how null the circumstances. As quickly, a Lethean stream washes through us and bereaves us of ourselves. . . .
>
> What a benefit if a rule could be given whereby the mind, dreaming amidst the gross fogs of matter, could at any moment east itself and find the sun. But the common life is an endless succession of phantasms. And long after we have deemed ourselves recovered and sound, light breaks in upon us and we find we have yet had no sane hour. Another morn rises on mid-noon.[29]

In discussing the implications of Romantic ideas for spirituality and social life, Emerson and other Transcendentalists drew on their own experience as well as their reading of Coleridge and Wordsworth. Though grounded in Unitarian theology, they were restless souls in search of a remedy for what they perceived to be its limitations. To be sure, the Transcendentalists were inspired by the literary Romantics, but their interest was not merely literary. Their primary intention was to foster a religious form of Romanticism by applying the insights gained from their acquaintance with British and continental Romantics to individual spiritual life and corporate worship. In doing so they came to develop and practice a form of spiritual discipline geared to enable the mind "to east itself and find the sun." Hedge referred to it as "the art of life," whereas the more common rubric for this pursuit was "self-culture," or the cultivation of the soul. Emerson gave a series of early lectures on the subject. Bronson Alcott penned a "Treatise on the Doctrine and Discipline of Human Culture." Clarke produced a best-selling book entitled *Self-Culture*. Fuller adopted the notion as her life's work. Thoreau's sojourn at Walden Pond was an experiment in self-culture.

This impulse, so widely shared among the Transcendentalists, came from the fact that, ministers or not, all of them were at heart spiritual seekers. They were not content merely to philosophize in the manner of Coleridge, nor to resign themselves to the loss of inspiration as Wordsworth seemed to do. Difficult though it might be "to keep heights which the soul is competent to gain," the Transcendentalists persisted in the effort. The myriad ways they sought to do this is the subject of a future chapter. As we shall also see, the cultivation of the soul was not merely for the purpose of spiritual elevation, but more important, for applying the wisdom gained from such experience to the conduct of everyday life and congregational worship.

2

THE TRANSCENDENTALIST
CRISIS OF FAITH

Waldo, as he preferred to be called, was not the first of the five Emerson brothers to prepare for the ministry; it was William, the eldest. William decided to study at the University of Göttingen in Germany—arguably the most advanced intellectual center anywhere—rather than at Harvard, his father's alma mater. Arriving in the spring of 1824 full of confidence and high hopes, he devoted twelve hours a day to his studies. More than anything what drew him there was the opportunity to attend the lectures of Johann Gottfried Eichhorn, the foremost biblical scholar in the world and a pioneer in the "higher criticism" of the Bible. "I have no desire to conceal my own admiration of this great man," William declared in a letter to a college classmate. "And I cannot but consider myself as very happy in being permitted to visit Göttingen while he yet lives."[1]

Before long, though, William began to have second thoughts about his decision to study at Göttingen. Like his father he considered himself a liberal Christian in the mold of William Ellery Channing, the spiritual and intellectual leader of the Unitarian movement. In Channing's famous sermon on "Unitarian Christianity," he had argued that "the Bible is a book written for men, in the language of men, and that its meaning is to be sought in the same manner as that of other books."[2] The Bible was to be understood in light of its historical context, not taken literally. The Unitarians were of the opinion that the Bible contained divine revelation but that it also included material that was fanciful. A historical approach promised to distinguish between revealed truth and literary fiction.

William was troubled by the skepticism that Eichorn's higher criticism seemed to engender. He soon became disillusioned, questioning his call to ministry and regretting his decision to study in Germany. In September, less than five months after beginning his studies, he visited Johann Wolfgang von Goethe in Weimar, seeking the renowned author's advice. Only years later did anyone learn how Goethe had counseled the young divinity student. In an endnote to Waldo Emerson's essay on Goethe in the centenary edition of his complete works, his son Edward wrote: "The German philosophy and the Biblical criticism shook his [William's] belief in the forms and teachings of the religion in which he had been brought up." William shared his doubts with "the wisest man of the age," hoping that Goethe might show him a way "he could honorably and sincerely exercise the priestly office." To his great disappointment all Goethe had to tell him was "to persevere in his profession, comply with the usual forms, preach as best he could, and not trouble his family and his hearers with his doubts." Goethe's advice seemed hypocritical to William and he dismissed it. Returning to Göttingen, he finished out the year, went back to America, and studied law instead.[3]

By the time William returned to Boston, his younger brother Waldo had enrolled in Harvard Divinity School to become a minister himself. William confided his misgivings to Waldo, especially concerning church rituals such as communion. Significantly, William's reservations had a strong influence on Waldo's decision to resign, in 1832, from his ministry at Boston's Second Church. In the meantime—between 1825, when William returned from Germany, and 1835, as Waldo embarked on a new career as a lecturer—the theological milieu that had shaped liberal religion in America was radically transforming. The consequences were profound, not only for Unitarianism, but also for American religious culture more broadly.

William Emerson's disillusionment with the ministry is indicative of a wide range of intellectual forces affecting religious belief in the late eighteenth and early nineteenth centuries. It illustrates the tensions that resulted in widespread skepticism and a search for new grounds for faith in an increasingly secular world. In William's case, new historical scholarship undermined the reliance on biblical scripture and the doctrines and rituals of the church as vehicles of divine revelation. The Bible was shown to be the work of many hands, a patchwork of myths and legends, rife with contradictions. Biblical scholars argued that doctrines such as the Trinity and rituals such as the Lord's Supper were not scripturally defensible. Historians were beginning to look at Christianity in a developmental context and in comparison with other religions. Three forces were together combining to dramatically alter the nature of religious consciousness in the Western world: empiricism in science and philosophy; the materialistic, utilitarian impact of the Industrial Revolution; and the new historical approach to religion among biblical scholars.

In many ways, the Transcendentalist revolt was simply the next stage in the development of Unitarianism. Liberal religion prided itself on offering a rational approach to religion but had worked itself into a corner theologically. While liberal Christians subjected the Bible to critical scrutiny, they continued to accept the accounts of Jesus's miracles at face value. Moreover, in reaction to the emotional fervor of the evangelical revivals sweeping the country at the time, Unitarians had swung far in the other direction, becoming hyper-rational, and offering little appeal to the emotions or spirit. On both of these points—the historical veracity of the New Testament and the emotional aridity of Unitarian theology and worship—some of the Transcendentalists were prepared to go further in their critique than others, but the Unitarian establishment regarded the Transcendentalist movement as a whole "the latest form of infidelity," in the words of biblical scholar and Harvard professor Andrews Norton.[4]

Well before they were identified as Transcendentalists, and prior to the controversy surrounding Emerson's "Divinity School Address" in 1838, young radicals among the Unitarian clergy were challenging the basis of Unitarian Christianity, even of religion itself. At the heart of their complaint was the influence of John Locke on Unitarian theology. But the dispute was not simply intellectual. It went much deeper. The radicals' breach with orthodox Unitarianism was precipitated by a crisis of faith. Locke insisted that knowledge comes by way of sense experience. Such a view presented two problems for the religious radicals. One the one hand, the empirical philosophy of Locke had led to the religious skepticism of David Hume, who attacked the notion of causality and, by extension, traditional arguments for the existence of God. On the other hand, the Unitarians' reliance on Locke's ideas was internally contradictory. They depended on the evidence of Jesus's miracles to establish his divine authority, but there was no empirical basis for such supernatural claims in the first place. Some termed the Unitarian position "supernatural rationalism." No doubt Hume would have considered the phrase an oxymoron. So far as he was concerned miracles were a violation of the laws of nature, depending for their authority on credulity, not physical evidence.

Some of the radicals felt that even if miracles had occurred, they were irrelevant because the truth of Jesus's message rested not on empirical proof, nor even on his divine authority, which the evidence was adduced to support, but rather on what Emerson called "the intuition of the moral sentiment." As Theodore Parker, the most prominent of the Transcendentalists who remained in the Unitarian ministry, insisted in his controversial 1841 sermon on "The Transient and the Permanent in Christianity," the teachings of Jesus would be true even if the man himself had never existed. For his part, Emerson thought the teaching of the church on miracles was "Monster," as he put it, and gave a false impression. If Jesus spoke of miracles it was not because he had performed them but because he taught that all of life was a miracle. Others among the radicals dismissed the notion of miracles altogether.

These radicals felt strongly that Unitarianism could not be sustained or defended on empirical grounds. In fact all religious faith was threatened by a tide of philosophical skepticism that was sweeping the Western intellectual world. In his 1819 sermon on "Unitarian Christianity," Channing had in fact affirmed the use of reason in correcting the errors of scripture and the doctrines of Christianity. But once reason was applied to faith, there was no stopping point. The Unitarian Christians were prepared to go only so far. The radicals did not disparage reason; rather, they took Locke and Hume seriously. And for this reason they did not believe that the Understanding alone was sufficient as a means either to advance Christianity or to shield it from skepticism.

As far as the Transcendentalists were concerned the hyper-rationality of the Unitarians was an impediment to faith. They found Unitarian preaching largely dry and dull. It did not awaken religious feeling. There is "a famine of our churches," Emerson said bluntly in speaking to the graduating seniors and their faculty in his Harvard Divinity School address. The primary duty of the preacher is not carried out. "In how many churches, by how many prophets, tell me, is man made sensible that he is an infinite Soul; that the earth and heavens are passing into his mind; that he is drinking forever the soul of God?"[5]

The response to Emerson's provocative address was swift and severe. Norton issued a warning in the *Boston Daily Advertiser* a month later. "The community know what they require when they ask for a Christian Teacher," he wrote; "and should any one approving the doctrines of [Emerson's] discourse assume that character, he would deceive his hearers; he would be guilty of a practical falsehood for the most paltry of temptations; he would consent to live, a lie, for the sake of being maintained by those whom he had cheated."[6]

Although Emerson had the temerity to speak spiritual truth to power, he was hardly alone in expressing such views. In 1859, looking back on his ministry at the end of his career, Parker observed that the Unitarian clergy had lacked religious feeling. "Preaching to the understanding," he wrote, "the cry was ever, 'duty, duty! work, work!' They failed to address with equal power the soul, and did not also shout, 'joy, joy! delight, delight!'" He went on to explain, "This defect of the Unitarians was a profound one.... [T]hey had broken with the old ecclesiastic supernaturalism.... But in general they had no theory which justified a more emotional experience of religion. Their philosophy, with many excellences, was sure of no great spiritual truth."[7]

The Unitarians were indeed facing declining membership, particularly in the churches that Emerson and Parker accused of lacking spirituality. Unitarianism had developed and spread in response to increasing urbanization and commerce in the port cities of New England, especially the Boston area. Harvard College and its Divinity School supplied the congregations of Massachusetts with liberal, well-educated ministers. These congregations were glad to be rid of Calvinism and readily embraced liberal Christianity— "the Boston Religion," some called it. Yet by subjecting Christian dogma to reason and excising emotional and spiritual experience, the liberal churches had inadvertently opened wider the gates to infidelity, hastening their own demise. By 1853 the historic First Church of Boston, where Emerson's own father had once served, had fewer than eighty active families in its congregation.[8] From the radicals' point of view the "commercial spirit," with its materialistic and utilitarian emphasis, was inimical to religious faith. The popularity of Parker's fiery preaching, which attracted an audience of thousands, only confirmed the negative trends.

Other forces also posed challenges to the churches and problems for believers. The historical criticism of the Bible, previously mentioned, was one of these. The radicals readily sensed the implications of such study for the Unitarian ministry and their own personal faith. Parker, who taught himself German so that he could read the writings of these biblical scholars, came to the following conclusion:

> I soon found that the Bible is a collection of quite heterogeneous books, most of them anonymous, or bearing names of doubtful authors, collected none knows how, or when, or by whom; united more by caprice than any philosophic or historic method, so that it is not easy to see why one ancient book is kept in the canon and another kept out. I found no unity of doctrine in the several parts; the Old Testament "reveals" one form of religion, and the New Testament one directly its opposite; and in the New Testament itself, I found each writer had his own individuality, which appears not only in the style, the form of thought, but quite as much in the doctrines, the substance of thought, where no two are well agreed.[9]

While Parker considered this discovery enlightening and ultimately liberating, for others, such as William Emerson, it had undermined their faith and call to the ministry.

During this same period scholars became increasingly aware of the texts and doctrines of other religious and philosophical traditions, particularly those of the Far East. This scholarship, too, came to the attention of a younger generation of religious seekers within the ranks of the Unitarian clergy. Unlike their elders in the Unitarian clergy who dismissed such teachings as inferior or heathenish, the young radical ministers read them for inspiration and combed them for commonly held spiritual truths. Parker's experience was typical:

> I studied the historical development of religion and theology amongst the nations not Jewish or Christian, and attended as well as I then could to the other four great religious sects—the Brahmanic, the Buddhistic, the Classic, and the Mahometan. As far as possible at that time, I studied the sacred books of mankind in their original tongues, and with the help of the most faithful interpreters. Here the Greek and Roman philosophers came in for their place there being no sacred books of the classic nations. I attended pretty carefully to the religion of savages and barbarians, and was thereby helped to the solution of many a difficult problem. I found no tribe of men destitute of religion who had attained the power of articulate speech.[10]

These studies challenged the notions of Christian exceptionalism and exclusivity. Those who took them seriously found it increasingly difficult to maintain the literal truth of Christian claims. Other religious and philosophical traditions had their saviors, saints, and sages too. Orthodox Christians, including many Unitarians, considered these faith traditions subordinate to Christianity, but the young radicals embraced them as part of their growing religious cosmopolitanism.

The very notion of religion was undergoing a radical revision. Once religion had been synonymous with Christianity; now Christianity was one religion among many. Once it seemed that the teachings of the church were immutable; now they were seen as a product of historical development. Prior to these developments, it would have been difficult if not impossible to speak of religion apart from any one of its historical manifestations. Now it was possible to view religion itself as an evolutionary process and the various faiths as ways in which the religious sentiment found representation in different cultures. In Parker's words, "religious consciousness was universal in human history." If religious truth could not be validated objectively, on empirical grounds, it could be vouched for subjectively, as a feature of consciousness itself. In his 1859 memoir, *Experience as a Minister,* he elaborated:

> Here, then, was the foundation of religion; laid in human nature itself, which neither the atheist nor the more pernicious bigot, with their sophisms of denial or affirmation, could move, or even shake. I had gone through the great spiritual trial of my life, telling no one of its hopes or fears; and I thought it a triumph that I had . . . devised a scheme which to the scholar's mind, I thought, could legitimate what was spontaneously given to all, by the great primal instincts of mankind.[11]

The conclusion that religion was grounded in human consciousness was a breakthrough for Parker and his fellow radicals. They felt keenly that faith was threatened by the steady encroachment of skepticism, materialism, rationalism, and secularism. It could not be defended on traditional grounds of belief; that is, the scriptures and the teachings of the church. The scriptures are contradictory and the teachings are fallible, subject to interpretation and change.

In addition to the quickly changing intellectual and cultural climate, larger societal forces were widening the breach between the Transcendentalists and the Unitarian establishment, contributing to a sense of alienation deeply felt among the younger generation of religious radicals. America was rapidly becoming more industrialized and urbanized. Factories displaced the artisan system of production. The rise of manufacturing, trade, and commerce drew workers from the farms to metropolitan areas. What had once been an agrarian economy was now an industrial one. These changes prompted Emerson to declare in his address "The American Scholar" that whereas once people had been whole, now they were divided and parceled out in so many pieces. "The state of society," he said, "is one in which the members have suffered amputation from the trunk, and strut about so many walking monsters,—a good finger, a neck, a stomach, and elbow, but never a man." Meaningful work had become lifeless routine, the soul subject to dollars. "The priest becomes a form; the attorney, a statute-book; the mechanic, a machine; the sailor, a rope of a ship."[12] This was the fragmented and divided state in which people now found themselves.

Emerson was speaking to an audience of scholars, members of the intellectual elite. The alienation of working people was fraught with more dire and personally felt consequences. Workers toiled for fourteen-hour days in difficult conditions with few educational opportunities. A dramatic increase in immigration during the 1830s and 1840s depressed the labor market. The financial panics of 1837 and 1839 led to a lengthy depression, long-term unemployment, civil unrest, and growing disparity between the wealthy and the poor. In addition to suffering economic hardships, American society was marred by social inequality and the oppression of Native peoples and African Americans.

The Transcendentalists had a number of concerns about how economic and social pressures affected spiritual life. One of these was the extent to which faith as well as the soul were suffering under such pressures. In their view, religious faith should inspire moral living and human betterment, goals that were compromised by the materialism, competitiveness, and instrumental values associated with "the commercial spirit." This was all too apparent in the Unitarian congregations in and around Boston. Unitarians made up a large share of the civic and mercantile elite. They were leaders in society. They tended to be conservative in their views, accepting of the slave economy and determined to preserve the social status quo. The clergy serving these congregations were often morally compromised in the same ways. The persecution of Universalist minister Abner Kneeland for blasphemy, resulting in a jail term in 1838, was an indication of just how far the liberal Christian establishment was willing to go to enforce their notion of religious conformity.[13]

The young radicals, on the other hand, were deeply affected by the unrest and injustice of their society. They were intellectually curious and spiritually restless, which often led to uncertainty about choosing a vocation. James Freeman Clarke intended to study law until his reading of Coleridge decided him on the ministry instead. Orestes Brownson was orphaned as a young child, raised without parental guidance or religious affiliation, and struggled "to lead a religious life," he said, "without faith, without hope, without love," not knowing what to believe or what to do.[14] In the course of a lengthy religious odyssey he became by turns a Presbyterian, a Universalist minister, a Unitarian minister, and a Transcendentalist before finally converting to Catholicism. Ralph Waldo Emerson was born into the clerical elite, but following his father's death when he was eight, he was raised in relative poverty. He tried teaching before turning to ministry. Then a personal crisis of faith led him to exchange his pulpit in the church for a podium on the lecture circuit. Margaret Fuller, Elizabeth Palmer Peabody, Caroline Healey Dall, and other women of the Transcendentalist group struggled with issues of role and identity in a society that accorded women few opportunities or political rights.

By virtue of their intelligence, education (some of them self-taught), and social status (some of them marrying into wealthy families), the Transcendentalists were among the elites. Yet they embraced reform and social change rather than clinging to the conservative status quo. Peabody and Bronson Alcott promoted reforms in education. Fuller championed women's rights. Thoreau advocated civil disobedience. Parker and Brownson sought to mobilize the laboring classes. George and Sarah Ripley conducted an experiment in cooperative communal living. Virtually all the Transcendentalists were actively involved in the abolition of slavery. Transcendentalism is often depicted as an intellectual or literary movement, albeit with reformist impulses. But it was also a religious revolt. The Transcendentalists were moving beyond the narrow confines of "the British Protestant inheritance," in Leigh Eric Schmidt's phrase. Yet even as they were raising serious critiques of the Unitarian establishment, in a sense they were also following a path laid down for them by the more progressive liberal Christians, William Ellery Channing foremost among them.

In his sermon "Humanity's Likeness to God," Channing, in many ways a bridge between the conservatives and the radicals, anticipates the Transcendentalist position by saying the spirit of God is within us and can be understood only by experience. "In proportion as we receive this spirit, we possess within ourselves the explanation of what we see. We discern more and more of God in everything, from the frail flower to the everlasting stars." By what means do we discern the spirit of God? "That unbounded spiritual energy which we call God," he insisted, "is conceived in us only through consciousness, through the knowledge of ourselves."[15] It is the religious progressivism of Unitarians such as Channing that made possible the rise of what Schmidt calls the "Spiritual Left" in America:

> Individualistic in their understanding of authority, religious liberals were generally contemptuous of creeds and scorned uncritical submission to scriptural texts as ignorance or even idolatry. Moving beyond mere toleration as an ideal, they led the way as eager sympathizers with other faiths. With a grand sense of human freedom and potentiality, they were committed to progress in the domains of spiritual consciousness, social organization, and scientific knowledge. For religious liberals, unlike their secular cousins, a deepened and diversified spirituality was part of modernity's promise. Materialism and scientism might challenge this unfolding religion of the spirit from one side and reactionary pieties and politics from the other, but, to its proponents, those perils only made the inward dimension of liberalism more important. Religious liberalism, with its motley bedfellows of romantics and reformers, led the way in redefining spirituality and setting out its essentials.[16]

At the heart of religious liberalism lies a fundamental paradox. The Unitarians were firmly committed to individual spiritual freedom, which Channing described as "the attribute of a mind, in which reason and conscience have begun to act, and which is free through its own energy, through fidelity to the truth, through resistance of temptation. . . . [I]t is moral energy or force of holy purpose put forth against the senses, against the passions, against the world, and thus liberating the intellect, conscience, and will, so that they act with strength and unfold themselves forever." The notion of spiritual freedom, as Channing defined it, is fundamentally disruptive of human institutions, religious as well as civic ones. Liberal religion is, ironically, susceptible to the unintended consequence of this principle; namely, a tendency to undermine its own institutions. Channing insisted that religion "must be viewed, not as a monopoly of priests, ministers, or sects, . . . but as the property of every human being, and as the great subject for every human mind."[17] Though not a Transcendentalist himself, Channing nevertheless validated the movement's spiritual striving.

3

TRANSCENDENTALIST
SPIRITUALITY

By the early 1840s the Transcendentalists had attracted considerable attention through their writings, lectures, sermons, and a variety of activities. Elizabeth Peabody established a salon and bookstore on West Street in downtown Boston. Margaret Fuller began a series of "Conversations" with women at Peabody's salon and, along with Emerson, started the *Dial* magazine. George and Sarah Ripley founded Brook Farm, a cooperative community in West Roxbury. Bronson Alcott's Temple School had opened to fanfare but closed amid controversy, after his educational methods and ideas were derided in the press. Emerson himself had gained notice and notoriety through the publication of his books *Nature* and *Essays: First Series,* and through the controversy surrounding his provocative address arguing in favor of moral intuition over religious doctrine at Harvard Divinity School several years earlier. The Transcendentalists were at the very center of the religious radicalism and social reform in and around Boston during the late 1830s and early 1840s.

Yet people were as confused then as they are today about what Transcendentalism meant. Emerson wryly noted in his journal at the time, "Transcendentalism means, says our accomplished Mrs. B., with a wave of her hand, *A little beyond.*"[1] Typical of comments made at the time was a brief anonymous article on Transcendentalism, appearing in August 1841 in the *Christian Register,* a Unitarian weekly, in which an unnamed writer asserted that "this term is but little understood. It seems to be commonly regarded as synonymous with *mysticism.*" The notion "that such speculations should be entertained in Germany can be no occasion of surprise," the author concluded, "but, that they should be received with much favor in our own country,—in the midst of ourselves—would be not less wonderful than alarming."[2]

Sensing the public needed a better explanation, Emerson addressed the subject of Transcendentalism in a lecture, one of a series he gave in the winter of 1841–42. No doubt the lecture attracted a curious public eager to hear what this central figure of the Transcendentalist circle had to say about the topic. Emerson noted, first of all, that Transcendentalist views are not in fact new, but are actually a modern expression of perennial wisdom. The light is always the same, whatever "shape" it takes by the objects it falls upon, he said. As we have seen, they are a form of idealism—"Idealism as it appears in 1842."[3]

Emerson contrasted idealism with materialism, asserting that materialism emerges from the data of the senses, idealism from intuition and inspiration. The Transcendentalist affirms the world of facts but doesn't stop there. Besides the fact itself, there's the consideration of what it means to us, what we make of it, the value it has, and the reality it assumes in our minds. Truth known by intuition, through consciousness, is greater than facts derived empirically from experience. For the Transcendentalist, it is mind, not matter, that is the true reality, because it is the mind that assigns things the *rank,* or importance they assume in our consciousness. How we think about the world affects our actions and our circumstances. Thus, materialism never has the final word.

In contrast to the empiricism of the materialist, the Transcendentalist believes in miracle, inspiration, and ecstasy; that is to say, a mystical form of perception open to the "influx of light and power." Hence, the appeal to truth is never from external authority but from personal experience. For this reason there can be no "Transcendental *party,*" per se, because there can never be a "party line" so far as truth is concerned. Nor, Emerson insisted, have there been any pure Transcendentalists, leaning entirely on the spiritual side, eating nothing but "angel's food."[4]

In response to the materialism and commercialism of the present day, he continued, many would-be Transcendentalists have pursued "a certain solitary and critical way." They hold themselves aloof, at once shunning what society expects of them and crying out for something worthy to do. Essentially a countercultural movement, Transcendentalism has incurred the censure of society, which considers their aloofness a reproach. Reformers and philanthropists, according to Emerson, consider them dropouts, who shirk their duty to society. However, these young men and women are not by nature unsocial or melancholy. To the contrary, they are joyous and hopeful, and they are moral perfectionists, skeptical of causes and institutions.

Probing more deeply, Emerson observed that these young people are also spiritually troubled. In particular, they believe that their faith differs from the faith of others. Theirs comes as the result of a mystical insight that has made a deep impression on them. Emerson described it as:

> a certain brief experience, which surprised me in the market, in some place, at some time,—whether in the body or out of the body, God knoweth—and made me aware that I had played the fool with fools all this time, but that law existed for me and for all; that to me belonged trust, a child's trust and obedience, and the worship of ideas, and I should never be fool more. Well, in the space of an hour probably, I was let down from this height; I was at my old tricks, the selfish member of a selfish society. My life is superficial, takes no root in the deep world; I ask, When shall I die and be relieved of the responsibility of seeing an Universe which I do not use? I wish to exchange this flash-of-lightening faith for continuous daylight, this fever glow for a benign climate.[5]

Such experiences are at once profound and transitory. The greatest challenge of the spiritual life, he concluded, is to integrate these fleeting moments—full of wonder and significance—with the realities of everyday life.

This is a recurring theme in Emerson's writing, which he referred to as the problem of "double consciousness." We seem to live two lives that bear little relation to each other, he observed. "One prevails now, all buzz and din; and the other prevails then, all infinitude and paradise; and, with the progress of life, the two discover no greater disposition to reconcile themselves." We have these moments of enlightenment and "presently the clouds shut down again." Nevertheless, "we retain the belief that this petty web we weave will at last be overshot and reticulated with veins of the blue, and that the moments will characterize the days."[6]

Emerson accepted some of the criticism leveled against the Transcendentalists. There are bound to be excesses and inconsistencies, he conceded. Nevertheless, it is better that youthful idealists obey their genius. Society has an obligation to them, too. Besides "farmers, sailors and weavers," there must also be "collectors of the heavenly spark, with power to convey the electricity to others." Society needs idealists who speak "for thoughts and principles not marketable and perishable" but such as shall enable us to achieve a "fuller union with the surrounding system," long after commercial improvements and mechanical inventions have outlived their usefulness.[7]

Who were these young people that Emerson describes? Perhaps one of them was his young protégé, Henry Thoreau, who was then twenty-four, or some of the younger members of the Brook Farm community. But most of the Transcendentalists familiar to the public with were hardly young—Parker, Ripley, Peabody, Fuller, Alcott and, of course, Emerson himself. It was a conceit on Emerson's part to describe the movement in the third person, as though he was a generation removed from it. He exaggerated the degree to which they withdrew from society, but not their moral idealism or their dissatisfaction with the prevailing views of religion and philosophy. All the Transcendentalists experienced crises in their personal and professional lives. All of them felt alienated from the growing commercialism and utilitarian tenor of the times. And all of them sought congruence between their visions and their vocations.

There was, indeed, a fundamental difference between their faith and that of others, as Emerson said. Robert Bellah explores this difference in his book *Religion in Human Evolution.* Religion can be approached in one of two ways, he says. It is perhaps most often understood in a conceptual way, as a system of beliefs and practices. However, it is also possible—and perhaps more valuable—to view it experientially, not as a system of beliefs and practices but as a kind of cognition or way of knowing.[8] This second way was how Emerson and the Transcendentalists understood it. Bellah describes this way of knowing as "Being cognition," or "B-cognition" for short—a term taken from the work of psychologist Abraham Maslow. This type of perception is in contrast to what Maslow calls "Deficiency cognition," or "D-cognition." To name the more common way of thinking as a "deficiency" is somewhat misleading, as it suggests there's something wrong with this mode of knowing. This way of seeing the world may indeed be a function of physical or psychological deficiencies, such as economic deprivation, poor self-esteem, addictive behaviors, or material desires. But for most people D-cognition is a function of living in the actual, everyday world. It helps us succeed in our work, provide for our families, meet deadlines and obligations; in short, to get things done.

The paramount reality for most people, most of the time, is what we think of as the world of daily life.[9] We relate to this world in a practical, pragmatic way, and we assume that this world is defined in terms of what we take to be standard measures of time and space. In order to function well, we need to analyze things, keep accounts, and plan for the future. While we take this world for granted, our existence in it is characterized by a certain amount of anxiety, because there are always pressures, expectations, losses, and uncertainties that we must deal with. And, whether or not we are consciously aware of it, the specter of death is always lurking in the background.

But we find it difficult to spend all of our time in the empirical world of everyday life. We also sleep and dream, play sports, watch television, listen to music, go for walks in the woods, and so on, engaging in activities that divert us from this mundane world of daily life. We find pleasure in these activities and sometimes feel guilty for allowing ourselves to be disengaged from our perceived responsibilities and obligations. Though we think of it as real, this world is actually a fiction maintained through effort and common consent. It lacks ontological reality. What "actually" is only *seems* to be.

B-cognition stands in marked contrast. Emerson alluded to this difference in the lengthy passage from "The Transcendentalist," quoted earlier. B-cognition is a type of perception associated with what Maslow calls *"peak experiences."*[10] Even though such experiences are of utmost importance, they cannot be summoned nor sustained for long. Peak experiences raise serious questions about the commonly assumed nature of reality and the way we choose to live our lives. Although he predated Maslow and Bellah by about a century, Emerson understood the difference between these two types of cognition and the significance this distinction has for our spiritual life. The effort to reconcile these two modes of consciousness is at the core of Transcendentalist spirituality. "Presently the clouds shut down again" and we go back to our accustomed habits and preoccupations. "Yet we retain the belief" that the ordinary affairs of everyday life, including its challenges and shortcomings, might be transformed by an awareness of the soul, such that these moments of insight might come to "characterize the days." Toward this end, Emerson and the Transcendentalists developed and practiced an informal spiritual discipline, which we will examine more closely in subsequent chapters.

It has long been debated whether the Transcendentalists were mystics in any meaningful sense of the word. Emerson would have been reluctant to accept that label, although fellow Transcendentalist James Freeman Clarke, in examining "The Mystics in All Religions," declared Emerson the prime example of an American mystic.[11] Whether they were full-fledged mystics or not, there is no question that Transcendentalist epistemology is essentially mystical in nature. If it is true, as William James argues in *The Varieties of Religious Experience,* that "personal religious experience has its root and centre in mystical states of consciousness," it is because mysticism is a form of B-cognition.[12] B-cognition is analogous to the Transcendentalists' usage of the term "Reason." By Reason, they meant intuitive reason rather than discursive reason. They did not disparage discursive reason, or the Understanding, but felt that it was limited to instrumental uses. Intuitive reason, on the other hand, gives access to the Universal Mind and thus to a different way of knowing. The Understanding is knowledge of the parts; the Reason is comprehension of the whole, revealed in moments of insight and expanded consciousness.

The Understanding and the Reason represent two different forms of cognition and two different ways of knowing: the empirical epistemology of the Understanding and the intuitive epistemology of the Reason. Although "The Over-Soul" does not include much of this terminology, this essay is Emerson's most sustained reflection on the revelations of the Reason. The essay begins by contrasting our everyday, habitual existence with moments of insight and inspiration. "There is a difference between one and another hour of life, in their authority and subsequent effect," he writes. "Our faith comes in moments; our vice is habitual. Yet there is a depth in those brief moments which constrains us to ascribe more reality to them than to all other experiences." The revelations of the Reason, though fleeting, are nevertheless authoritative. They refuse to be dismissed by the Understanding and the standards of everyday experience. If we feel that our life is superficial, where does this feeling come from? And how can we tell? The "philosophy of six thousand years" has searched for but failed to find the answers to these questions. And yet, deep down, we feel compelled to acknowledge "a higher origin" for such occurrences than the human will.[13] Indeed, it is only by surrendering our will and putting ourselves in a receptive frame of mind that these visions come to us.

Whence do these visions come? And what do they tell us? Their source, Emerson says, is "that great nature in which we rest, as the earth lies in the soft arms of the atmosphere; that Unity, that Over-soul, within which every man's particular being is contained and made one with all other." They tell us that we live divided, partial, and superficial lives. Yet deep within "is the soul of the whole; the wise silence; the universal beauty, to which every part and particle is equally related; the eternal ONE. . . . We see the world piece by piece, as the sun, the moon, the animal, the tree; but the whole, of which these are the shining parts, is the soul." Insight into this oneness is the highest sort of wisdom that we can aspire to, and it is available, intuitively, to each of us. It is difficult to understand much less acknowledge the wisdom of these remarks. For those whose sense of reality is conditioned by the Understanding, or Deficiency cognition, such language makes little sense. At the same time, it is difficult for one who has had a unitive experience to describe it. "My words do not convey its august sense," Emerson says; "they fall short and cold."[14]

The individual soul, which, as Emerson says, is part and parcel of the Over-soul, is not a physical entity, but a spiritual reality. "The soul in man is not an organ," he says, "but animates and exercises all the organs; is not a function, like the power of memory, of calculation, of comparison, but uses these as hands and feet; is not a faculty, but a light; is not the intellect or the will, but the master of the intellect and the will; is the background of our being, in which they lie—an immensity not possessed and that cannot be possessed."[15] In sum, the soul gives itself to those who are receptive to it and worthy to receive it. It can come to anyone, of high or low estate, who will receive it humbly and simply, without let or hindrance. Approaching the soul requires no intermediaries, no rites or priesthood. Those who revere it "will come to see that the world is the perennial miracle which the soul worketh; that there is no profane history; that all history is sacred; that the universe is represented in an atom, in a moment in time. He will weave no longer a spotted life of shreds and patches, but he will live with a divine unity."[16]

Emerson's essay "The Over-Soul" was a response to the spiritual condition of his day, and, I would say, it relates to ours as well; namely, to a lack of congruity between Deficiency consciousness and Being consciousness, the horizontal axis of life and the vertical; or, as Emerson expressed it, between the Understanding and the Reason. Because "the axis of vision is not coincident with the axis of things," he wrote in *Nature*, we are disunited within ourselves.[17] I believe, as Emerson did, that the solution to this problem lies in "the redemption of the soul," that is to say, subordinating the Understanding to the Reason, instead of the other way around.

This essay is Emerson at his most transcendental. Although many of his essays and lectures deal with spiritual themes and issues, "The Over-Soul" is his most cogent expression of religion, not as a system of beliefs, but as a matter of personal experience. He was well aware, as he said in his lecture on "Man the Reformer," that "the community in which we live will hardly bear to be told that every man should be open to ecstasy or a divine illumination, and by his daily walk elevated by intercourse with the spiritual world."[18] The world we live in is governed by practical considerations and empirical methods, and is loath to give credence to the claims of intuition.

To what degree is Emerson the "representative man"—to use a term he applied to exemplary individuals in his book *Representative Men*—of the Transcendentalist movement? Were his conceptions of the soul and the nature of enlightenment shared by others in the group? Perhaps the biggest difference of opinion was over the nature of God. For Emerson, God was impersonal. For Theodore Parker, God was personal. But the Transcendentalists generally agreed that spiritual truth is known intuitively by the use of Reason and that, if they were not pantheists as Emerson and Thoreau sometimes appeared to be, they were panentheists who believed that God is transcendent as well as immanent in the world and human nature. Nor was Emerson alone in attesting to the significance of moments of inspiration and insight. The word most commonly used by the Transcendentalists to describe such experiences is *"ecstasy."* It comes from the Greek *ekstasis,* meaning to stand outside oneself. This experience may be of greater or lesser intensity, as Emerson notes, but it involves seeing the world and life from the selfless perspective of the Reason, as opposed to the egocentric point of view of the Understanding. To use Maslow's terminology, these ecstasies are peak experiences, in which the universe is "perceived as an integrated and unified whole."[19]

There is nothing esoteric about such experiences. They are natural even if they are not common or ordinary, and many if not most people have had them to some degree. "I hold that ecstasy will be found normal," Emerson insists, "or only an example on a higher plane of the same gentle gravitation by which stones fall and rivers run."[20] They are not experiences of a different world; they are experiences of this world viewed differently, from a holistic perspective rather than an atomistic one. The mode of consciousness is perceptual, not conceptual. They are experiences of a different reality, to be sure, but not a supernatural one. They are experiences of the world as it really is or could be. It is this world, not the *actual* world, the world of *maya* (Sanskrit for "*illusion*") or appearances, but instead the *real* world, the world seen *sub specie aeternitatis* (Latin for "from the perspective of eternity"), in its essential state. It is a world in which we are not estranged from nature, but one with it; in which we are not divided within ourselves, but whole. Ecstatic or peak experiences may come unbidden and unexpectedly, as in a "silent walk by the way-side," or they may come after a period of personal struggle.[21] However and whenever they come, they typically bring a sense of renewal, serenity, confidence, and efficacy in everyday life.

Emerson frequently alluded to such experiences in his lectures and essays, and described them in his journals. Many of the other Transcendentalists also had them and wrote about them. Theodore Parker, best known for his prodigious intellect and passion for social justice, experienced periods of depression. In an 1841 letter, he lamented, "Oh, how our life is streaked with sadness! I shall begin to believe, with some weeper, that all the birds sing in the key of grief, for the stars look melancholy to me now." A few months later the bird of grief was singing in a different key: "There is no end to the development of the soul. I feel the bird element is wakened in me anew. Wants of my nature never satisfied, but drugged to sleep by the will, open now their beaks, flutter their wings, and try the thin air. I feel a new development of youth. I thought once it would never return . . . there is a resurrection of myself."[22]

Margaret Fuller, a woman of singular talents, struggled to find a place for herself in a male-dominated society that allowed women few opportunities for advancement or self-expression. In her journal Fuller wrote of having been distraught, "wearied out with mental conflicts, and in a mood of . . . child-like sadness." She felt that her gifts were unrecognized and unappreciated. In a vision she "saw there was no self, that selfishness was all folly, and the result of circumstance; that it was only because I thought self real that I suffered; that I had only to live in the idea of the ALL, and all was mine. This truth came to me, and I received it unhesitatingly; so that I was for that hour taken up into God. In that true ray most of the relations of earth seemed mere films, phenomena. My earthly pain at not being recognized never went deep after this hour."[23] She went on to become, by turns, a teacher, an editor of the *Dial* magazine, an investigative journalist and cultural critic for Horace Greeley's *New-York Tribune,* a foreign correspondent, and a revolutionary in Italy's fight for independence and unification.

Although Thoreau didn't suffer from despondency, he had similar ecstatic experiences and lamented that they occurred all too seldom and passed all too quickly. As a youth he experienced intimacy with nature and "ecstasies begotten of the breezes!" which he alluded to in a journal entry on July 16, 1851. At one point, he suddenly felt an "indescribable, infinite, all-absorbing, divine, heavenly pleasure, a sense of elevation and expansion." He perceived he was "dealt with by superior powers" and felt "a pleasure, a joy, an existence" that he had not brought on himself. "I speak as a witness on the stand, and tell what I have perceived," he attested:

> When I detected this interference I was profoundly moved. For years I marched to a music in comparison with which the military music of the streets is noise and discord. I was daily intoxicated, and yet no man could call me intemperate. With all your science can you tell how it is, and whence it is, that light comes into the soul?[24]

For Wordsworth, these priceless moments lingered in the memory. As we saw in chapter 1, he felt they were the high water mark of our spiritual lives: "Those shadowy recollections, / Which, be what they may, / Are yet the fountain light of all our day, / Are yet a master light of all our seeing."[25] If they are difficult to summon, still "the memory of those rarer moods," in Thoreau's words, "comes to color our picture and is the permanent paint pot as it were into which we dip our brush. Thus no life or experience goes unreported at last; but if it be not solid gold it is gold-leaf, which gilds the furniture of the mind. It is an experience of infinite beauty on which we unfailingly draw, which enables us to exaggerate ever truly. Our moments of inspiration are not lost though we have no particular poem to show for them; for those experiences have left an indelible impression, and we are ever and anon reminded of them."[26]

These peak experiences reveal how superficial much of everyday life is and show us how our lives could be enriched. They do not scorn the mundane, but redeem it. The lesson they teach us is conveyed in this passage from the conclusion of Thoreau's essay "A Walk to Wachusett":

And now that we have returned to the desultory life of the plain, let us endeavor to import a little of that mountain grandeur into it. We will remember within what walls we live, and understand that this level life too has its summit, and why from the mountain-top the deepest valleys have a tinge of blue; that there is elevation in every hour, as no part of the earth is so low that the heavens may not be seen from, and we have only to stand on the summit of our hour to command an uninterrupted horizon.[27]

Fuller made a similar point in one of her letters. We go on "an undulating course," she wrote, "sometimes on the hill, sometimes in the valley." But one is only enlightened who "in the valley forgets not the hill-prospect, and knows in darkness that the sun will rise again. That is the real life which is subordinated to, not merged in, the ideal; he is only wise who can bring the lowest act of his life into sympathy with its highest thought. And this I take to be the only aim of our pilgrimage here. I agree with those who think that no true philosophy will try to ignore or annihilate the material part of man, but will rather seek to put it in its place, as servant and minister to the soul."[28]

Importing the wisdom gained from peak experiences into the affairs of everyday life is the essence of Transcendentalist spirituality. The Transcendentalists endeavored to do this by various means, which they termed "self-culture," the subject of the next chapter. Transcendentalist spirituality is mystical in nature, but only in the broadest sense of the term. A mystic is most often thought of as one who leads a secluded life of quiet contemplation, focused on the love of God, and not concerned with the world's affairs. This devotional form of mysticism is much more common than the philosophical mysticism of the Transcendentalists. They were contemplative to some degree, but they did not live secluded lives, despite Thoreau's two years at Walden Pond. He was never the hermit he has been made out to be, but active in world, as were his fellow Transcendentalists. Theirs is a mysticism not of cloisters or caves, but of everyday life, available to anyone attentive to the strains of the spirit.

In the chapter from *Walden* "Where I Lived, and What I Lived For," Thoreau offers a picture of Transcendentalist spirituality in symbolic terms. He took up residence in his cabin near the pond on the Fourth of July, as if to say that the spiritual life requires a measure of freedom and independence. He wrote his book, he said, for the purpose of waking his neighbors up, crowing "as lustily as chanticleer in the morning." The morning is symbolic of spiritual awakening. Much of the time we appear to be asleep. We must rouse ourselves from our spiritual lethargy, not by external or artificial means, but by aspirations from within summoning us to a higher mode of life. Sadly, most people are alert enough only for physical labor; considerably fewer for intellectual exertion; fewer still for "a poetic or divine life."[29] Only when we are awake are we fully alive.

Thoreau was convinced that we can elevate our lives by a conscious effort, though it may be difficult. He didn't advocate resignation, but he did insist that it was necessary for us to slow down and simplify our lives. Too much of life is frittered away by detail, and society as a whole lives too fast. "When we are unhurried and wise," Thoreau insisted, "we perceive that only great and worthy things have any permanent and absolute existence, that petty fears and petty pleasures are but the shadow of the reality."[30] We are like the prince in the Hindu fable who was raised by a forester, ignorant of his true estate. He imagined himself to belong to a lowly caste until one of the king's ministers discovered him and revealed to him who he truly was, thereby dispelling the misconception of his character. We think that our estate, too, is mean, but only because we confuse appearance with reality. We will explore the themes Thoreau raises—awareness, simplicity, nature, leisure, solitude, spiritual practice—in the chapters to come.

4

THE ART OF LIFE

S elf-culture was "the defining characteristic of the age," according to literary scholar Mark G. Vasquez, referring to the 1820s to 1850s.[1] When and under what circumstances the term "self-culture" first came into use is uncertain. It may have derived from the Prussian educator Wilhelm von Humboldt's early-nineteenth-century notion of *bildung,* or self-cultivation, which regarded education as a lifelong process of human development rather than mere training in knowledge or skills.[2] The goal of education, according to von Humboldt, was to continually expand the individual's spiritual and cultural sensibilities. The idea of self-culture may also have been inspired by Joseph Marie, baron de Gérando, whose book *Self-education; or, the Means and Art of Moral Progress,* was translated from the French by Elizabeth Peabody in 1830 as a favor to a small circle of friends, including William Ellery Channing. Peabody wrote in her preface that Gérando's emphasis was on "moral self-culture, adapted to minds which shrink from metaphysical disquisition"; in other words, spiritual growth for the masses.[3]

The Unitarians viewed self-culture in a similar way. The notion was perfectly aligned with the Arminian theology of the liberal Christians, which emphasized human agency and effort in the process of conversion, in contrast to Calvinism, which asserted that salvation could come only by divine grace.[4] In the words of David Robinson, conversion was no longer seen "as a single intense experience, but rather as a continuing process of character

40

formation and cultivation."[5] This represented a decisive break with the Calvinist theology of the New England churches. Rejecting the doctrines of predestination and innate depravity, the Unitarians affirmed free will and human dignity. The formation of character was substituted for the notion of divine election. Self-culture was the process by which moral character was developed and maintained.

This view is perhaps best reflected in Henry Ware, Jr.'s treatise on *The Formation of Christian Character*, published in 1831. Ware was Emerson's predecessor as minister of the Second Church in Boston, prior to teaching on the faculty of Harvard Divinity School. His treatise was a manual for the cultivation of piety though submission to God by means of devotional practices such as reading, meditation, prayer, worship, and partaking of the Lord's Supper. Though in some ways sympathetic to Transcendentalism, Ware criticized Emerson's Divinity School address for denying the personality of the deity.

While the term "self-culture" may suggest elitist connotations for us today, Channing and Peabody, among others, insisted that it was available to everyone. It was widely promoted, not only in Unitarian churches but also in lecture halls and mechanics institutes. In 1838 Channing delivered a lecture on the subject to a working-class audience of laborers and artisans at the Franklin Institute in Boston. He defined self-culture as "the care which every man owes to himself, to the unfolding and perfecting of his nature." Everyone is capable of pursuing it and benefiting both spiritually and practically, he said, "not only because we can enter into and search ourselves. We have a still nobler power, that of acting on, determining and forming ourselves."[6]

Channing likened self-culture to the agrarian practice of cultivation. "To cultivate any thing, be it a plant, an animal, a mind, is to make grow," he observed. "Growth, expansion, is the end. Nothing admits culture, but that which has a principle of life, capable of being expanded. He, therefore, who does what he can to unfold all his powers and capabilities, especially his nobler ones, so as to become a well-proportioned, vigorous, excellent, happy being, practices self-culture."[7] Self-culture does not mean accumulating information but "building up a force of thought which may be turned at will on any subjects, on which we are called to pass judgment."[8] Self-culture is not a selfish, individual matter, he argued, but answers a social need, cultivating the affections "which bind a man to friends and neighbors, to his country, and to the suffering who fall under his eye, wherever they belong."[9]

Some people may say that the masses "need no other culture than is necessary to fit them for their various trades," Channing observed, but "the ground of a man's culture lies in his nature, not his calling."[10] Self-culture is not a means to another goal but is an end in itself, pursued for its own sake, for the perfection of the self. Some may say the laboring classes have no time for self-culture, he continued, but anyone committed to the idea, regardless of class, will find or make time for it: "It seizes on spare moments, and turns larger fragments of leisure to golden account."[11] And some may say the working classes deserve relaxation more than "the toils of the mind," but Channing argued that self-culture actually increases one's capacity for enjoyment. Reading and lectures, for instance, can be pleasurable and gratifying at the same time.

In 1830 Ralph Waldo Emerson had preached on the same topic to his congregation at Boston's Second Church and then, a year prior to Channing's address, had offered a popular series of public lectures on "Human Culture."[12] For Emerson, also, self-culture was a natural and necessary process in our development as a person. "His own culture,—the unfolding of his nature, is the chief end of man," Emerson said. "A divine impulse at the core of his being impels him to this." But the pursuit of culture was not like going to a finishing school, he pointed out. Culture "does not consist in polishing and varnishing" the self, nor is it akin to "the trimming and turfing of gardens." Rather, self-culture aims to reconcile or harmonize the individual with the universal. We are so intimately related to everything, he observed, that "the laws of nature and the soul unite their energies in every moment and every place."[13]

The union of the individual with the universal "consists in a systematic abandonment to the highest Instinct," Emerson continued. It cannot be predicted or produced. "True growth is spontaneous in every step. The mind that grows could not predict the times, the means, the mode of that spontaneity. God comes in by a private door into every individual: thoughts enter by passages which the individual never left open." Our spiritual growth is an unfolding, like that of a flower. We must "trust the instinct to the end though you cannot tell why or see why. It is vain to hurry it. By trusting it, it shall ripen into thought, into truth, and you shall know why you believe."[14]

Emerson urged his listeners to reflect on this process to discern, if possible, "the secret law" by which it operates. "A certain wandering light comes to us and is the distinction, the principle we wanted. But the oracle comes because we had previously laid siege to the shrine." "Laying siege to the shrine" is the key to self-culture and to resolving one of the perennial paradoxes of the spiritual life, namely, how to command what is essentially spontaneous, and thereby tap "that endless, silent stream ever flowing in from above."[15]

He offered several suggestions for the practice of self-culture. The first is to have a place to yourself, "though you sell your coat and wear a blanket." Second, he advised keeping a journal:

> Pay so much honor to the visits of Truth to your mind as to record those thoughts that have shone therein. . . . It is not for what is recorded, though that may be the agreeable entertainment of later years, and the pleasant remembrances of what we were, but for the habit of rendering an account to yourself of yourself in some more rigorous manner and at more certain intervals than mere conversation or casual reverie of solitude require.

His third recommendation was to practice contemplation in solitude. He advised his listeners to develop mindfulness:

> The simple habit of sitting alone occasionally to explore what facts of the moment lie in the memory may have the effect in some more favored hour to open to the student the kingdom of spiritual nature. He may become aware that there around him roll new at this moment and inexhaustible the waters of Life; that the world he has lived in so heedless, so gross, is illumined with meaning, that every fact is magical; every atom alive, and he is the heir of it all.[16]

Finally, Emerson urged his audience to take walks in nature. "We need Nature, and cities give the human senses not room enough. The habit of feeding the senses daily and nightly with the open air and firmament, presently becomes so strong that we feel the want of it like water for washing."[17]

For Emerson, the moments when we experience inspiration and insight are the pinnacle of our spiritual life. "The mind is then all light," he said:

> These moments are the years of the mind; for they are epochs from which we date. . . . Yet are these moments not the privilege of any class of men: they come to all men. They are the foundation on which religion rests in the world. The forms, the books, which are called religions, are nothing

but the monuments and landmarks men have erected to commemorate these moments, and to fix, if it were possible, their too volatile Spirit.[18]

Although such moments happen unexpectedly and infrequently, the aim of self-culture is to prepare the mind for their reception. While they may be difficult to summon or sustain, such experiences are not necessarily one-time events in the course of any person's life. The disciplines that Emerson advised—and additional practices that he and other Transcendentalists developed—were intended both to cultivate awareness and to apply it to the affairs of everyday life.

Self-culture was often described as "the art of life." In 1840 Frederic Henry Hedge wrote an article by that title for the *Dial* magazine. Hedge, a charter member of the Transcendental Club, was a noted scholar who had studied in Germany. He traveled all the way from his parish in Bangor, Maine, to attend the meetings. (Emerson himself preferred to call it Hedge's Club.) In this article he stated, "The work of life, so far as the individual is concerned, is self-culture—the perfect unfolding of our individual nature." It is a prize worth seeking, he explained, but it comes at a price. We must be single-mindedly devoted to achieving it. Too often we feel we are getting ready to live, but not living. We are distracted by material goods, false goals and trivial concerns. Society promotes "not the highest culture, but the greatest comfort," he wrote. But the aim of self-culture "is to live now, to live in the present, to live in the highest."[19] Self-culture is a not a selfish pursuit. Its influence on society is just as beneficial as its influence on the individual. In self-culture are the ground and condition of all reform.

Hedge's vision of self-culture was more strenuous than Emerson's. Whereas Emerson emphasized abandonment and spontaneity, Hedge stressed abstinence and renunciation. Both advocated detachment from the superficial and proximate goods of a profit-centered society and a focus on the true and ultimate ends of life. And both recommended contemplation in solitude—or "retirement," as Hedge put it—as a means of engaging in "the art of life." For Emerson, Hedge, and the other members of the Transcendentalist group, self-culture was the essential to spiritual growth.

A perfect example of self-culture, in both its spontaneous and strenuous forms, was Henry David Thoreau. Like so many young people then and now, Thoreau graduated from college with uncertain career prospects. He lived with his parents and for a time worked as a teacher in Concord and as a tutor to the children of Emerson's brother, William, on Staten Island.

He aspired to write, but felt torn between making a living and making a life. He found himself drawn into a quagmire that had already engulfed his contemporaries—the search for wealth and social status. But he was determined to chart a different course. Taking a page from Hedge, he "retired" to Walden Pond to contemplate the means and ends of existence. "When we consider what, to use the words of the catechism, is the chief end of man, and what are the true necessaries and means of life," he wrote in *Walden,* the account of his experience there, "it appears as if men had deliberately chosen the common mode of living because they preferred it to any other. Yet they honestly think there is no choice left. But alert and healthy natures remember that the sun rose clear. It is never too late to give up our prejudices."[20]

Walden is one of the most memorable treatises ever written on the art of life. Thoreau went to Walden Pond for a variety of reasons—to find a quiet place to write; to "drink in the soft influences and sublime revelations of Nature" in the woods and fields;[21] to practice the yogic teachings of the Bhagavad Gita, and, most of all, to conduct an experiment in the art of living. "I went to the woods because I wished to live deliberately," he wrote, "to front only the essential facts of life, and see if I could not learn what it had to teach, and not, when I came to die, to discover that I had not lived."[22] The question he asked of himself and his readers was: Will we live a life of "quiet desperation"—as the mass of humans appears to do—or will we choose to "live deliberately"?

In his experiment Thoreau reduced life to its essentials, cultivated an aware-ness of nature and his inner self, and used leisure to its greatest benefit. His regimen included contemplation; walking in nature (or, as he called it, "saun-tering"); bathing in the pond; keeping a journal; and abstaining from meat, tea, and coffee. He aimed to make his life a steady progression, "yielding inces-santly to all the impulses of the soul," while making sure that "every stroke of the chisel" entered his "own flesh and bone" in creating "such a masterpiece, as you may imagine a dweller on the table lands of central Asia might produce, with three score and ten years for canvass, and the faculties of man for tools—a human life. . . . For such a masterpiece as this, whole galleries of Greece and Italy are a mere mixing of colors and preparatory quarrying of marble."[23]

Like Thoreau, Margaret Fuller also made a conscious effort to practice self-culture. Fuller took her motto, "Extraordinary generous seeking," from her literary hero, Johann Wolfgang von Goethe. Goethe (1749–1832) was a major figure in German literature. More than anyone else, he influenced the Transcendentalists' notion of self-culture as the primary goal in life. Fuller was his champion, having studied his works and translated several of them for his American audience. Tiffany K. Wayne, author of *Woman Thinking: Feminism and Transcendentalism in Nineteenth-Century America*, writes, "In Margaret Fuller's reading of Goethe . . . were the foundation and aims of her own feminism: a belief that the main human goal was to grow and develop as individuals to our highest potential."[24]

In everything she applied herself to—writing, editing, teaching, social reform, and her own self-creation—Fuller aspired to grow and develop. "*Very early I knew the only object in life was to grow,*" she wrote. "I was often false to this knowledge, in idolatries of particular objects, or impatient longings for happiness, but I have never lost sight of it, have always been controlled by it, and this first gift of thought has never been superseded by a later love."[25] Commenting on this passage in her *Memoirs*, Clarke noted, "Margaret's life *had an aim*. . . . This aim, from first to last, was SELF-CULTURE." It was, he said, a "profound desire for a full development of her whole nature, by means of a full expression of life."[26]

Fuller struggled, as Thoreau did, with discerning a vocation. Finding few outlets for her energy and talents, she also turned to teaching initially, one of the few occupations open to women. Through her series of Conversations in Boston, in which she urged women to pursue self-culture, Fuller was able to gain a wider audience. She drew on her vast knowledge of classical mythology and literature to raise the consciousness of a large number of well-educated women who had previously been confined to domestic roles.

Fuller wrote prodigiously in the form of books, reviews, and articles, always bringing in her perspective of self-culture. She was a regular member of the Transcendental Club and, along with Emerson, wrote a considerable number of the *Dial's* articles and reviews. Her first book, *A Summer on the Lakes,* published in 1844, chronicled her trip to the Midwest. Here she sympathetically described the plight of women on the prairie and the degraded condition of Native Americans. Shortly after writing this book, she took a job as columnist and literary critic for Horace Greeley's *New-York Tribune,* becoming the first woman to have a front-page byline. While living in New York, she published her most influential work, *Woman in the Nineteenth Century,* another significant treatise on self-culture from a woman's perspective. She next accepted an offer to become the first foreign correspondent, male or female, for an American newspaper. She sent dispatches to the *Tribune* describing European culture and politics, and the conditions that led to the Revolutions of 1848. She was on the front lines covering the unsuccessful Italian uprising to overthrow control of Italy by France and Austria. Returning home in 1850 with her Italian husband and their child, all three were drowned in a shipwreck off Long Island.

Fuller's ability to invent herself as a public intellectual in a society that shut women out of most occupations was remarkable. From an early age she knew she "was not born to the common womanly lot" and would need to find her own way in life, "a pilgrim and sojourner on earth."[27] The path she found was a life-long pursuit of self-culture, which for her meant the unfolding of a higher, spiritual nature. Similarly to other Transcendentalists, her practice consisted of reading, contemplation, journal writing, conversation, walks in nature, and periods of solitude. She did not aspire to social success but to an active, thoughtful life, always "seeking to be wise."[28]

Self-culture, as practiced by the Transcendentalists, was the underpinning of social reform as well as individual development. Sermons, lectures, articles, essays, and books were all devoted to the subject. Self-culture was key to Bronson Alcott's educational theories, which he wrote about in the introduction titled "The Doctrine and Discipline of Human Culture" to his book *Record of Conversations on the Gospels*. It was also the title of Clarke's most popular book, which went through twenty-two editions between 1880 and 1897. "We are put here to grow," Clarke wrote, "and we ought to grow, and to use all the means of growth according to the laws of our being."[29]

But not everyone agreed. In a lengthy article about Brook Farm, Orestes Brownson criticized self-culture as a selfish and misguided pursuit. The cultivation of the self is a luxury that many hard-working people cannot afford and does nothing to alleviate society's problems, Brownson said. "Cultivation to any considerable extent is compatible only with leisure and easy circumstances. Instead, then, of enjoining culture as the means of social amelioration, we should effect the amelioration as the condition of the culture."[30] Moreover, social ills are systemic, he argued, requiring collective will to address them, not just cultivation of private virtues. Critics like Brownson identified self-culture with radical individualism, and they viewed the cultivation of the soul as a feckless response to society's most pressing needs. More recent critics have acknowledged that some proponents of self-culture—like Emerson, Thoreau, and Fuller—did in fact engage with political and social issues, but argue that their activism represented a departure from their original Transcendentalist views.[31]

We know now that Emerson, Thoreau, Fuller, and other proponents of self-culture were in fact agents of change. And we can see that self-culture was key not only to their personal growth, but to their political empowerment as well. The pursuit of self-culture accounts for Thoreau's retreat to Walden Pond, as well as the radicalism of his essay on "Civil Disobedience." It accounts for Fuller's construction of herself as an individual, as well as her revolutionary fight for Italian independence. David Robinson explains the relationship between self-culture and social reform as a dialectical one:

> Transcendentalist ideals pointed not only to otherworldly values but also to worldly abuses, and the transcendentalists' lament over such abuses served both to reaffirm those ideals and to enliven the commitment to their realization. A complex dialectic is at work here, but in a sense each of its poles necessitates the other: the ideal demands embodiment while the process of social transformation must have the guidance of an ideal. Fuller, who embodied her ideal in the commitment to self-culture, discovered that self-culture as an end required social reform as a means, that the fulfillment of woman necessitated the concerted action of women.[32]

The Transcendentalists were activists, not in spite of their idealism but because of it. As a critic of Transcendentalism, Brownson may have been able to separate self-culture from social reform, but none of the committed Transcendentalists did or would have wanted to. Clarke wrote in *Self-Culture,* "God has placed us here to grow, just as he placed the trees and flowers. The trees and flowers grow unconsciously, and by no effort of their own. Man, too, grows unconsciously, and is educated by circumstances. But he can also control those circumstances, and direct the course of his life. He can educate himself; he can, by effort and thought, acquire knowledge, become accomplished, refine and purify his nature, develop his powers, strengthen his character. And because he can do this, he ought to do it."[33] This may sound quaint to the modern ear. But the popularity of contemporary books such as *The Road Less Traveled,* by M. Scott Peck; *Care of the Soul,* by Thomas Moore; and *Wherever You Go, There You Are,* by Jon Kabat-Zinn, to name just a few, demonstrates that the cultivation of the soul is as important now as it ever was. As Clarke maintained, our nature is to grow spiritually, as well as physically, intellectually, and morally.

The cultivation of the soul is an ongoing, lifelong process of unfolding development and growth. But we must make a deliberate choice to be active participants in this process. Active learners, those who exercise their powers of self-searching and self-forming, or introspection and agency, are in alignment with God's purpose, which is growth. Clarke put it this way: "To grow higher, deeper, wider, as the years go on; to conquer difficulties, and acquire more and more power; to feel one's faculties unfolding, and truth descending into the soul—this makes life worth living."[34]

Some people are more motivated to cultivate the soul than others. Spiritual discipline, like physical exercise, requires us first to overcome our own inertia. We need to see a practical benefit, which is harder with the spirit than the body. We may fear the change, anxiety, and pain that often accompany spiritual growth. Very often the impetus for spiritual growth requires a catalyst in the form of a crisis, a mid-life passage, or a feeling of ennui or emptiness that just won't go away. With all the stresses and strains of daily life—the demands of work, family obligations, financial worries, the hectic " pace of the world today—we try very hard to stay within a spiritual comfort zone. But we are not here simply to experience pain-free living. Change, like life itself, is difficult. But satisfaction, joy, vitality, and a sense of power can come from meeting life's challenges. Indeed, this is what it means to grow.

Peck has written that "the healthy spiritual life consists of progressively growing out of narcissism."[35] Self-centeredness is a major impediment to the cultivation of the soul. It causes us to confuse the desires of the ego with the needs of the soul. All of the major religions and great wisdom traditions teach that the path away from selfishness and egotism is the path toward greater depth and meaning in life. Peabody coined the term *"egotheism"* for mistaking the ego for the soul. Channing, Emerson, and others in Peabody's circle advised disinterestedness, or detachment, as a guard against worshiping the ego rather than cultivating the soul. "Self-culture is part and parcel with how a human life unfolds," writes philosopher John Lysaker in his book *Emerson and Self-Culture*. "The question is thus not *whether* to pursue self-culture, but how best to do so."[36] How the Transcendentalists did this will be the subject of subsequent chapters.

5

THREE PREREQUISITES OF
THE SPIRITUAL LIFE

The art of life!" Thoreau exclaimed in his journal. "Was there ever anything memorable written upon it? By what disciplines to secure the most life, with what care to watch our thoughts. To observe what transpires, not in the street, but in the mind and heart of me! I do not remember any page which will tell me how to spend this afternoon."[1] In their quest for "the art of life" the Transcendentalists developed a rich and varied spiritual practice. This was predicated, however, on three necessary conditions: nature, leisure, and self-reliance.

NATURE

As we have seen, the Romantics had given a new signification to nature, beautifully expressed in Wordsworth's "Tintern Abbey":

> Therefore am I still
> A lover of the meadows and the woods,
> And mountains; and of all that we behold
> From this green earth; of all the mighty world
> Of eye and ear—both what they half create,
> And what perceive; well pleased to recognize
> In nature and the language of the sense,
> The anchor of my purest thoughts, the nurse,

> The guide, the guardian of my heart, and soul
> Of all my mortal being.[2]

Wordsworth approached Tintern Abbey as "a worshipper of Nature," not God. It is as if the ruins of the abbey represented the ruins of Christianity itself. The revelations of Nature had replaced the revelations of the Bible. Gone, too, was the notion that nature was subservient to humans needs. In the Romantic view, nature was sacred, intrinsically good, and not merely valuable for the commercial uses it could be put to. The Transcendentalists shared this conception of nature because they desired "an original relation to the universe," as Emerson put it, unmediated by centuries of Christian tradition.

As Unitarian ministers, the religious radicals of the Transcendentalist movement had inherited a theological distinction between two types of religion: natural and revealed. Natural religion was based on all that could be known about God, morality, and immortality from observations of the natural world. Observing the appearance of design, for instance, one could presume the existence of God. Observing the abundance of natural resources, one could presume His benevolence. And so on. Revealed religion, on the other hand, was based on what God had directly communicated to the writers of the Christian scriptures. The authority of the Bible was confirmed by the authenticity of Jesus's miracles. For liberal Christians, revealed religion completed natural religion. Natural religion could be pantheistic or polytheistic. In their view, revealed religion corrected such errors.

Because the Transcendentalists believed miracles were a violation of the laws of nature, they did not accept them as evidence of the authority of the scriptures. The Transcendentalists did not deny revelation; rather, they claimed that it was known intuitively, on the basis of Reason and not by empirical evidence. From their studies of the Bible and the history of religions, they concluded that the forms of religion varied in time and place. Ultimately, revealed religion rested on natural religion rather than the other way around. Thus Emerson argued that nature "lends all her pomp and riches to the religious sentiment. Prophet and priest, David, Isaiah, Jesus, have drawn deeply from this source."[3] Nature was the ultimate source of religious revelation, replacing scripture.

The first in-depth expression of this view is Emerson's earliest work, *Nature,* published anonymously in 1836. Among its avid readers was young Henry David Thoreau, then a student at Harvard College. The book is an example of what Thomas Carlyle had termed "natural supernaturalism," the use of scriptural language to convey the sacredness of nature. Indeed, Emerson's rhetoric in *Nature* has a biblical ring to it, which was intended to add weight to his argument. For example, when Emerson asked why we should "grope among the dry bones of the past," he employed an image from Ezekiel's symbolic account of a disheartened nation.

Emerson wanted to distinguish between traditional views of nature and nature perceived afresh, in an unprejudiced way. Properly seen—that is, when our "inward and outward senses are . . . truly adjusted to each other"—the manifold objects of nature awaken in us a sense of reverence and delight, suggesting what Emerson termed an "occult" or hidden relationship between us and the natural world. In moments of rapture we experience "the currents of Universal Being" circulating through us and feel that we are part and parcel of the whole. "In the woods," he wrote, "we return to faith and reason."[4]

Nature ministers to us in a multitude of ways, and Emerson introduced a hierarchy of nature's ministry from its lowest to highest forms. At the most basic level, that of *commodity,* nature provides resources for human needs, from food clothing and shelter to the raw materials for trade and commerce. "A nobler want" than commodity that nature serves, he said, is that of *beauty.* Natural objects "give us a delight *in and for themselves.*" They also restore our spirits through "their eternal calm." We find beauty as well in virtuous action and, higher yet, in the productions of art, according to Emerson.[5]

On the next level, nature provides us with the source of *language.* "Words," he said, "are signs of natural facts"; for instance, "*right* means *straight; wrong* means *twisted.*" Moreover, every aspect of nature has symbolic meaning. "Who looks upon a river in a meditative hour," Emerson asked, "and is not reminded of the flux of all things?" If nature is symbolic it is because there is a "radical correspondence between visible things and human thoughts." By contemplating nature, human beings can read the mind of God. "A life in harmony with Nature," Emerson insisted, "will purge the eyes to understand her text. By degrees we may come to know the primitive sense of the permanent objects of nature, so that the world shall be to us an open book, and every form significant of its hidden life and final cause."[6]

Higher still is *discipline.* Nature educates both the Understanding and the Reason. Dealing with sensible objects—weighing, measuring, comparing, for example—exercises the intellect. Nature educates the Reason by demonstrating that natural laws are also moral laws: "The moral law lies at the centre of nature and radiate to the circumference. It is the pith and marrow of every substance, every relation, and every process. All things with which we deal, preach to us." Because we are infinitely related and part of the unity of nature, nature's laws apply to us as well. "A leaf, a drop, a crystal, a moment of time," Emerson wrote, "is related to the whole, and partakes of the perfection of the whole. Each particle is a microcosm, and faithfully renders the likeness of the world."[7]

Up to this point Emerson has been dealing with the ministry of nature in its material form. Where, he asked, does matter come from? He did not dispute what his senses told him, but neither did he believe that the material world represents the ultimate reality. It is more like "a great shadow pointing always to the sun behind us." We should not think "the world is a divine dream" because to do so would mean that we are not a natural part of it ourselves. We live much of our lives estranged from nature and alienated from God. The intellect cannot resolve this condition. We can only address it "by untaught sallies of the spirit, by a continual self-recovery, and by entire humility."[8]

The cause of this condition is a denial of our kinship with nature. We relate to it on the basis of the Understanding alone, mastering it "by a penny-wisdom." Here and there we have "gleams of a better light." But the problem lies in our lack of perception. "The ruin or blank that we see when we look at nature, is in our own eye," Emerson said. "The axis of vision is not coincident with the axis of things, and so they appear not transparent but opaque. The reason why the world lacks unity, and lies broken and in heaps, is because man is disunited with himself." The marriage of matter and spirit is not celebrated. However, with new eyes we may come to see a unity rather than a dualism. Emerson was convinced that a resolution of this dichotomy would be revolutionary in all areas of life.[9]

Emerson made several important claims in *Nature,* the first being that nature is a unity because every aspect of it "betrays its source in universal Spirit."[10] Human beings know intuitively that they, too, are "part or parcel" of the Universal Spirit, and thus there exists "an occult relation" between themselves and the natural world. Because of this intimate relationship and common origin, nature can be for us both an ethical teacher and a spiritual guide. From the revelations of nature "we learn that the highest" is present to the human soul and pervades all of creation. As plants are nurtured by the spirit, human beings are likewise "nourished by unfailing fountains" and draw "inexhaustible power" from the same source.[11] The ultimate function of nature, then, is to feed the spirit that is in us and liberate its capacities.

The tradition of American nature writing arguably began with the Transcendentalists, and today's deep ecology perspective can be traced to their influence.[12] Others, perhaps, had spoken *about* nature; the Transcendentalists—Emerson and Thoreau especially—spoke *for* nature. Whereas Emerson is often rather abstract in his defense of nature, Thoreau is refreshingly concrete. For both nature was sacred. Both believed that the sanctity of nature was threatened by the encroachment of civilization and material values. The locomotive, for example, that invades Thoreau's sanctuary at Walden Pond, disturbing the contemplative atmosphere and drowning out the sounds of the forest, is a symbol of the commercial spirit. In the "Sounds" chapter of *Walden* Thoreau marveled at the speed and punctuality of the railroad, and how much it has transformed economic and social life. These changes, however, come at the expense of spiritual growth and peace of mind nurtured by contact with the natural world. "So is your pastoral life whirled past and away," Thoreau lamented. "But the bell rings, and I must get off the track and let the cars go by."[13]

Richard Louv writes in his book *The Nature Principle* that people today suffer from "nature-deficit disorder," a diminished sense of physical and spiritual well-being resulting from a lack of connection with the natural world.[14] The woods are much less accessible, the stars harder to see at night, the sounds of birds drowned out by the noise of traffic. As America has become more urbanized and consumer-oriented, experiences of the natural world become fewer and farther between. This sentiment echoes Emerson's wise observation in one of his lectures on "Human Culture": "We build street on street all round the horizon and shut out the sky and the wind; false and costly tastes are generated for wise and cheap ones; thousands are poor and cannot see the face of the world; the senses are impaired, and the susceptibility to beauty; and life made vulgar."[15]

What would Emerson make of the fact that so many people today, walking outside, never look up from their smartphones? The remedy for nature deficit disorder is obvious enough. "What is the pill which will keep us well, serene, contented?" Thoreau asks. "For my panacea, instead of one of those quack vials of a mixture dipped from Acheron and the Dead Sea . . . let me have a draught of undiluted morning air. Morning air! If men will not drink of this at the fountain-head of the day, why, then, we must even bottle up some and sell it in the shops, for the benefit of those who have lost their subscription ticket to morning time in this world."[16]

LEISURE

In the "Sounds" chapter of *Walden,* Thoreau gives us an account of a day spent at his house in the woods:

> There were times when I could not afford to sacrifice the bloom of the present moment to any work, whether of the head or hands. I love a broad margin to my life. Sometimes, in a summer morning, having taken my accustomed bath, I sat in my sunny doorway from sunrise till noon, rapt in a revery, amidst the pines and hickories and sumachs, in undisturbed solitude and stillness, while the birds sang around or flitted noiseless through the house, until by the sun falling in at my west window, or the noise of some traveller's wagon on the distant highway, I was reminded of the lapse of time. I grew in those seasons like corn in the night, and they were far better than any work of the hands would have been. They were not time subtracted from my life, but so much over and above my usual allowance. I realized what the Orientals mean by contemplation and the forsaking of works.[17]

The broad margin he refers to is the amount of space around the text on the page of a book. It is a metaphor for the amount of leisure required for the cultivation of the soul. The more, the better, he believed. This is probably the reason some people consider him a hypocrite and a freeloader, sneaking off from his cabin in the woods to have dinner with the Emerson family.

Too often people then and now find it hard to experience leisure even in the narrowest margins of their existence. Many people live difficult if not desperate lives, but that does not mean leisure is a luxury they can ill afford. The pursuit of leisure is not an elitist activity any more than is going to church on Sunday. The idea of a Sabbath, as the Transcendentalists understood it, is an invitation to leisure. The word "leisure" suffers from several misunderstandings. For some it suggests indolence and slacking off from one's responsibilities. Others misconceive it as referring to hobbies and free-time activities. In both these senses, the notion of leisure has been deformed through increasing commodification and consumerization. Nowadays, to loaf on one's porch is a sign of indolence; to loaf on a beach in the Caribbean is a mark of affluence.

For the Transcendentalists, leisure had little to do with either recreation or mere idleness. From childhood their education was steeped in the Greek and Roman classics. To classical authors, such as Plato, Aristotle, the Epicureans, and the Stoics, leisure was not the same as free time. It was understood that people needed a break from work. Recreation was important because it was restorative. It left one refreshed, relaxed and renewed, ready for another round of the daily grind. Time off in this sense was on a plane with work, two sides of the same coin. But leisure was not an amount of time at all. It was the antithesis of time, since it was not ruled by the clock. It had more to do with the quality of the time one had to one's self, not the quantity of it. According to Aristotle, leisure is freedom from the necessity of being occupied by other things. Work and recreation serve a utilitarian purpose. They are equally important, but they serve more limited ends. Leisure, on the other hand, is a state of being in which activity is done for its own sake or as its own end.

Aristotle considered two activities in particular worthy of the name "leisure" (*skole* in Greek): the arts and contemplation.[18] The arts are enjoyed for their own sake, and they are central to the cultivation of the self. Contemplation is prized above all. In contemplation one looks upon the world from a disinterested point of view, without the aim of manipulating others, making money, or winning fame. Only in this way can we gain wisdom and discover true happiness, both of which come from having a tranquil mind. Only in contemplation are we truly free, since we have no attachment to things. Because of this sense of detachment, contemplation is considered the essence of the good life.

Leisure was important for the Stoics also. This school of philosophy had its roots in Greece but flourished in the early years of the Roman Empire with the teachings of Epictetus, Seneca, and Emperor Marcus Aurelius. Seneca was a noted lawyer and playwright as well as a philosopher. We should take care of the mind, he said, and "from time to time give it the leisure that serves as its sustenance and strength." He advised outdoor walks to refresh and raise our spirits as we breathe the open air. He took nature as his guide, believing that a life in accordance with nature was best for the well-being of the soul. To Aristotle's list of leisure pursuits Seneca added stimulating conversation, occasional changes of scenery, and generous amounts of wine.[19] For both Seneca and Aristotle, contemplation is how we find the detachment and peace of mind necessary for directing our lives.

As the ideal of leisure developed in Greece and Rome, it came to include the liberal arts as well as the fine arts, the pursuits associated with culture and the cultivation of the mind. Religion was also considered a leisure activity, as it provided opportunities for contemplation and self-reflection. All of these activities were pursued for no other purpose than achieving wisdom and happiness, and one's own vision of the good life.

The classical ideal of leisure persisted throughout the Middle Ages, the Renaissance, and the Enlightenment. Our nation's founders and the Transcendentalists also sang its praises. But the rise of the Protestant work ethic, followed by the Industrial Revolution in the nineteenth century, put an end to leisure as an essential cultural value. Work in the mines and mills was tedious and unrelenting. Nowadays, Americans pride themselves on their industriousness and take little time for leisure. In our current economy many can support themselves only by taking on two or more jobs. Any free time that people have is more likely used for recreation or passive entertainment than leisure in the classical sense of the term.

Thoreau's admonition in *Walden* seems still, after more than 150 years, to speak directly to us today:

> Most people, even in this comparatively free country, through mere ignorance and mistake, are so occupied with the factitious cares and superfluously course labors of life that its finer fruits cannot be plucked by them. Actually, working people have not leisure for a true integrity day by day. They have no time to be anything but a machine. The finest qualities of our nature, like the bloom on fruits, can be preserved only by the most delicate handling. Yet we do not treat ourselves nor one another thus tenderly.[20]

Thoreau urged even those who had families to care for and thus "no time to be anything but a machine," to nevertheless continue to seek out leisure. Speaking to an audience of manual laborers in 1838, William Ellery Channing asked, rhetorically, "How can the laboring classes find time for self-culture?" His answer was, "an earnest purpose finds time or makes time. It seizes on spare moments, and turns larger fragments of leisure to golden account."[21] He advised reading, walking in the out-of-doors, and attending worship services and lectures.

American society today is more consumer-oriented and materialistic than ever. But standard of living and quality of life are not the same. We are physically and mentally overworked and spiritually undernourished.

Taking Thoreau's view, we can see that our technological innovations—the ubiquitous smartphones and ever more portable computers—are nothing more than improved means to as yet unimproved ends. We sense a lack of intimacy and depth in our relationships. Because we confuse stimulation with fulfillment, nothing ever quite measures up to our expectations. We need Thoreau's broad margin of leisure now more than ever:

> Keep the time, observe the hours of the universe, not of the [railroad]. What are threescore years and ten hurriedly and coarsely lived to moments of divine leisure in which your life is coincident with the life of the universe? We live too fast and coarsely, just as we eat too fast, and do not know the true savor of our food. . . . That aim in life is highest which requires the highest and finest discipline. How much, what infinite, leisure it requires, as of a lifetime, to appreciate a single phenomenon![22]

A life that is lived "too fast and coarsely" cannot take its own measure. It cannot hear the voice within. That's what leisure is for. Instead of saving time, we consume it, both in work and in play. To be sure, there are legitimate demands on our time, and yet the sheer busyness of our lives reflects a measure of self-avoidance. Creative work, meaningful relationships, and peace of mind can be accomplished only with a broad margin of leisure. Only in leisure can we consider life's possibilities from a higher vantage point.

SELF-RELIANCE

"Self-reliance" is another term that is frequently misunderstood. Emerson's essay of that title is easily his most popular, and the doctrine of self-reliance was central to his teaching from his earliest sermons to his last lectures. The term has often been confused with individualism, but that's not what Emerson meant by self-reliance. Nor does it mean independence or self-sufficiency. The worst mistake of all would be to equate it with narcissism, which many of his detractors continue to do.[23]

The self that Emerson refers to is not the ego or isolated self of modern philosophy. Emerson was well aware of the perils of individualism resulting from a distorted understanding of the true nature of the self. What he meant by the self is the Soul, which, though individually incarnated in each person, is commonly shared by all human beings. Thus, self-reliance is not reliance on the self in *isolation,* but the self in *relation* to that larger Self which "makes us receivers of its truth and organs of its activity."[24] Because all selves are equally related to this larger Self, each person possesses inherent human rights.

Emerson and the Transcendentalists put great store in genius. But the word "genius" also meant something different for them than it usually does for us. For us genius connotes great intelligence or talent; for the Transcendentalists it had one or another of two meanings. A person who had genius was receptive to the influx of the Divine or Universal Mind. In the second sense of the term, taken from the Greeks, genius was a *daemon*, or spirit guide, unique to each human being, offering wise advice. Emerson and Thoreau often urged readers to heed their own genius.

Emerson used "genius" in the first sense of the term when he declared, "To believe your own thought, to believe that what is true for you is true for all men,—that is genius." Paradoxically, the thoughts that are most unique to us are also the most universal, since they represent the Universal Mind speaking through us. Moses, Plato, and Milton are considered geniuses because they said what they were inspired to say, not what others thought. And so should we. "Imitation is suicide," Emerson wrote in "Self-Reliance." We must till the soil that is given to us alone. "The power which resides" in each of us "is new in nature," and no one but us knows what we can do until we have tried. The failure to assert ourselves renders us impotent. Our genius, or guardian spirit, deserts us and leaves us without hope. "Trust thyself: every heart vibrates to that iron string," he declared.[25]

In their innocence, children are naturally self-reliant. As we grow up, however, there is increasing pressure to conform. The inner voice that guides us grows faint as we enter the world. "Society everywhere is in conspiracy against the manhood of every one of its members," Emerson announced. "The virtue in most request is conformity. Self-reliance is its aversion." To preserve our individuality, we must refuse to conform. The problem with conformity, in his view, is that "it scatters your force." One then becomes a cipher rather than an individual. If we conform we are predictable, false and partial persons. Still, the pressures to conform are great, and if we fail to do so, "the world whips you with its displeasure." The desire for consistency also undermines our self-trust. We should not be afraid to question past judgments, even if it would seem that we contradict ourselves. So what? Emerson would ask. "A foolish consistency is the hobgoblin of little minds, adored by little statesmen and philosophers and divines."[26]

If we are true to ourselves then our integrity or authenticity as a person will be apparent. In the end "we pass for what we are," Emerson wrote. Actions that are honest and natural will also be harmonious. Each one reveals who we are in a way that conformity and consistency alone can never do. Great people are those who have the courage to be themselves, no matter what. We, too, must be our own persons, and not mendicants or sycophants. Self-reliance is reliance on Spontaneity or Instinct. Intuition of the Universal Mind is the prerequisite of what is true for each of us, Emerson insisted. Behind this we cannot go. There is a unity that we discern intuitively "in calm hours," a sense of oneness that includes us and proceeds from the same source that we do.[27] This source is what Emerson called the Over-soul, the fountain of all action and thought.

Thus, for Emerson, self-reliance is not deference to the ego, but trust in the Over-soul, "the ever-blessed ONE." Because the individual soul is a reflection of the One, it may be trusted. "God," Emerson wrote, "is within." Instead of putting ourselves "in communication with the internal ocean," however, we go "abroad to beg a cup of water of the urns of other men." We must go alone, éven if it means a break from our accustomed ways. If we do not follow what is dictated by our own nature, we risk being hypocrites. Some may say that rejecting popular standards means breaking with all standards, and that "the bold sensualist will use the name of philosophy to gild his crimes." Being true to our nature is not the easy way out. As Emerson put it, "If any one imagines that this law is lax, let him keep its commandment one day."[28]

The present state of society suggests that people are afraid to assert themselves, Emerson observed. Society needs self-reliant persons, but most people "cannot satisfy their own wants," he said. So many decisions are made *for* us, not *by* us. A greater self-reliance would revolutionize our thinking, our relationships, and our modes of living. "Insist on yourself," Emerson admonished his readers, "never imitate. Your own gift you can present every moment with the cumulative force of a whole life's cultivation; but of the adopted talent of another you have only an extemporaneous half-possession." Society advances only when people learn to be self-reliant and to measure the worth of each other by what each is, not what each has. Our fortunes may rise or fall. Things may for a time seem to go our way. However, Emerson warned, "Nothing can give you peace but yourself. Nothing can bring you peace but the triumph of principles."[29]

There is much to admire in Emerson's gospel of self-reliance, and a few concerns to consider. One has to do with the nature of authority. Several of his critics claim that self-reliance gives us license to do as we please. This is the charge of antinomianism, the view that divine inspiration is difficult to distinguish from selfish impulse. In reply, Emerson stressed the importance of discerning the difference between the soul and the ego, and deferring to the "public" or impersonal self rather than the "private" or personal self. As he expressed it in another of his essays, "the Soul's emphasis is always right," but "the individual is always mistaken."[30]

Some charged that Emerson was insensitive to the plight of the poor and the efforts of social reformers. Indeed, his comments on this topic are harsh and grating to the contemporary ear. He believed that reform needed to begin with each person, and that associations, even benevolent ones, should not dictate the actions of individuals. However, as he became more involved in cause of abolition, largely at the prompting of the women of the Concord Female Anti-Slavery Society, he came to realize that, while reform must always begin with the individual, it couldn't end there.[31] Self-reliance doesn't mean that one should remain aloof from politics or the need for change. In fact, it is because we all have something of the divine within us, Emerson argued, that slavery is "the unpardonable outrage that it is." Unfortunately, the myth of Emerson's apolitical individualism has persisted.

I believe the reason why the essay "Self-Reliance" resonates with so many people is that it addresses a loss of selfhood, which Parker Palmer describes in his book *Let Your Life Speak:*

> We arrive in this world with birthright gifts—then we spend the first half of our lives abandoning them or letting others disabuse us of them. As young people, we are surrounded by expectations that may have little to do with who we really are, expectations held by people who are not try-ing to discern our selfhood but to fit us into slots. In families, schools, workplaces, and religious communities, we are trained away from true self toward images of acceptability; under social pressures like racism and sex-ism our original shape is deformed beyond recognition; and we ourselves, driven by fear, too often betray true self to gain the approval of others.
>
> We are disabused of original giftedness in the first half of our lives. Then—if we are awake, aware, and able to admit our loss—we spend the second half of life trying to recover and reclaim the gift we once possessed.[32]

More than anything else, "self-reliance" is about finding our true self and living a life of wholeness and authenticity. Similarly, the contemporary spiritual writer Thomas Moore observes, "Far beneath the many thick layers of indoctrination about who we are and who we should be lies an original self, a person who came into the world full of possibility and destined for joyful unveiling and manifestation. . . . Chronically trying to be someone other than this original self, persuaded that we are not adequate and should fit some norm of health or correctness, we may find a cool distance separating us from that deep and eternal person, that God-given personality, and we may forget both who we were and who we might be."[33]

This is precisely the dilemma faced by the young Margaret Fuller as she struggled to find her voice and place in a society that marginalized women. In the mystic vision described in a previous chapter, she saw herself on a stairway, wondering who she was and what she might do with her life. Afraid of displeasing her father and "wearied out with mental conflicts," she felt suffocated by the pressures from her church and its minister to conform. She thought about all the times she had felt this way and how long it must take "before the soul can learn to act under [the] limitations" that were placed on her. This vision was a breakthrough moment for her. "The statue has been emerging, though slowly, from the block," she wrote. "Others may not see the promise even of its pure symmetry; but I do, and am learning to be patient. I shall be all human yet."[34] Fuller was certainly not alone in feeling that her original self was buried beneath layers of indoctrination and pressures to conform. The women who attended her Boston Conversations were likewise individuals of intelligence and talent, frustrated by a society that constrained them.

These women—and many others then and since—were determined to follow their genius, as Emerson had advised. Thoreau put it even more emphatically: "If one listens to the faintest but constant suggestions of his genius, which are certainly true, he sees not to what extremes, or even insanity, it may lead him; and yet that way, as he grows more resolute and faithful, his road lies. The faintest assured objection which one healthy man feels will at length prevail over the arguments and customs of mankind."[35] People are never misled by their genius. Only by hearing and heeding that voice deep within one's self can we become the person we really are and were meant to be.

6

SOLITUDE, CONTEMPLATION, SAUNTERING, AND SIMPLE LIVING

The Transcendentalists developed an array of spiritual practices they found helpful in their goals of transforming self and society. Not everyone in the Transcendentalist circle engaged in all these practices, nor with the same enthusiasm or regularity. In some cases, they did not think of them as a spiritual regimen at all, even as they were recommending practices such as walking and simple living, as Emerson and Thoreau did in lectures and various writings. Some of them came to them naturally, simply by paying attention to what fed their own spirits. Some they developed from their knowledge of classical philosophy and Eastern religion. Their practices still speak to the question of how to live well today.

The Transcendentalists received a classical education, unlike most students today. Beginning at an early age, they learned Latin and Greek and read classical literature. They were familiar with the philosophic schools on which Catholicism had based its own mysticism, spirituality, and contemplation. As they distanced themselves more and more from traditional Christianity, they gravitated toward classical views. Philosophy scholar

Arnold Davidson describes spiritual exercises in various schools of Greek and Roman philosophy this way:

> Rather than aiming at the acquisition of a purely abstract knowledge, these exercises aimed at realizing a transformation of one's vision of the world and a metamorphosis of one's personality. The philosopher needed to be trained not only to know how to speak and debate, but also how to live. The exercise of philosophy "was therefore not only intellectual, but could also be spiritual." . . . Its goal was nothing less than an art of philosophical life. Spiritual exercises were exercises because they were practical, required effort and training, and were lived; they were spiritual because they involved the entire spirit, one's whole way of being. The art of living demanded by philosophy was a lived exercise exhibited in every aspect of one's existence.[1]

As the Transcendentalists practiced and promoted their own version of the art of living, they looked to examples in the classical traditions—the Stoics, the Epicureans, and Neoplatonists in particular. As they learned about religions and wisdom traditions from other parts of the world, India and China especially, they drew on models from these as well.

In the next chapters, we will examine a number of Transcendentalist spiritual practices—some of them with classical antecedents, others developed by the Transcendentalists themselves. Human beings, after all, have been pondering and pursuing the art of living for millennia. Transcendentalist spirituality is one expression of this universal human desire for spiritual growth and the cultivation of the soul.

SOLITUDE

Anyone who has heard of Henry David Thoreau is likely to know that he lived for a little over two years at Walden Pond. His withdrawal to Walden Pond is one of the iconic acts of American cultural history. Even today, an estimated 700,000 visitors from the United States and other countries make pilgrimages to the pond and the site of Thoreau's cabin. But his deed also has invited puzzlement, misunderstanding, and even derision. Teenagers I have taught over the years often can't imagine why anyone would want to do such a thing. Young people are typically so deeply enmeshed in their peer relationships and social networks, and so consumer-oriented, that Thoreau's retreat seems to them like exile or death. Adults sometimes think he was an asocial recluse who shirked his obligations to society.[2]

Thoreau's decision to go to Walden in 1845 did not come as a surprise to those who knew him. He had long been considering such a move. In April 1841 he wrote in his journal, "I will build my lodge on the southern slope of some hill, and take there the life the gods send me."[3] Later that year he noted in his journal, "I want to go soon and live away by the pond, where I will hear only the wind whispering among the reeds. It will be success if I have left myself behind. But my friends ask what I will do when I get there. Will it not be employment enough to watch the progress of the seasons?"[4] Some years previously, perhaps in 1837, he had lived for six weeks with a college roommate in a shanty on the shore of nearby Flint's Pond.

For several years, while he was considering the possibility of a retreat, Thoreau found various means of employment. He lived with the Emersons as a handyman for two years. Then for six months, as we learned earlier, he tutored the children of Waldo's brother, William Emerson, on Staten Island. Returning to Concord, Thoreau assisted his father in his thriving pencil business and in building a new home for the Thoreau family. By that time, though, Thoreau was tired of working for others and was determined to live for himself instead. Emerson had recently purchased a woodlot on Walden Pond in 1844 and invited Thoreau to build his cabin there. With the help of friends, he constructed a 10-by-15 foot house on the south-facing shore, cutting a few pine trees for corner posts and using recycled building materials for siding. He moved in on July 4, 1845. Although he said the date was coincidental, it marked the beginning of his period of greatest independence.

What Thoreau did was not so unusual at the time. During the 1830s and 1840s writers had promoted the idea of a literary hermitage in the woods or by the shore of a lake.[5] At one time Emerson planned to build one for himself on the far side of Walden Pond. A close friend, Ellery Channing, had previously lived for some months in a small cabin in the Illinois country-side. The rustic retreat in nature had, in fact, a long history, going back to the Roman philosophers, including Cicero and Seneca. The fourteenth-century poet Petrarch advocated the same in his *Life of Solitude*. Swiss philosopher Johann Georg Zimmermann's *Solitude*, published at the turn of the nineteenth century, was one of the few books Thoreau owned. It was full of examples of solitary retreats from classical and humanist literature. Thoreau is certain to have noticed the following passage:

Thus rural retirement dries up those streams of discontent which flow so plentifully through public life; changes most frequently the bitterest feelings into the sweetest pleasures; and inspires an ecstasy and content unknown to the votaries of the world. . . .

The Solitude which is necessary to produce this advantage cannot in towns be conveniently practiced. It seems, indeed, no very difficult task for a man to retire into his chamber, and, by silent contemplation, to raise his mind above the mean consideration of sensual objects; but few men have sufficient resolution to perform it; for, within doors, matters of business every moment occur, and interrupt the chain of reflection; and without, whether alone or in company, a variety of accidents may occasionally happen, which will confound our vain wisdom, aggravate the painful feelings of the heart, and weaken the finer powers of the mind.[6]

Thoreau had many reasons for seeking solitude at Walden Pond. He wished to complete a book he was writing and he wanted to withdraw from the "restless, nervous, bustling, trivial Nineteenth Century." He found solace and sanity in the tranquility of nature. The contrast between the tone of the chapters "Economy" and "Solitude" is extraordinary. The first chapter is didactic, truculent even, in its critique of Americans' habitual modes of living. "The mass of men lead lives of quiet desperation," he insisted. "What is called resignation is confirmed desperation." By the fifth chapter, however, his mood has completely changed. It is soothing and sensual:

This is a delicious evening, when the whole body is one sense, and imbibes delight through every pore. I go and come with a strange liberty in Nature, a part of herself. As I walk along the stony shore of the pond in my shirt-sleeves, though it is cool as well as cloudy and windy, and I see nothing special to attract me, all the elements are unusually congenial to me. The bullfrogs trump to usher in the night, and the note of the whippoorwill is borne on the rippling wind from over the water. Sympathy with the fluttering alder and poplar leaves almost takes away my breath; yet, like the lake, my serenity is rippled but not ruffled. These small waves raised by the evening wind are as remote from storm as the smooth reflecting surface.

Here, a mile from any neighbor, he had, as he put it, "my own sun and moon and stars, and a little world all to myself."[7]

This attunement with nature sets Thoreau's restless spirit at ease. "There can be no very black melancholy to him who lives in the midst of nature and has his senses still." Only once, he said, and for just an hour, did he feel lonely. Otherwise, even during inclement weather, he felt serene and at home. "Why should I feel lonely?" he asks; "is not our home in the Milky Way?" Such serenity cannot be found in the thick of society—not in "the bar-room, the meeting-house, the school-house, the grocery, Beacon Hill [center of Boston society], or the Five Points [a disreputable section of New York City], where men most congregate"—but only in the solitude of nature. There we encounter a divine presence, a spiritual reality common to all religions, and conditions favorable to "awakening or coming to life."[8] Immersed in nature, we can detach from the affairs of daily life and put emotional distance between ourselves and others. And we can identify with the earth and its processes.

As much as he valued solitude and enjoyed the respite from village life that his sojourn at Walden Pond afforded, Thoreau was not a hermit by any means. He often walked to town to socialize with friends and neighbors. He took dinners with his family and the Emersons. He did odd jobs and offered help to those who needed it. He went to Maine for a couple of weeks and spent a memorable night in the city jail for refusing to pay his taxes. And he reported that he had more visitors at Walden than he'd ever had before. Modern writers have often disparaged Thoreau as a hypocrite for espousing solitude while "sneaking" into town for his mother's cookies. But Thoreau never claimed that the solitude and quiet he sought at Walden required complete isolation.[9]

He understood that solitude and society should alternate in any well-balanced life. He would have agreed with Zimmermann who exhorted his "readers to listen to the advantages of *occasional retirement*," but warned them "against that dangerous excess into which some of the disciples of this philosophy" had fallen.[10] "Society is the school of Wisdom, and Solitude the temple of Virtue," Zimmermann wrote. "In the one we learn the art of living with comfort among our fellow creatures; and, in the other, of living with quietude by ourselves." Too often we are caught up in the affairs of the world, "*the perpetual drunkenness of life*," as he put it. Those who "mingle rational Retreat with worldly Affairs" will not be "whirled round, and rendered giddy, by the agitations of the world," but from that "sacred Retirement" will return calm and collected.[11]

Thoreau found solitude at Walden; others found it elsewhere. For example, while Emerson enjoyed his walks to Walden Pond as much as Thoreau did, he found solitude primarily in his study. Rising early, he broke his fast

with a slice of pie and two cups of coffee and then retired to his library
to contemplate, to write, and to make entries in his journal, undisturbed
until lunchtime. For Emerson, it was not the solitude of place, like Thoreau's cabin in the woods, but the solitude of soul that mattered. Solitude
was a vital part of every person's education, Emerson noted in his journal,
"because it gives a breathing space, a leisure, out of the influence of dazzling
delusions, the pomp, and vanity of the wicked world," and sends the soul
back on itself.[12] In a later journal entry Emerson echoed Zimmermann's
thoughts on balancing solitude with society:

> Solitude is naught and society is naught. Alternate them and the good
> of each is seen. You can soon learn all that society can teach you for one
> while. . . . Then retire and hide; and from the valley behold the moun-
> tain. Have solitary prayer and praise. Love the garden, the barn, the
> pasture, and the rock. There digest and correct the past experience, blend
> it with the new and divine life, and grow with God. After some interval
> when these delights have been sucked dry, accept again the opportunities
> of society. The same scenes revisited shall wear a new face, shall yield a
> higher culture. And so on. Undulation, Alternation, is the condition of
> progress, of life.[13]

Seekers of solitude always have to contend with critics who charge them
with being selfish, irresponsible, or hypocritical. Anne Morrow Lindbergh
offers this observation in her book *Gift from the Sea:*

> If one sets aside time for a business engagement, a trip to the hairdresser,
> a social engagement, or a shopping expedition, that time is accepted as
> inviolable. But if one says: I cannot come because that is my hour to be
> alone, one is considered rude, egotistical or strange. What a commentary
> on our civilization, when being alone is considered suspect; when one
> has to apologize for it, make excuses, hide the fact that one practices it—
> like a secret vice![14]

This is why Thoreau has been so misunderstood, both by his neighbors and
by modern critics. Society considers solitude suspect, a reproach as well as
a waste of time. The biggest obstacle to an appreciation of solitude is the
emphasis placed on attachment; that is, on intimate relationships and the
sense of belonging to a community. According to Ester Schaler Buchholz in
The Call of Solitude, "Both needs—to be alone and to engage—are essential
to human happiness and survival, with equally provocative claims. Without
solitude existing as a safe place, a place for long sojourns and self-discovery,

we lose the important sense of being self-regulating individuals."[15] One of the paradoxes of the human condition, recognized in all philosophies and religions, is that one must be connected to the world and to other people, but must also seek spiritual growth through solitude and contemplation.

If it is difficult for society to accept individuals' need for solitude, it is also hard for us as individuals to be still or alone for any length of time. We are not accustomed to it. We would rather check our e-mail or read Facebook posts. Thoreau recognized the same compulsion in "Life without Principle": "In proportion as our life fails, we go more constantly and des- perately to the post-office. You may depend on it, that the poor fellow who walks away with the greatest number of letters, proud of his extensive corre- spondence, has not heard from himself for quite a while."[16] The prospect of solitude makes us uncomfortable, afraid perhaps that we might be lonely, or worse yet, discover something about ourselves that we would prefer to ignore. Yet how important solitude is amidst "the perpetual drunkenness of life." As William Wordsworth wrote in his masterpiece *The Prelude:*

> When from our better selves we have too long
> Been parted by the hurrying world, and, droop,
> Sick of its business, of its pleasures tired,
> How gracious, how benign, is Solitude.[17]

Solitude enriches the soul. It is essential to mental health, creativity, self- discovery, and spiritual growth. "I have often said that all the misfortunes of men spring from their not knowing how to live quietly at home, in their own rooms," the seventeenth-century philosopher Blaise Pascal wrote.[18] We may be very productive, but without solitude and the introspection it invites, it is unlikely that we will be reunited with "our better selves."

Whether in a study, an attic garret, or a cabin in the woods, solitude was an essential component of the Transcendentalists' spiritual practice. Most of them were authors and ministers and needed solitude for reading, reflecting, and writing. But the importance of solitude went beyond practical, voca- tional considerations. It is a human need and a universal value. One cannot become an individuated, self-reliant person in Emerson's sense of the term without it. Zimmermann wrote that solitude did not imply a total retreat from the world. But it is vital to spiritual growth. As Thoreau noted in his journal: "You think that I am impoverishing myself by withdrawing from men, but in my solitude I have woven for myself a silken web or chrysalis, and, nymph-like, shall ere long burst forth in a more perfect creature, fitted for a higher society."[19]

CONTEMPLATION

Contemplation was another important spiritual practice for the Transcendentalists, though it was a less formal discipline than concentration or meditation, similar practices often associated with the cultivation of the soul. While the word "contemplation" appears in a number of places in the Transcendentalists' writings, the topic is not treated as extensively as solitude, for example. Nevertheless, there are several things we can observe regarding their use of the word. As was the case with mysticism and spirituality, their understanding of contemplation differed from the traditional meaning of the term. In the Christian tradition it had come to mean a beholding or awareness of God, and was considered a form of mental prayer. The Transcendentalists thought of it in a more classical sense, as a kind of intuitive perception of truth or reality. It is seeing with "the mind's eye" (or *nous,* as the Greeks called it), as opposed to knowledge gained from the physical senses. Today we might call it a form of mindfulness.

In an early lecture series, Emerson prescribed contemplation as one of the disciplines of self-culture:

> The simple habit of sitting alone occasionally to explore what facts of moment lie in the memory may have the effect in some more favored hour to open to the student the kingdom of spiritual nature. He may become aware that all around him roll new at this moment and inexhaustible the waters of Life; that the world he has lived in so heedless, so gross, is illuminated with meaning, that every fact is magical; every atom alive, and he is the heir of it all.[20]

Emerson believed that we live on different planes or platforms. There is an external life that we learn in school, the workplace, and everyday life. We are taught to be useful and agreeable and to develop our talents. Contemplation acquaints us with the inner life, which is not practical and pragmatic, but is insightful, holistic, and wise. Contemplation corrects our tendency to allow the presumed facts of the external world determine how we perceive reality. It is the attempt to go beneath the clutter of the mind and of everyday life in search of "the waters of Life."

Thoreau often described contemplation as reverie or musing, shown in this passage from *A Week on the Concord and Merrimack Rivers:*

> We occasionally rested in the shade of a maple or a willow, and drew forth a melon for our refreshment, while we contemplated at our leisure the lapse of the river and of human life; and as that current, with its floating twigs and leaves, so did all things pass in review before us, while far away in cities and marts on this very stream, the old routine was proceeding still. There is, indeed, a tide in the affairs of men, as the poet says, and yet as things flow they circulate, and the ebb always balances the flow. All streams are but tributary to the ocean, which itself does not stream, and the shores are unchanged, but in longer periods than man can measure.[21]

Notice how the imagery of the river flowing to the ocean becomes symbolic of the infinite and the eternal. As we find so often in Thoreau's writing, particular sights and sounds, contemplated in leisure, trigger a cosmic consciousness beyond time and place.

"Sauntering" was one of Thoreau's favorite words, and he uses it not only in reference to walking but also to one's faculties. "I must let my senses wander as my thoughts, my eyes see without looking," he wrote. "What I need is not to look at all, but a true sauntering of the eye."[22] We must learn to see not just with our eyes, that is, not just with our senses, but with "the eye of the mind" as well. Indeed, for Thoreau contemplation could be defined as a sauntering of the mind, akin to Wordsworth's notion of "wise passiveness."[23] As shown in the passage on leisure from the "Sounds" chapter of *Walden,* quoted in the last chapter, contemplation is best described as mindfulness, a relaxed awareness of the sounds of birds singing or flitting through the house, the sight of hawks circling overhead and fish jumping in the pond. It is a timeless mood for Thoreau, broken only by the intrusion of the locomotive and the commerce of daily life.

Emerson's use of the term is somewhat different from Thoreau's. Although Emerson enjoyed nature and the out-of-doors, he did not seek out reverie in nature the way Thoreau did. His was the contemplation of the study rather than the forest retreat. For Emerson, it was an act of the mind associated with Reason rather than Understanding. It is by means of contemplation that inchoate perceptions lying in the unconscious are rendered into meaningful concepts. He described this process in his "American Scholar" address. A new event occurs, Emerson observed, and "remains for a time immersed in our unconscious life. In some contemplative hour it detaches itself from the life like a ripe fruit, to become a thought of the mind. Instantly it is raised, transfigured; the corruptible has put on incorruption. Henceforth it is an object of beauty, however base its origin and neighborhood."[24]

Twentieth-century Trappist monk Thomas Merton distinguishes between two types of contemplation, passive and active. Both are essentially intuitive processes, yet the first involves receiving impressions from without through a "sauntering of the mind," while the second involves mentally engaging with impressions that lie in the unconscious and bringing them into consciousness. In Merton's view each requires some element of the other. "Active contemplation depends on ascesis of abandonment," Merton wrote, "a systematic relaxation of the tensions of the exterior self and a renunciation of its tyrannical claims and demands."[25] Passive contemplation is not wholly passive but requires what Thoreau calls a "prepared mind," on the alert for the promptings of the spirit.[26] Thoreau's is the more passive form of contemplation, Emerson's the more active, but they represent two routes to the same goal.

Unlike practitioners of Buddhism and other Eastern religions, the Transcendentalists did not seek to achieve release or enlightenment through contemplation. They didn't set aside a special time or do it in a specific way. The contemporary mindfulness teacher Jon Kabat-Zinn defines meditation as "the process by which we go about deepening our attention and awareness, refining them, and putting them to greater practical use in our lives."[27] This is certainly the spirit in which the Transcendentalists practiced contemplation.

Contemplation is a vital discipline of the spiritual life. It is practiced in some form in every religious tradition. It is the effort to bring greater awareness to all aspects of life. Yet contemplation is not just a pathway to serenity; it is also a springboard to social action. Through contemplation we are able to rise above "the servitude to wealth and a pursuit of mean pleasures" and perceive moral truth, Emerson asserted.[28] Because contemplation is an act of the Reason, it is a revelation of higher laws, such as justice and freedom, which should govern human behavior. Contemporary writer and educator Parker Palmer, in his book *The Active Life,* makes the relationship between contemplation and action even more clear. He understands *"contemplation to be any way that we can unveil the illusions that masquerade as reality and reveal the reality behind the masks"* [author's emphasis]. The illusions he refers to are those intended to keep things as they are: that violence solves problems; the poor have earned their fate; young people who die in wars to defend corporate interests are heroes rather than victims, and so on. "This is why the contemplative moment, the moment when illusion is stripped away and reality is revealed, is so hard to come by; there is a vast conspiracy against it." Far from being a luxury or a form of escapism, contemplation is a way of changing consciousness, and it has more impact than action divorced from contemplation. "The only thing we have to bring to community is ourselves," Palmer writes, "so the contemplative process of recovering our true selves in solitude is never selfish. It is ultimately the best gift that we can give to others."[29]

SAUNTERING

The Transcendentalists were devoted walkers, and they elevated the activity to a spiritual practice. There was ample precedent for this. French philosopher Jean-Jacques Rousseau in the eighteenth-century was the first of the "peripatetic philosophers," to use a term Bronson Alcott applied to Thoreau.[30] A deeply troubled man, Rousseau found that only his solitary walks gave him happiness and peace of mind, as recounted in his book *Reveries of the Solitary Walker.* "These hours of solitude and meditation are the only ones in the day when I am completely myself and my own master," he wrote; "the only ones when I can truly say that I am what nature meant me to be."[31] A nearer precursor to the Transcendentalists was William Wordsworth, whose devotion to the art of walking was legendary. He walked nearly every day of his long life, logging an estimated 175,000 miles.[32] His walks inspired his poetry; if he could not walk, he could not write.

The Romantics, including Wordsworth, worshiped nature, and walking brought them into intimate contact with it. Walking in the natural landscape as a contemplative, spiritual, or aesthetic experience was relatively unknown in the West before the late eighteenth century. Until then, walking was a form of transportation, not an experience in itself. Thoreau is the Transcendentalist who most exemplifies a walker in the Romantic sense. His essay "Walking" is a classic expression of the activity as a spiritual practice. He prefers the word "sauntering," derived, he believes, either from the French phrases *á la Sainte Terre* (to the Holy Land) or *sans terre* (without a land or home). The etymologies of these terms invest the relatively simple act of walking with spiritual capital. "I think that I cannot preserve my health and spirits, unless I spend four hours a day at least," Thoreau writes, "sauntering through the woods and over the hills and fields, absolutely free from all worldly engagements."[33]

Thoreau preferred the word "sauntering" to "walking" to distinguish between walking as transportation or exercise and walking as a form of contemplation. Sauntering is walking mindfully, with awareness, linking sights and sounds to higher thoughts. One "must walk like a camel," he said, "the only beast which ruminates when walking." Those who are confined to their houses or walk only in gardens or malls cannot develop the spiritual richness that Thoreau believed exposure to wild nature fosters. To saunter one must leave the village and mental preoccupations behind. "What business do I have in the woods," he asked, "if I am thinking of something out of the woods?"[34] The intrusion of civilization on nature—cutting down forests to make room for houses—deforms the landscape, making life tamer and cheaper.

He walked in every season of the year, and in all types of weather, preferably in the afternoon. He especially liked moonlight strolls, enjoying the altered perspective the nighttime afforded. In summer he often went for "fluvial" walks, wearing only a hat and wading, chin deep, in rivers and streams. He used the word "sauntering" to describe his daily walks near Concord. He called his longer walks to distant locations "excursions." He usually walked alone, but he had several walking companions, especially for the longer hikes. He jotted down his observations of nature, including daily temperatures and dates when flowers bloomed and birds returned from their migrations. These notes, along with the ruminations stimulated by his walk, filled the pages of his journal. The amount of his writing each day was roughly equivalent to the length of his walks; the farther he walked the more he wrote. His walks, he said, were "the adventure of the day."[35] Even on a cold and bleak winter day he still extolled the spiritual qualities of walking:

> There is nothing so sanative, so poetic, as a walk in the woods and fields even now, when I meet none abroad for pleasure. Nothing so inspires me and excites such serene and profitable thought. The objects are elevating. In the street and in society I am almost invariably cheap and dissipated, my life is unspeakably mean. No amount of gold or respectability would in the least redeem it. . . . But alone in distant woods or fields, in unpretending sprout-lands or pastures tracked by rabbits, even in a bleak and, to most, cheerless day, like this, when a villager would be thinking of his

inn, I come to myself. I once more feel myself grandly related, and that cold and solitude are friends of mine. I suppose that this value, in my case, is equivalent to what others get by churchgoing and prayer. I come to my solitary woodland walk as the homesick go home.[36]

If Thoreau was "born into the family of the Walkers," then Emerson was certainly a brother Walker.[37] In an early journal entry Emerson noted that he had a "strong propensity for strolling," deliberately shutting up his books on a July afternoon to "slink away" unobserved, picking blueberries in the woods. "I seldom enjoy hours as I do these. I remember them in winter; I expect them in spring."[38] Like Wordsworth—and Thoreau, too, for that matter—Emerson alternated the reading of books with walking in nature. In his own essay on walking, "Country Life," Emerson observed that few people know how to take a walk:

> It is a fine art, requiring rare gifts and much experience. No man is sud-
> denly a good walker. Many men begin with good resolution, but they
> do not hold out, and I have sometimes thought that it would be well to
> publish an Art of Walking, with Easy Lessons for Beginners. These we
> call apprentices. Those who persist from year to year, and obtain at last an
> intimacy with the country, and know all the good points within ten miles,
> with the seasons for visiting each, know the lakes, the hills, where grapes,
> berries and nuts, where the rare plants are; where the best botanic ground;
> and where the noblest landscapes are seen, and are learning all the time;—
> these we call professors.[39]

Visitors to the Emerson family home in Concord today will not fail to notice "Professor" Emerson's hat and walking stick on a stand near the front door.

Today the word *"pedestrian"* has come to mean something dull and mundane, implying that the practice Thoreau and Emerson found so spiritually uplifting is nothing more than the meanest form of transportation. As Rebecca Solnit, author of *Wanderlust*, observes, "Suburban sprawls generally make dull places to walk."[40] And the lengthy commutes required of working people living in the suburbs leave little time for leisurely strolls. People are more likely to walk on a treadmill at the gym than to walk on the street.

In recent years many people have indeed taken up walking for fitness, frequently with companions. But how often do we practice the kind of walking the Transcendentalists advised—sauntering or strolling in nature, regularly, mindfully, and observantly? Walking in the woods by lakes and streams is therapeutic and inspirational. It fosters a sense of serenity and wholeness that can hardly be found in any other way. "The walking of which I speak has nothing in it akin to taking exercise," Thoreau chides us, "but is itself the enterprise and adventure of the day. If you would get exercise, go in search of the springs of life."[41] The benefits of walking far exceed mere health and physical fitness. In nature one can discover "the springs of life." It is walking that gets us there.

SIMPLE LIVING

The expression that best characterizes Transcendentalism is "plain living and high thinking," a phrase from Wordsworth's poem "Written in London," and often used by Emerson.[42] Transcendental "high thinking"—contemplation, reading, conversation, journal writing, leisure, solitude, and walks in nature—required a simple life style. In the Transcendentalists' view, seeking wealth was a hindrance, not an aid, to self-culture. They sought to reform existing modes of living—especially those they deemed exploitative and dehumanizing, such as market capitalism—not succumb to them. They prized ideas more than things. Their goal was to develop an alternative way of life that reduced their material needs so that they could pursue spiritual, moral, and aesthetic aims. In a letter to his friend Margaret Fuller, William Henry Channing, nephew of William Ellery Channing, described his "scheme of life":

> to live content with small means; to seek elegance rather than luxury, and refinement rather than fashion; to be worthy, not respectable; and wealthy, not rich; to study hard, think quietly, talk gently, act frankly; . . . to listen to stars and birds, to babes and sages, with open heart; to bear all cheerfully, do all bravely, await occasions, hurry never; . . . in a word, to let the spiritual, unbidden and unconscious, grow up through the common. This is to be my symphony.[43]

The life the younger Channing aspires to is one of spiritual wealth, not material riches. The same could be said of his fellow Transcendentalists.

In *Walden,* Thoreau articulated his own "scheme of life." Living "content with small means" was an important part of it. Living simply was not merely a practical matter of reducing his expenses. It was also an ethical issue concerning the best way of spending his life. How much does one need? What are the basic necessities of life? Why do we work? Where do we find happiness?

The "Economy" chapter of *Walden* raises all these questions. It consists largely of observations on the common way of life in Thoreau's day. "I have travelled a good deal in Concord," he wrote, "and everywhere, in shops, and offices, and fields, the inhabitants have appeared to me to be doing penance in a thousand remarkable ways." People seem so burdened with responsibilities and labor that they can't enjoy the finer fruits of life. Lacking leisure, they have no time to be anything but a machine. Worst of all, they are driving themselves as if they had no other choice, resigned to their apparent lot in life. Unfortunately, what we think of ourselves determines our fate, leading most people, as Thoreau observed, to endure "lives of quiet desperation."[44]

Change *is* possible, in spite of our habits and anxieties. When we have obtained the necessities of life, there is an alternative to going after the superfluities, Thoreau argued, and that is "to adventure on life now, [our] vacation from humbler toil having commenced."[45] Once our physical needs are met, it's time to seek a deeper, more spiritual kind of fulfillment. Thoreau doesn't quarrel with those who feel well employed. He's mainly concerned with those who feel otherwise, complaining of their lot in life when they might actually take steps to improve it. However, most people are not satisfied with merely securing the necessities, and reach for the luxuries, which Thoreau considers positive hindrances to our spiritual elevation. But the wisest, he says, have always lived in voluntary poverty.

This is not the poverty of the oppressed but the cultivation of simplicity so that we can reap spiritual growth. As we have seen, for Thoreau, going to Walden was an experiment in living deliberately, confronting "the essential facts of life," and learning what lessons the experiment had to teach. At the end of his two-year stay, he tells us what he learned:

> I learned this, at least, by my experiment; that if one advances confidently in the direction of his dreams, and endeavors to live the life which he has imagined, he will meet with a success unexpected in common hours. . . . In proportion as he simplifies his life, the laws of the universe will appear less complex, and solitude will not be solitude, nor poverty poverty, nor weakness weakness. If you have built castles in the air, your work need not be lost; that is where they should be. Now put the foundations under them.[46]

Other Transcendentalists also experimented with new modes of living. In 1841, four years before Thoreau went to Walden Pond, George and Sophia Ripley founded The Brook Farm Association in West Roxbury, which is now part of Boston. It was a co-operative community primarily consisting of a farm on approximately two hundred acres. They sold shares to raise capital, constructed buildings, and established a school there. In a letter inviting Emerson to join the community, Ripley described his intentions

> to insure a more natural union between intellectual and manual labor than now exists; to combine the thinker and the worker, as far as possible in the same individual, to guarantee the highest mental freedom, by providing all with labor, adapted to their tastes and talents, and securing to them the fruits of their industry; to do away with the necessity of menial services, by opening the benefits of education and the profits of labor to all; and thus to prepare a society of liberal, intelligent, and cultivated persons, whose relations with each other would permit a more simple and wholesome life, than can be led amidst the pressure of our competitive institutions.[47]

Emerson politely declined. He had consulted a farmer he knew, who advised him the plan was unworkable.

The scheme proposed equal pay for all types of work, and allowed each person to choose tasks and amount of time for doing them. The goal was for members of the community to achieve a balance between labor and leisure. As Elizabeth Peabody reported in the *Dial* magazine, "This community aims to be rich, not in the metallic representative of wealth, but in the wealth itself, which money should represent; namely, LEISURE TO LIVE IN ALL THE FACULTIES OF THE SOUL."[48] Brook Farm was an earnest attempt at pursuing simplicity in a communal setting. For a variety of reasons—including a fire that destroyed the new Phalanstery, a large building with rooms to meet most of the community's needs—the experiment in communal simple living officially ended in 1849.

Both these experiments—at Walden Pond and at Brook Farm—fell short of their initiators' aims to transform the existing modes of living. Thoreau concluded that even he could not be entirely self-sufficient without sacrificing more leisure than he was willing to allow. Brook Farm could not be financially self-sustaining on the basis it was established. This is not to say that their critique of society was unwarranted or that their advice was misguided. Indeed, their example has inspired generations of Americans to seek a balance in their lives between labor and leisure by reducing their wants and living more simply.

"Plain living and high thinking" did not require ascetic self-denial. It meant cultivating a life that was both creative and gracious, as William Henry Channing expressed it in his letter to Margaret Fuller. To view life as an art, to see the beauty in simple things, to live within flowing rhythms at a human pace, free from over-riding anxiety and constant striving, are indispensable to voluntary simplicity. The challenge is to make our living poetic. "If it is not poetic," Thoreau said, "it is not life but death we get."[49] To live poetically is to appreciate what one has and to view the world from the perspective of plentitude rather than poverty. As Thoreau stated in a letter to a friend, "I am grateful for all I am and have. My thanksgiving is perpetual. Oh how I laugh when I think of my vague, indefinite riches. No run on my bank account can drain it—for my wealth is not possession but enjoyment."[50]

One does not need to live in a rustic cabin in the woods as Thoreau did to enjoy life. He felt that each person should go his or her own way, but that everyone could profit from settling accounts, so to speak, in order to live a richer life. We still face today the challenge that Thoreau and the Transcendentalists faced: to find a way to live simply, graciously, and well without an excessive dependence on money.

7

READING, CONVERSATION, AND JOURNAL WRITING

Virtually all the Transcendentalists regarded reading, conversation, and journal writing as essential elements of their spiritual practice and pursuit of self-culture. Some of them can be considered spiritual masters for their accomplishments in one or more of these areas: Parker for his prodigious reading; Fuller for her famous conversations, and Thoreau for his remarkable journal. Though they didn't often call attention to these activities, there was nothing casual about them. They undertook them quite intentionally for the cultivation of their souls.

READING

The Transcendentalists were devoted readers. They were scholars as well as nature mystics and political firebrands. Historian Henry Steele Commager wrote of Theodore Parker, "In breadth of intellect, in range of information, in catholicity of interests, he stood alone."[1] But Parker was none of these without his library. As Commager described it, "The books sprawled over on to the floor, crowded on to the great oaken table, . . . flooded out of the study and down the stairs, swarmed up into the attic, filled the closets, the bedroom and the parlor. There were thousands and thousands of them . . . but he knew them all."[2] Many of the books were in foreign languages, which Parker taught himself to read, especially Greek and Roman classics and works of German theologians and philosophers. He read literature, mythology, history, science, and travel books. He used his lecture fees to purchase even more volumes. After he died his books became the core collection of the newly opened Boston Public Library.

Tutored by her domineering father, Margaret Fuller began reading works in Latin at age six. By nine she had read the major Roman authors and had begun reading French literature, too. In her teens, she added Spanish, Italian, and German literatures. Her favorites in English were Shakespeare and the Romantic poets. Her real passion, however, was for German literature, especially, as previously mentioned, the writings of Goethe. During her twenties she made a concerted effort to fill the gaps in her reading. Without doubt, she was the most well-read woman in America and, as editor of the *Dial* and later book critic for the *New-York Tribune,* she became an arbiter of the nation's literary tastes.

The list could go on and on—Frederic Hedge, Elizabeth Peabody, George Ripley, Caroline Healey Dall—all of them considered reading essential to self-culture. As Emerson expressed it: "When shall I be tired of reading? When the moon is tired of waxing and waning, when the sea is tired of ebbing and flowing, and when the grass is weary of growing, when the planets are tired of going."[3] Emerson, too, was "a man in love with and addicted to books. He seems to have read everything," according to scholar Robert D. Richardson.[4] Readers of his essays struggle with his references to ancient and modern literature, history, science, mythology, current affairs, and world religions.

Even though the Transcendentalists read widely, they also chose carefully. In his essay "Reading," in *Society and Solitude,* Emerson estimated that the Paris Library contained about a million volumes and calculated that after reading from dawn to dusk for sixty years, one would die only in the first alcoves. In the lottery of reading there are, he noted, "at least fifty or a hundred blanks to a prize." The best books, he said, are those that "impart sympathetic activity to the moral power" and those that stimulate the imagination. At the top of this list were "the Bibles of the world, or the sacred books of each nation," including the Hebrew and Greek scriptures; Hindu, Buddhist, and Chinese sacred writings; and the works of the Stoic philosophers and

Christian mystics. "All these books are the majestic expressions of the universal conscience," he observed, "and are more to our daily purpose than this year's almanac or this day's newspaper. But they are for the closet, and to be read on bended knee."[5]

Emerson offered advice on *how* to read as well as *what* to read. In his journal he noted Coleridge's four classes of readers: the "Hour-glass," "all in and all out"; the "Sponge," "giving it all out a little dirtier than it took in"; the "Jelly-bag," "keeping nothing but the refuse," and the "Golconda," "sieves picking up the diamonds only."[6] Golconda referred to a place in India noted for its diamonds and thus a source of great wealth. Emerson was clearly in the last category, a "high-grader," mining for the richest ore only.[7] Elsewhere he had recommended reading for "lustres," as he called them, those bits of wisdom that attract our attention because we are somehow attuned to recognize them when we see them. "'Tis the good reader that makes the good book; a good head cannot read amiss; in every book he finds passages which seem confidences or asides hidden from all else and unmistakably meant for his ear."[8]

Emerson was also aware that reading had its dangers. In his "American Scholar" address, he warned against becoming a bookworm who reverences writings of the past more than his own thoughts. "Books are the best of things, well used; abused, among the worst. What is the right use? What is the one end, which all means go to effect? They are for nothing but to inspire. . . . Books are for the scholar's idle times," Emerson insisted. "When he can read God directly, the hour is too precious to be wasted in other men's transcripts of their readings. But when the intervals of darkness come, as come they must,—when the soul seeth not, when the sun is hid, and the stars withdraw their shining,—we repair to the lamps which were kindled by their ray to guide our steps to the East again, where the dawn is."[9]

Thoreau's library consisted largely of unsold copies of his first book, but he too was a devoted and disciplined reader. He borrowed books from Emerson and, as an alumnus, had access to the Harvard library as well. "Reading" is the first chapter of *Walden* in which Thoreau describes his day-to-day life at the pond, signifying that reading was an important activity during his time there. Reading was a means for studying the truth, and he considered his solitary residence more conducive to this pursuit than any university. For him, reading was not to fill idle hours, but carefully chosen for his own self-culture:

To read well, that is, to read true books in a true spirit, is a noble exercise, and one that will task the reader more than any exercise which the customs of the day esteem. It requires a training such as the athletes underwent, the steady intention almost of the whole life to this object. Books must be read as deliberately and reservedly as they were written.

He mainly recommended the ancient classics and religious scriptures because they represented the treasured wealth and cumulative wisdom of the human race. Thoreau believed that we will be truly rich when we have filled our libraries with "Vedas and Zendavestas and Bibles, with Homers and Dantes and Shakespeares, and all the centuries to come shall have successively deposited their trophies in the forums of the world. By such a pile we may hope to scale heaven at last."[10]

Thoreau viewed reading "as a noble intellectual exercise." The best literature speaks directly to our condition, whatever it may be, lifts us up and opens new perspectives for us. "How many a man has dated a new era in his life from the reading of a book! The book exists for us, perchance, which will explain our miracles and reveal new ones." Reading makes us liberal and broad-minded. Yet we do too little to promote our self-culture in this way. We need to be provoked, "goaded like oxen," into expanding our horizons of learning. We should have schools and educational opportunities for adults, just as we do for children:

> It is time that villages were universities, and their elder inhabitants the fellows of universities, with leisure . . . to pursue liberal studies the rest of their lives. . . . [The village] can spend money enough on such things as farmers and traders value, but it is thought Utopian to propose spending money for things which more intelligent men know to be of more worth. . . . Instead of noblemen, let us have noble villages of men. If it is necessary, omit one bridge over the river . . . and throw one arch at least over the darker gulf of ignorance which surrounds us.[11]

We read for pleasure, for information, and for work, but we also read for inspiration, delight, and our own transformation. These are the real lures of reading. In a letter to a young friend, Emerson wrote, "It happens to us once or twice in a lifetime to be drunk with some book which probably has some extraordinary relative power to intoxicate us . . . and having exhausted that cup of enchantment we go groping in libraries all our years afterwards in the hope of being in Paradise again."[12] Emerson and Thoreau placed sacred scriptures, classical literature, poetry, drama, and certain works of fiction at the top of their lists. Nowadays our reading tastes are perhaps broader than theirs, but I suspect that we, too, especially relish the books that change us and signal a new era in our lives.

CONVERSATION

Much of the drama of the Transcendentalist movement was communicated orally, in the meetings of the Transcendental Club, in lectures and sermons, and, above all, in the celebrated Conversations of Margaret Fuller and Bronson Alcott. The role of conversation in the Transcendentalists' pursuit of self-culture cannot be overstated. They would have readily agreed with the words of French essayist Michel de Montaigne, who wrote, "In my opinion the most profitable and most natural exercise of our mind is conversation. To me it is a more agreeable occupation than any other in life." Reading, he said, is a passive activity, whereas "conversation instructs and exercises us at the same time."[13]

Yet oral communication is evanescent. Words are spoken, then often lost forever. We have some cursory descriptions of what was said on these occasions but little to convey their impact on those who participated in them. The original model for conversation as a spiritual practice was the symposium, described by Plato as a gathering of friends for reciting poetry and discussing philosophy. "The Symposium" was the name first proposed for what became known as the Transcendental Club, which met intermittently between 1836 and 1840. There are no transcripts of those meetings, but we do have lists of their high-minded discussion topics: "What is the essence of religion as distinct from morality?" "Does the Species advance beyond the individual?" "Is Mysticism an element of Christianity?" "Wonder and Worship," and "Esoteric and Exoteric doctrine," among others.[14]

In eighteenth-century Europe literary salons were enormously popular. These gatherings were often led by women such as Germaine de Stael, whose Paris salon attracted famous writers and intellectuals. It was through the journals and letters of Madame de Stael that Margaret Fuller got her introduction to the titans of German literature—Johann Wolfgang von Goethe, Friedrich Schiller, and Johann Gottfried Herder, whose writings were instrumental in her own self-culture. Madame de Stael was also surely an inspiration for Fuller's own salon at Elizabeth Peabody's bookshop in Boston.

In nineteenth-century America, clubs, parlors, and salons were popular venues for promoting self-culture through conversation, or table talk, as it was sometimes called. In his essay "Domestic Life," Emerson wrote, "Let us then come out of the public square and enter the domestic precinct. Let us go to the sitting-room, the table-talk, and the expenditure, of our contemporaries."[15] As much as he extolled the virtues of solitude, Emerson prized conversation even more highly. It was a favorite subject of his essays and lectures. In his essay "Circles," Emerson likened conversation to the Pentecostal experience of speaking in tongues. "Conversation is a game of circles. In conversation we pluck up the *termini* which bound the common of silence on every side," he noted. "Yet let us enjoy the cloven flame whilst it glows on our walls. . . . O, what truths profound and executable only in ages and orbs are supposed in the announcement of every truth!"[16]

Similarly, in "The Over-Soul," Emerson drew on the imagery of Jesus's appearance to his disciples on the road to Emmaus to describe the process by which, in conversation, people became "wiser than they were":

> In all conversation between two persons, tacit reference is made as to a third party, to a common nature. That third party or common nature is not social; it is impersonal; is God. And so in groups where debate is earnest, and especially on high questions, the company become aware that the thought rises to an equal level in all bosoms, that all have a spiritual property in what was said, as well as the sayer. They all become wiser than they were. It arches over them like a temple, this unity of thought, in which every heart beats with nobler sense of power and duty, and thinks and acts with unusual solemnity. All are conscious of attaining to a higher self-possession. It shines for all.[17]

In "Table Talk," one of his later lectures, Emerson wrote that conversation must adhere to certain "mechanics," or rules: "You shall not be leaky," meaning confidences must be kept; "You shall not be opinionative and argumentative"; "Beware of jokes," since humor punctures the mood; and "You shall not be negative, but affirmative." When these conditions are met, conversation becomes a kind of collective "*maietucs,*" or midwifery, by which each participant helps to bring the latent thoughts of others to consciousness:

> This is the true school of philosophy, the college where you learn what Thoughts are: What powers lurk in those fugitive gleams, and what becomes of them; how they make history. A wise man goes to this game to play upon others, and to be played upon, and at least as curious to know

what can be drawn from himself, as what shall be drawn from them. For, in discourse with a friend, our thought, hitherto wrapped in our consciousness, detaches itself, and allows itself to be seen as a thought, in a manner as new and entertaining to us, as to our companions.[18]

Emerson's conversation was that of the parlor and the club. Margaret Fuller and Bronson Alcott brought conversation into the salon and the classroom to promote self-culture and provide for their own livelihood. Beginning in 1839, and continuing for five years, Fuller led her series of Conversations, primarily for women, at Peabody's bookstore. These were essentially a form of spiritual consciousness-raising, facilitated by Fuller, on a variety of topics, including literature, mythology, and women's issues. Each series was offered by subscription and consisted of two-hour sessions over a period of three months.

These were not simply intellectual discussions, and their purpose was not educational in the usual sense of the term. Fuller sought, first, to integrate the head and the heart, the intellect and the affections. Second, she wished to connect learning with living by applying thought to the problems of life. How, for example, might the myth of Athena, the Greek goddess of wisdom and strength, be a model for the empowerment of women?[19] As she expressed it, the aim of these Conversations was "to pass in review the departments of thought and knowledge and endeavor to place them in due relation to one another in our minds. To systematize thought and give a precision in which our sex are so deficient, chiefly, I think because they have so few inducements to test and classify what they receive. To ascertain what pursuits are best suited to us in our time and state of society, and how we may make best use of our means for building up the life of thought upon the life of action." These conversations were guided by two fundamental questions, "What were we born to do? How shall we do it? which so few ever propose to themselves 'till their best years are gone by."[20]

Alcott, who taught young children at the Temple School in Boston, used conversation as a pedagogical method in drawing out his students' thoughts on a variety of topics. In 1837 he decided to apply the theory of conversation to the education of adults and offered Conversations courses on the "Theory and Practice of Self-Culture" in nearby towns. "I deem this as the most direct and ready means of quickening the mind of the people. I should gather all the best minds in the village, and guide their thoughts to the worthiest topics," he announced in his journal. He was following in the footsteps of Pythagoras,

Socrates, and Jesus—in his mind the three greatest teachers of all time—who also used the method. In his view, conversation was "the natural organ of communicating, mind with mind. It is the method of human culture. By it I come nearer the hearts of those whom I shall address than by any other means."[21]

Fuller's Conversations ended in 1844, when she moved to New York to write for Greeley's *Tribune.* But Alcott continued to offer Conversations until 1878, when he started the Concord School of Philosophy—which, had he lived that long, Thoreau would have welcomed as a village opportunity for adult education. Over the years Alcott traveled throughout New England and the Midwest, leading conversations, often in Unitarian churches and colleges, including at Harvard Divinity School in 1873. The format, similar to Fuller's, was fairly simple. He presented a carefully prepared summary of the topic, then opened the floor for conversation. He served as facilitator, drawing out participants' thoughts, keeping the discussion on topic, and offering his own commentary from time to time. By all accounts, Alcott's Conversations were popular and well received, even if they were never highly profitable.

Conversation today is seldom so high-minded. Little thought is given to Emerson's "mechanics" or the purpose of conversation. Those in pursuit of self-culture may attend lectures or worship services, but there is seldom much in the way of group discussion. Book clubs and study groups do serve a similar function as the great intellectual clubs of the nineteenth century, and many churches offer adult education programs and what are called "small-church ministries." As a minister and religious educator I have seen that adults still long for these kinds of discussions and the spiritual and intellectual stimulation they derive from them.

Sociologist Sherry Turkle argues that conversation is "where we develop the capacity for empathy. It's where we experience the joy of being heard, of being understood. And conversation advances self-reflection, the conversations with ourselves that are the cornerstone of early development and continue throughout life." In her book *Reclaiming Conversation: The Power of Talk in a Digital Age,* Turkle cites the image of the three chairs Thoreau described in his Walden cabin: "one for solitude, two for friendship, three for society," as he put it.[22] We still need conversation on all levels—with oneself, with family and friends, and with others in social settings. But meaningful conversation is difficult, she says, when people are constantly sneaking peeks at their smartphones and using social media to substitute for in-person social interaction.[23] She offers a few general rules: put away your phone; slow down to a more human pace; create a sacred space for conversation; allow the conversation to unfold, and remember what you know about life. Like the slow food movement that began in the 1980s, it behooves us to take time to both create and savor conversation for the spiritual nourishment it gives us.

JOURNAL WRITING

We know as much as we do about the Transcendentalists in large part because they kept journals. Bronson Alcott's journal consisted of five million words, possibly more. Caroline Healey Dall kept a diary for seventy-five years, perhaps the longest diary of its kind in existence. Although she didn't make entries every day, her remarkable memory enabled her to reconstruct lectures and conversations almost verbatim, giving us the most vivid accounts we have of these events that would otherwise be lost. She also chronicled her mother's mental illness, her father's unreasonable expectations, her husband's failure as a minister, and his abandonment of his family in order to establish a Unitarian mission in India. No doubt her diary brought relief from her troubles and disappointments, but it also served another purpose. Elizabeth Peabody, her first female intellectual mentor, told her that her diary should be a journal of self-discovery and spiritual growth. She took that advice.

Emerson began his journal at age sixteen while a student at Harvard, and made his last entries at about age seventy-three, when his mind began to fail. His early journals contain quotations, lists of the books he read, notes from his classes, opinions on poetry and literature, and advice from his remarkable aunt Mary, a faithful diarist herself. His entries reveal theological doubts, personal insecurities, and, after the death of his first wife, the crisis of faith that led to his resignation from the ministry. During the 1840s and 1850s it documents his transition from aloofness *regarding* the issue of slavery to ardent advocacy of abolitionism and the cause of John Brown. He called his journal his "savings bank," a repository of thoughts he drew on in composing his lectures and essays. The journal played a large role, not only in his career as a writer, but also in the cultivation of his soul: "Each young and ardent person writes a diary, in which, when the hours of prayer and penitence arrive, he inscribes his soul. The pages thus written are to him burning and fragrant; he reads them on his knees by midnight and by the morning star; he wets them with his tears; they are sacred."[24]

Emerson recommended keeping a journal to the auditors of his 1837 Human Culture lecture series: "Pay so much honor to the visits of Truth to your mind as to record those thoughts that have shone therein. It is not for what is recorded, though that may be the agreeable entertainment of later years, and the pleasant remembrances of what we were, but for the habit of rendering an account to yourself of yourself in some more rigorous manner and at more certain intervals than mere conversation or casual reverie of solitude require."[25] Presumably, he also gave this advice to Thoreau. On October 22, 1837, his young friend sat down at his desk and wrote, "'What are you doing now?' he asked. 'Do you keep a journal?' So I make my first entry to-day." Thus began what became one of the most extraordinary journals ever kept by an author, which is especially notable for its faithful recordkeeping of Thoreau's observations of the natural world, interwoven with his spiritual insights.

Thoreau's journal may be his best writing. His published works tend to keep their readers at arm's length. While his journal contains little that is personal, it does chronicle his inner life, and it was an important element of his spiritual practice. It was the ongoing record of his spiritual transformation in and through his communion with nature. The sights and sounds of the natural world were the stimulus for mystic flights and philosophical musings. "A journal," he said, is "a book that shall contain a record of all your joy, your ecstasy."[26] We are fortunate to have the chance to read these journals today. He wrote them not for human eyes, he said, but for the gods:

> My Journal is that of me which would else spill over and run to waste, gleanings from the field which in action I reap. I must not live for it, but in it for the gods. They are my correspondent, to whom daily I send off this sheet postpaid. I am clerk in their counting-room, and at evening transfer the account from day-book to ledger. It is as a leaf that hangs over my head in the path. I bend the twig and write my prayers on it; then letting it go, the bough springs up and shows the scrawl to heaven.[27]

The journals of the Transcendentalists—Emerson, Thoreau, Fuller, Dall, and others—were a daily record of soliloquies or inner dialogues of the self. Though the Transcendentalists wrote journals primarily for their own self-culture, they often shared them with friends as a way of establishing intellectual intimacy and spiritual kinship. They reveal the spiritual lives of those who kept them, similar to the *Meditations* of Marcus Aurelius and the *Confessions* of Saint Augustine. The late French historian of philosophy, Pierre Hadot, wrote this about Aurelius's *Meditations,* and it is true of the Transcendentalists' journals also: "The goal is to reactualize, rekindle, and ceaselessly reawaken an inner state which is in constant danger of being numbed or extinguished. The task—ever renewed—is to bring back to order an inner discourse which becomes dispersed and diluted in the futility of routine."[28] In addition to their practical purposes, their journals served as a reminder of truths revealed and wisdom gained that might otherwise have been lost or forgotten. Alcott remarked of his journal that it contained his "inmost thoughts, feelings, purposes, speculations, and confessions."[29] Today we can read many of these journals ourselves as sources of insight and inspiration.

Few people keep ongoing handwritten journals any more, likely because blogs and social media provide such ready means of brief self-expression. We send messages to the "cloud" perhaps, but not exactly to the heavens, as Thoreau put it. Several contemporary writers, like Emerson, recommend taking up journal writing and have indeed found followers. Julia Cameron, in *The Artist's Way,* advises beginning each day with "morning pages," making brief entries on awakening. "It is impossible to write morning pages for any extended period of time without coming into contact with an unexpected inner power," she writes. "Anyone who faithfully writes morning pages will be led to a connection with a source of wisdom within."[30] Janet Conner, in *Writing Down Your Soul,* describes the process as a dialogue between self and soul. "Once you start engaging in rich, deep conversation with something higher, bigger, deeper, and wiser than yourself, you'll find yourself contemplating ideas you've never considered, saying things you've never said, and asking questions you've never asked."[31] These writers suggest that keeping a journal is a form of meditation. The Transcendentalists would certainly have agreed.

8

Religious Cosmopolitanism

The Transcendentalist movement started when a group of young religious radicals in the early nineteenth century began moving away from Protestant Christianity, even the more liberal brand of Unitarian Christianity. All of them were theists and, if asked, probably would have said they were Christians, too. Some of their departures from orthodoxy were more pronounced than others, leading them to explore other religions and, in some cases, reject their own religious upbringing and training. But they all shared an intuitive epistemology and an orientation toward an ethical form of mysticism. Their conservative critics, however, considered them unorthodox if not heretical in their views.

One significant development that arose from Transcendentalism is a sense of religious cosmopolitanism. This may well be the most enduring legacy of the movement. The Transcendentalists' rejection of tradition in favor of an intuitive approach to religion led them to consider the essence of religion apart from its manifold (and therefore conditional) manifestations. Some of them called it natural or universal religion. Parker's term was "absolute religion." As spiritual seekers, they were attracted to the scriptures of other faith traditions, looking for inspiration and evidence of common ground. Some were drawn to progressive, developmental views of religion. Some continued to privilege Christianity, while others became more universal in their religious sentiments and outlook.

Under the heading of religious cosmopolitism, then, there were several types of Transcendentalist responses to these other traditions as they became increasingly familiar with them. One was the Unitarian Transcendentalism of those such as James Freeman Clarke and Elizabeth Peabody. Clarke, a minister who became secretary of the American Unitarian Association, initiated significant reforms in congregational life. He was also Professor of Ethnic Religions and the Creeds of Christendom at Harvard Divinity School, and published a two-volume work called *Ten Great Religions*. Clarke viewed other faiths as "ethnic religions" and considered them arrested or partial in relation to the progressive and universal qualities of Christianity.

Like so many of the Transcendentalists, Elizabeth Peabody was a person of extraordinary gifts and boundless energy. She published the *Dial* magazine; ran the West Street Bookstore, a center for Transcendentalist salons and conversations; taught at Bronson Alcott's Temple School; served as secretary to William Ellery Channing, the leading Unitarian minister of the day; and agitated for many reforms during her long and eventful life. And like her Transcendentalist friends, she shared an interest in other religions, especially Buddhism. She even studied Sanskrit so that she could read original texts. She can be credited with introducing Buddhism to an American audience. In 1844 she published in the *Dial* extracts from the Lotus Sutra, which she had translated from the French, under the heading "The Preachings of the Buddha." But she continued to feel that Buddhism and Hinduism were inferior to liberal Christianity.

These Unitarian Transcendentalists recognized that Christianity was one among many of the world's faiths, each of which have their own scriptures and traditions. But they retained their Unitarian bias, even though they were more open than many Christians to Asian religions. Some years later a younger group of American radicals, including Samuel Johnson, John Weiss, and others, rejected the idea that Christianity was superior. They embraced what we might term a universalist Transcendentalism.

The religious cosmopolitanism of Emerson and Thoreau is more difficult to label. It could perhaps be called, simply, Concord Transcendentalism. They took Asian religions, especially Hinduism, more seriously than any of the other Transcendentalists, allowing their own thinking and spirituality to be influenced by them. Their knowledge of Eastern religions, however, was piecemeal, coming from the scattered information available at the time, including extracts from anthologies, texts in European languages, and articles in American journals about ethnic religious beliefs and practices. Those articles were mostly derogatory, however, labeling them "oriental superstition."

In 1822, the Unitarian *Christian Register* published a lengthy positive article about the Bengali religious reformer Ram Mohan Roy, a Hindu, that piqued Emerson's curiosity. He began to read whatever Hindu scriptures he could get his hands on, a fascination that continued for decades. His first book, *Nature,* had been largely influenced by his reading of the Neoplatonic philosophers, Plotinus in particular. But he began to find Indian idealism more congenial to his temperament and evolving point of view.

Scholars have often raised the question of whether his study of Indian literature may have helped him form his notion of an "Over-soul," the title of one of his *Essays: First Series,* published in 1841. The term does not appear in any of his writings prior to 1845, when he told a friend how delighted he was to receive at last a copy of the Bhagavad Gita, extracts of which he had read and "often admired." According to at least one of his contemporaries there was little doubt that the term came from the eighth chapter of that book.[1] The distinction Emerson makes between the individual soul and the Over-soul is akin to the relationship, in Hindu teaching, between Atman (the individual soul) and Brahman (the universal soul). In his reading of Hindu texts he found analogues to many key concepts he already espoused. For example, *karma* was similar to Emerson's notion of compensation, *maya* to his use of illusion, and *samsara* to his belief in metamorphosis.

The high point of Emerson's embrace of Indian philosophy came in his poem "Brahma," written in 1856:

> If the red slayer thinks he slays,
>   Or if the slain thinks he is slain,
> They know not well the subtle ways
>   I keep, and pass, and turn again.
> Far or forgot to me is near;
>   Shadow and sunlight are the same;
> The vanished gods to me appear;
>   And one to me are shame and fame.
> They reckon ill who leave me out;
>   When me they fly, I am the wings;
> I am the doubter and the doubt,
>   And I the hymn the Brahmin sings.
> The strong gods pine for my abode,

> And pine in vain the sacred Seven;
> But thou, meek lover of the good!
> Find me, and turn thy back on heaven.[2]

In this poem Emerson has taken the concepts and many words and phrases directly from the Bhagavad Gita, particularly in the second chapter, in which Krishna says, "He who thinks this self a killer and he who thinks it killed, both fail to understand; it does not kill, nor is it killed. It is not born, it does not die; having been, it will never not be; unborn, enduring, constant, and primordial, it is not killed when the body is killed."[3]

While Emerson found much to appreciate in Hindu scriptures, he was also a critical reader of them. He realized that Indian culture could be repressive, and he expressed this ambivalence in his essay "Plato; or, the Philosopher," in *Representative Men:*

> The country of unity, of immovable institutions, the seat of a philosophy delighting in abstractions, of men faithful in doctrine and in practice to the idea of a deaf, unimplorable, immense fate, is Asia; and it realizes this faith in the social institution of caste. On the other side, the genius of Europe is active and creative: it resists caste by culture; its philosophy was a discipline; it is a land of arts, inventions, trade, freedom. If the East loved infinity, the West delighted in boundaries.[4]

In virtually every instance of polarities—society and solitude, Understanding and Reason, contemplation and action—Emerson sought a synthesis or balance. In this case it was a synthesis between the views of the East and those of the West—the one characterized by Unity or Identity, and the other by Variety. "It is impossible to speak, or think without embracing both," he said. For Emerson, the "representative man" is "the balanced soul."[5]

In addition to Hindu texts, Emerson read widely in all kinds of Asian and Near Eastern literature. In his writings he made frequent references to Sufi poetry, Buddhist scripture, and the Confucian classics. But, most of all, he absorbed and integrated the Hindu teachings of the *Bhagavad Gita* and the Upanishads, from a Vedantist or philosophical perspective. One may find fault with his comprehension and his use of these texts, but in his desire to assimilate them to his own spiritual growth, Emerson went well beyond most of his peers, whose interest was more scholarly.

Thoreau went even further than Emerson. Fourteen years younger, Thoreau expressed a less biased view of Hinduism, and more accurate information about it was available to him. Plus, he was not as influenced early in his life by Neoplatonic philosophy as Emerson was. In his early twenties Thoreau began enthusiastically studying Indian teachings with some tutoring from Emerson. In his journal entry on "The Laws of Menu" in 1841, he commented, "When my imagination travels eastward and backward to those remote years of the gods, I seem to draw near to the habitation of the morning, and the dawn at length has a place. I remember the book as an hour before sunrise."[6]

Thoreau took the Bhagavad Gita—in fact, Emerson's own copy—with him to Walden Pond. He copied passages from it into the manuscript of his first book, *A Week on the Concord and Merrimack Rivers,* which he had gone to the woods to write. The teachings of the Gita and Indian philosophy also figure in his personal life and in the composition of his next work, *Walden,* which wasn't completed until 1854.

In a letter to a friend, Thoreau wrote, "Rude and careless as I am, I would fain practice the *yoga* faithfully."[7] And, to a degree, that is what he did in going to Walden Pond. By "yoga," he didn't mean the practice of physical postures, or *asanas,* now familiar to Western audiences. In Hindu teaching "*yoga*" means a way or practice. There are four forms: action, devotion, philosophical speculation, and the physical form. Thoreau paid attention mainly to *karma,* the yoga of action or work. The sixth chapter of the Gita instructs practitioners to release themselves from petty affairs of daily life. The yogi should withdraw to a solitary place and live alone, exercise control over mind and body, dispense with personal possessions, and meditate on the *Atman.* "He should fix for himself a firm seat in a pure place, neither too high nor too low."[8] Compare this instruction to these two passages from *Walden:*

> Wherever I sat, there I might live, and the landscape radiated from me accordingly. What is a house but a *sedes,* a seat?—better if a country seat.[9]
> I was seated by the shore of a small pond, about a mile and a half south of the small village of Concord and somewhat higher than it, . . . but I was so low in the woods that the opposite shore . . . was my most distant horizon.[10]

In 1841, before going to Walden, he had written in his journal, "I want to go soon and live away by the pond, where I shall hear only the wind whispering among the reeds. It will be success if I shall have left myself behind."[11] Four years later, that's precisely what he did.

Paul Friedrich, in *The Gita within Walden,* remarks on the parallels between the Bhagavad Gita and *Walden:*

The protagonists in both texts, Arjuna and Thoreau, move from situations of despondency, or desperation in the midst of battle, literal, literary, or metaphorical—the field of Kuru or the mortgaged farm fields of Concord—to a denial of this and an affirmation of the opposite pole of peace and harmony through identification with Krishna or Nature. To move from one situation to its denial to the affirmation of its diametrical opposite in terms of absolute values is perhaps the most basic tension in both texts.[12]

In motivation, structure, and message, *Walden* indeed bears a strong resemblance to the Bhagavad Gita. The theme of both works is the perfection of self through a transcendence of the ego. The parable of the Artist of Kouroo in the final chapter of *Walden* epitomizes the theme. In it a woodcarver decides to make a staff, "perfect in all respects." Although it took him many years to find a suitable piece of wood, he didn't appear to grow any older. "His singleness of purpose and resolution, and his elevated piety, endowed him, without his knowledge, with perennial youth." As he carved the staff, it seemed that many eras of time had passed. Yet, as he completed his work, he discovered "the lapse of time had been an illusion."[13] The parable communicates on several levels. First, it represents karma yoga, the path of work or action. Second, it exemplifies Thoreau as an artist whose work when he went to Walden Pond was to write his first book. And, third, the staff that is fashioned is a metaphor of the self, seeking congruence with the transcendent dimension of life that the staff symbolizes. The staff is an example of what historian of religion Mircea Eliade calls the *axis mundi*, often depicted as a tree, mountain, or pole standing at the center of the world, "a spot where one can pass from one cosmic zone to another."[14]

While Thoreau admired Hindu scripture for its pure intellectuality, he found the New Testament remarkable for its pure morality. He commended Christianity for being "humane, practical, and, in a large sense, radical."[15] In contrast, he considered the argument of the Gita defective. "No sufficient reason is given why Arjoon [or Arjuna] should fight," he concludes. "Arjoon may be convinced, but the reader is not."[16] Thoreau proves to be, like Emerson, an endless seeker, for whom the wisdom of India provided refreshment but did not quench his spiritual thirst: "Every sacred book, successively, has been accepted in the faith that it was to be the final resting-place of the sojourning soul; but after all, it was but a caravansary which supplied refreshment to the traveler, and directed him farther on his way to Isphahan or Bagdat."[17]

In assimilating the wisdom of the Hindu tradition, Emerson and Thoreau became pioneers and paradigmatic figures among the restless souls of the Spiritual Left in America. They clearly felt those ideas resonated with their own experience and enriched their spiritual lives. If they engaged in some intellectual colonization—taking from other religions what suited them—their explorations in any case were the first effort to treat them sympathetically.

The religious cosmopolitanism of the Transcendentalists went through a second phase, beginning with the publication, in 1856, of the three-volume *Progress of Religious Ideas through Successive Ages,* written by Lydia Maria Child. Child was well known as a novelist, a feminist, an anti-slavery activist, and author of numerous books of advice and counsel for women. Her work on *The Progress of Religious Ideas* is one of the first attempts at comparative religion in America and is remarkable for its sympathetic treatment of other faiths. Notably, she placed the Christian religion on the same level as the others she studied. She took a progressive stance, believing that the moral standards of religion had steadily improved, and that the trend was toward what she called "that Eclectic Church of the Future which shall gather forms of holy aspirations from all ages and nations, and set them on high in their immortal beauty, with the broad sunlight of heaven to glorify them all."[18]

The most ambitious and scholarly work of this kind was Samuel Johnson's three-volume opus, *Oriental Religions and Their Relation to Universal Religion.* The first volume, on the religions of India, was published in 1872. Johnson, a second-generation Transcendentalist, studied all that was then known about the faiths of India, China, and Persia. Like Child's, his approach was both sympathetic and progressive. He rejected the idea of Christian exceptionalism, insisting that "revelation has in no wise been confined to one person, race, or religion." All religions had imperfections and superstitions they struggled to overcome. Insofar as they succeeded in divesting themselves of exclusive claims, he argued, they approached the ideal of Universal Religion. "Universal Religion," Johnson wrote, "cannot be any one, exclusively, of the great positive religions of the world. Yet it is really what is best in each and every one of them; purified from baser inter-mixture and developed in freedom and power."[19]

Thomas Wentworth Higginson, whose productive years spanned both earlier and later phases of Transcendentalism, advocated a "sympathy of religions." He took a sympathetic approach to other religions and also looked for sympathy or likeness among them. In his 1871 essay of that title, which was reprinted numerous times as a tract of the Free Religious Association, he wrote: "Every year brings new knowledge of the religions of the world, and every step in knowledge brings out the sympathy between them. They all show the same aim, the same symbols, the same forms, the same weaknesses, the same aspirations. Looking at these points of unity, we might say there is but one religion under many forms."[20] In his view, each of the world's religions had at its heart a universal core, which was "Natural Religion," and added its own sectarian or cultural bias. Like Child and the later Transcendentalists, Higginson envisioned a future church of the spirit with shared aspirations and a commitment to benevolence.

Preaching to Parker's former congregation in 1861 on the "Essential Principles of Religion," Emerson had taken a similar approach. From his study of the major religions he distilled several core principles: (1) find your true self, (2) develop your individuality through self-trust, (3) root yourself in nature and draw strength from that source, (4) cherish moments of extraordinary experience, (5) practice right action, and (6) resist conformity. All these principles were grounded in Divine Nature. Emerson envisioned a meeting of the greatest spiritual minds—the Buddha, Confucius, Dutch philosopher Baruch Spinoza, as well as Muslim, Stoic, and Christian thinkers—who would agree on these principles, to the consternation, he adds, of their followers.[21]

As spiritual seekers, the Transcendentalists were drawn to the mystical and moral teachings they found in other traditions. They sought to understand these traditions on their own terms and to look for similarities among them rather than dwell on their differences. Thoreau offered this suggestion:

> It would be worthy of the age to print together the collected Scriptures or Sacred Writings of the several nations, the Chinese, the Hindoos, the Persians, the Hebrews, and others, as the Scripture of mankind. The New Testament is still, perhaps, too much on the lips and in the hearts of men to be called a Scripture in this sense. Such a juxtaposition and comparison might help to liberalize the faith of men. This is a work which Time will surely edit, reserved to crown the labors of the printing-press. This would be the Bible, or Book of Books, which let the missionaries carry to the uttermost parts of the earth.[22]

Some, including William Rounseville Alger and Moncure Conway, took Thoreau's advice to heart, compiling anthologies of quotations from the world's religions for use as readings in worship services and as meditations in their spiritual practice.

Their knowledge was limited. Not much was known about Buddhism, for example, before the 1860s. Though serious, their scholarship was questioned by later scholars. They have since been accused of dilettantism and, worse, of intellectual colonialism. They were naïve in believing that religions were progressing toward a synthesis of faiths or a universal church of the future. The search for an "essence" of religion, natural, absolute, universal, or otherwise, proved to be elusive. And the notion of "orientalism"—the assumption that the religious traditions of Asia could be subsumed under such a catch-all and culturally distorted term—has long been discredited.

Nevertheless, the Transcendentalists contributed greatly to how successive generations of Americans have received other religions, particularly those from Asia. They made the teachings of other faiths accessible as never before, as resources for spiritual growth. The Transcendentalists' exploration of Asian religions, according to Schmidt in *Restless Souls,* led directly to the first World's Parliament of Religions in 1893, organized in large part by Higginson and representatives of the Free Religious Association. That Chicago event proved to be the springboard for the dissemination in America of spiritual teachings and practices representing all manner of spiritual traditions in America, including Zen Buddhism, Vedanta Hinduism, Sufi Islam, and many others.

Today's religious climate has been deeply infused by the religious cosmopolitanism of the Transcendentalists. Few of the writings of the Transcendentalists—with the notable exception of Emerson and Thoreau— are read today. Yet in virtually every account about Eastern religions in America there is a chapter or two on the influence of Transcendentalism. Their deep interest in seeking wisdom and inspiration from the world's faiths and philosophies continues to be a model for successive generations of spiritual seekers.

9

SELF-CULTURE AND
SOCIAL CHANGE

S cholars of Transcendentalism have hotly contested the relationship in the movement between self-culture and social change. Some insist the Transcendentalists were indifferent to social change, while others hold that the activism of the Transcendentalists grew directly out of their notion of self-culture. These judgments have been shaped as much by intellectual trends as anything else. To understand this debate we need to consider whether there is a fundamental contradiction between self-culture and social change, or whether there is a necessary relationship between the two. Were the Transcendentalists social activists? Did members of the group approach the issue of reform differently? Did these differences mean that some Transcendentalists were activists and some were not? And was their social activism consistent with their Transcendentalist principles or a deviation from them?

When it comes to social reform, some historians and critics have argued that the Transcendentalists were indifferent, insignificant, or complicit with the status quo. In the mid-twentieth century, American historian Arthur Schlesinger, Jr., argued that the Transcendentalists "from their book-lined studies, or their shady walks in cool Concord woods" found "the hullabaloo of party politics unedifying and vulgar."[1] Some decades later, literary scholar John Carlos Rowe wrote in his book *At Emerson's Tomb* that "transcendentalism reveals itself to be at fundamental odds with the social reforms" of the mid-nineteenth century.[2] Contemporary historian Anne C. Rose, author of *Transcendentalism as a Social Movement,* wrote that by 1850 the Transcendentalists had ceased their reform activities and that they were not especially active in the abolitionist movement.[3] Other critics attempt to de-Transcendentalize the movement, arguing that only after they ceased to be Transcendentalists did they became activists.[4] Some define Transcendentalism in such a way as to preclude any possibility of social engagement. For example, the late sociologist Robert Bellah classified Emerson's idea of self-reliance as "ontological individualism," a solipsism of the self, precluding concern for others.[5] Finally, some writers divide the Transcendentalists into two separate camps, the mystics and the social activists.[6]

In my view, the Transcendentalists were unquestionably activists. They advocated and worked toward reforms in many areas—education, church life, labor relations, women's rights, the abolition of slavery, and the treatment of the natural environment. They did not abandon their Transcendentalist views when they became active in these reforms. Rather, they applied them. Transcendentalism cannot be limited to a certain snapshot in time, say the 1830s, or to a very narrow definition. Movements, as the word implies, are not static, but dynamic, and so are individuals. The Transcendentalists changed and developed over time, but this does not mean they lost their identity.

A diverse, loose-knit group of individuals, the Transcendentalists were not all activists in the same ways or to the same degree. The reforms they advocated were not always successful. Yet they believed that every person shares a divine nature, a belief that provided the basis for both individual self-reliance and collective social identity. They sought to remove impediments to human flourishing and to reform social structures inimical to human freedom and equality. Properly understood, self-culture, the process by which self-reliance is developed, implied the transformation of both individuals and society. Only one member of the group, Orestes Brownson, ever publicly repudiated these beliefs.

Their actions were motivated by the injustices they witnessed all around them: the oppression of laborers, women, and African Americans; a rigid social hierarchy; inequality in marriage; harsh educational methods, and an economy that marginalized its poorest and weakest members. Their idea of self-culture implied the transformation of both individuals and society. Contemplation and social action were both necessary to achieve that end. As to the significance of their efforts, the Transcendentalists have had their defenders as well as their critics, as noted by C. S. Griffin in his study *The Ferment of Reform: 1830–1860:*

> Some historians urged that New England transcendentalism was largely responsible for the reform impulse [of the antebellum period]. To an "astonishing degree," said Henry Steele Commager in *The Era of Reform,* the reform movement was the "product of . . . Transcendentalism." In *The Idea of Progress in America, 1815–1860,* . . . Arthur A. Ekirsh alleged that in the 1840s transcendentalism became the "popular reform philosophy of the day." . . . Arthur Y. Lloyd, in *The Slavery Controversy, 1831– 1860,* claimed that "humanitarianism, idealism, and transcendentalism dominated the philosophy of the time."[7]

Since the 1980s interest in Transcendentalism and its major figures has quickened as scholars have reassessed the movement's impact on American history and social thought. This reappraisal has been prompted, in part, by the publication of letters, journals, and lectures not readily available before. To some extent it is due to a changing climate of intellectual and social thought since the 1960s, stimulated, at least in part, by the civil rights, women's liberation, and protest movements of the period. In the past four decades numerous significant biographies and critical commentaries have focused on Transcendentalism and the Transcendentalists, including, Emerson, Thoreau, Fuller, Parker, and Peabody. Much of this scholarship has focused on self-culture and the role it played in their personal lives and thinking, the impact of Transcendentalism on social reform and democratic theory, and the importance of religion to their views.

Contemporary scholars are generally in agreement with historian Robert D. Richardson's assessment of the movement in his book *Henry Thoreau: A Life of the Mind.* He argued that the significant achievement of the Transcendentalists was "in working out the ethical implications of transcendentalism and making them widely accessible and, above all, livable":

> It is therefore ironic that as a group they were thought—then as now—to have their heads in the clouds, to be impractical and otherworldly, vague, dreamy, and concerned with things that were neither real nor tangible. . . . The transcendentalists were, singly and as a group, more radical and more socially and politically activist than such writers as Poe, Hawthorne, or Melville, who held older, darker views of man and nature. Most of the

transcendentalists found that the ethical consequences of transcendental idealism impelled them to social, political, and intellectual reform.

New England transcendentalists stressed individual autonomy and freedom rather than individual isolation or solipsism. . . . [W]hile it was of course always possible for one to become lost or alienated, wandering in the "splendid labyrinth of [his] perceptions," it was neither desired nor approved. Instead, the strong ethical imperatives of New England transcendentalism led its members more often into the world than away from it.[8]

The Transcendentalists viewed self-culture as a process of spiritual growth, guided by introspection and self-examination, that was necessary for ethical action. Self-culture was not an exclusive pursuit, focusing on the self alone. It was for forming character and becoming a better, more moral person. The spiritual practices of self-culture were not performed in isolation from the realities of everyday life. Solitude was not sought to exclude society but to enable the self to become more individuated and authentic, and thus less conforming and compliant. Self-reliance did not mean avoiding relationships with other people but rather strengthening them by establishing them on an equal basis. In "The American Scholar" lecture, Emerson noted that the world imagines the scholar to be a recluse, "as unfit for any handiwork or public labor." But self-culture is not a form of quietism or inaction, he insisted. "Action is with the scholar subordinate, but it is essential. Without it, he is not yet a man. Without it, thought can never ripen into truth. . . . Inaction is cowardice, but there can be no scholar without the heroic mind."[9] Self-culture was for the purpose of developing self-reliance and promoting action from principle. Action is necessarily subordinate to moral principles, "but it is essential."

From the beginning, the Transcendentalists envisioned that their "new views" would transform society. In his 1836 book *New Views of Christianity, Society, and the Church,* Brownson prophesied that when these views became universally accepted, people would no longer wrong one another; slavery would be abolished; wars would end; education would dispel ignorance; freedom and equality would prevail; the church would side with progress; work would be reverenced; the earth would be deemed sacred; the body would be holy, and the church and state would be united.

This millennialist outlook, characteristic of Romantic idealism, inspired utopian visions and schemes, such as Brook Farm and the experiment in collective living in West Roxbury, Massachusetts. As George Ripley, a founder of the association, wrote in a letter to Emerson:

Our objects, as you know, are to insure a more natural union between intellectual and manual labor than now exists; to combine the thinker and the worker, as far as possible, in the same individual; to guarantee the highest mental freedom, by providing all with labor, adapted to their tastes and talents, and securing to them the fruits of their industry; to do away with the necessity of menial services, by opening the benefits of education and the profits of labor to all; and thus to prepare a society of liberal, intelligent, and cultivated persons, whose relations with each other would permit a more simple and wholesome life, than can be led amidst the pressure of our competitive institutions.[10]

Emerson declined Ripley's invitation to join Brook Farm, but the Transcendentalists made similar efforts to put individuals into right relations with one another, with society, and with nature, such as Bronson Alcott's short-lived Fruitlands commune in Harvard, Massachusetts, and Thoreau's experiment in simple living at Walden Pond. None of these schemes were ultimately successful, and each had fatal flaws. But they were earnest undertakings, and taught some valuable lessons even in failure. Even today, they continue to inspire ways of living—individually and communally—that are richer, simpler, more equitable, and more sustainable.

The religious radicalism of the 1830s that spawned Transcendentalism, in turn led to the reform efforts of the 1840s. As the movement developed, the Transcendentalists began working out the social implications of the "new views." In November 1840, a Convention of Friends of Universal Reform assembled in the Chardon Street Chapel in Boston for three days. Reformers came from all over New England and the Middle States. The Transcendentalists, including Parker, Alcott, and Emerson, among others, were well represented. Emerson gave this account of the proceedings in an article for the *Dial:* "If the assembly was disorderly, it was picturesque. Madmen, madwomen, men with beards, Dunkers, Muggletonians, Come-outers, Groaners, Agrarians, Seventh-day Baptists, Quakers, Abolitionists, Calvinists, Unitarians, and Philosophers,—all came successively to the top, and seized their moment, if not their *hour,* wherein to chide, or pray, or preach, or protest."[11] The spirit of reform was in the air.

Early the next year Emerson gave an address before the Mechanics' Apprentices' Library Association called "Man the Reformer." The lecture echoes the critical tone of the "Economy" chapter in Thoreau's *Walden,* but with an even sharper social message. Thoreau went to the woods in an individual effort to escape from a life of quiet desperation. Emerson said we cannot escape from "the ways of trade . . . grown selfish to the boarders of theft." Corruption is so pervasive that, even if we did not create the abuse, we are implicated in it. Even sugar came at the expense of misery and the abomination of the slave trade. Commerce is a system of selfishness and distrust, from which it is nearly impossible to extricate oneself. Perhaps if we returned to self-sufficient farming we might restore our virtue, but "the doctrine of the Farm" will not work for everyone. Short of that, we can examine our modes of living with a view to simplicity. "We spend our incomes for paint and paper, for a hundred trifles, I know not what, and not for the things of a man. Our expense is almost all for conformity. It is for cake that we run in debt; 't is not the intellect, not the heart, not beauty, not worship, that costs so much." It is better to go without luxuries than to have them at too great a cost. We should learn the true meaning of economy: "Can anything be more elegant as to have few wants and serve them one's self, so as to have somewhat left to give, instead of being always prompt to grab?"[12]

We cannot abstain from everything nor absolve ourselves of responsibility. Emerson put it this way: "If we suddenly plant our foot, and say,—I will neither eat nor drink nor wear nor touch any food or fabric which I do not know to be innocent, or deal with any person whose whole manner of life is not clear and rational, we shall stand still. . . . But I think we must clear ourselves each one by the interrogation, whether we have earned our bread to-day by the hearty contribution of our energies to the common benefit? and we must not cease to *tend* to the correction of these flagrant wrongs, by laying one stone aright every day." Even more important than reforming "our daily employments [and] our households," he said, we need to radically restructure our whole society—"the state, the school, religion, marriage, trade, science, and explore their foundations in our own nature." After all, Emerson asked,

> What is man born for but to be a Reformer, a Re-maker of what man has made; a renouncer of lies; a restorer of truth and good, imitating that great Nature which embosoms us all, and which sleeps no moment on an old past, but every hour repairs herself, yielding us every morning a new day, and with every pulsation a new life? Let him renounce everything which is not true to him, and put all his practices back on their first thoughts, and do nothing for which he has not the whole world for his reason.[13]

If the situation seems hopeless, Emerson wishes to remind us that people have always raised themselves by the power of principles, and every great improvement in the human condition is the triumph of some enthusiasm.

"Our age and history, for these thousand years, has not been the history of kindness, but of selfishness," Emerson continued. That has cost us dearly. We spend great sums for courts and prisons, only to make felons worse. We alienate laboring people and permit the rich to rule over them. It would be better, Emerson said, to "let our affection flow out to our fellows; it would operate in a day the greatest of all revolutions." The state must give preference to relieving the plight of the poor, and all should voice their support. "Every child that is born must have a just chance for his bread," he insisted. "Let the amelioration in our laws of property proceed from the concession of the rich, not from the grasping of the poor. Let us begin by habitual imparting. Let us understand that the equitable rule is, that no one should take more than his share, let him be ever so rich."[14]

The true reformer is a "mediator between the spiritual and the actual world," putting moral principles into practice, not in intermittent "impulses of virtue," but consistently, and by making personal sacrifices for the greater social good. At the beginning of his lecture, Emerson observed that "the community in which we live will hardly bear to be told that every man should be open to ecstasy or a divine illumination, and his daily walk elevated by intercourse with the spiritual world." Yet this "opening of the spiritual senses" is precisely what is needed to curb the desire for power and fame.[15]

With this address, Emerson made clear the social implications of self-culture. "The internal logic of Emerson's program of self-culture inevitably dictated social justice as a means of the willed enactment of the ideal," David Robinson writes in his commentary on this lecture.[16] Emerson understood that the "new views" of the Transcendentalists included new views of politics and society and the necessity for taking action. Self-reliance did not lead to self-centered individualism, as some critics have said.

This lecture "illustrates Emerson's desire to translate individualistic self-culture into a workable ethical praxis,"[17] according to Robinson. Here we see that Emerson's idealism signifies a criterion or higher law with which to critique society. It's not something vague and impractical. In another address given later the same year, Emerson said, "The history of reform is always identical; it is the comparison of the idea with the fact."[18]

This viewpoint was typical of the Transcendentalists as a whole—Ripley, Parker, and Brownson, as well as Emerson, Thoreau, and Fuller. "The popular conception of the transcendentalists as aloof or withdrawn does not fully account for their tendency to regard responsibility for the nurture of the contemplative life as part of a social agenda," Robinson argues.[19] They did have differences of opinion, however, on whether the reform of individuals or the reform of institutions by collective means was the better way to correct social ills. In "The Laboring Classes," an article in the *Boston Quarterly Review* during this same period, Brownson argued forcefully that personal reform was ineffective in dealing with social evils—which some took as a public repudiation of core Transcendentalist values. Such evils as slavery, wealth inequality, and oppression of the working classes cannot be wiped out by reform of the self alone. These are "inherent in all our social arrangements, and cannot be cured without a radical change of those arrangements," he wrote. Systemic problems require systemic solutions. Brownson did not think such change "will ever be effected peaceably. It will be effected only by the strong arm of physical force. It will come, if ever it come at all, only at the conclusion of war, the like of which the world has yet ever witnessed."[20]

Brownson was especially critical of those who argued that individual repentance and reform were sufficient to solve social problems. He dismissed the idea that social change was at all dependent on "the spiritual growth of the soul." Still, the other Transcendentalists and Brownson agreed on many points. Emerson, too, believed that social ills were systemic in nature and required structural changes. Authentic change could not succeed through piecemeal tinkering with the mechanics of society but must begin with shaking "their foundations in our own nature." Although Emerson maintained that self-examination and self-reformation were essential to social change, he came to the view that, in the face of intractable evils like slavery, personal change was not sufficient; collective effort was required—but by self-reliant persons. Otherwise, you have a mob rather than a social movement. Fuller, too, came to the conclusion that collective effort was required to address the issue of urban poverty. But she, like Emerson, held that "we must have units before we can have union."[21]

Emerson was a reluctant warrior when it came to social action. Some of his critics feel he came late to the anti-slavery cause and then merely gave speeches. In his journal and to his friends, he did not feel cut out for the role. But, with others' prompting and his own outrage over slavery, he became increasingly involved. Emerson's example raises the question, What constitutes social activism? The range of activities the Transcendentalists engaged in, whether writing, protesting, or organizing—Ripley's Brook Farm; Thoreau's night in jail in protest of the war with Mexico and subsequent lecture on "Civil Disobedience" (undoubtedly the most influential political document of the era); Alcott's Temple School; Fuller's investigative reporting and editorializing on poverty, prostitution, and prison reform; Parker's powerful preaching in support of abolition and women's rights; Peabody's advocacy of early childhood education; Emerson's defense of John Brown (the list could go on and on)—all give evidence of the many ways they applied their principles to solving the social problems of the day.

10

ABOLITION AND WOMEN'S RIGHTS

The abolition of slavery and the fight for women's suffrage were the most pressing issues of civil rights during the nineteenth century. Viewing the role of the Transcendentalists in relation to these major efforts is key to understanding the connection between their brand of idealism and social action. Their actions were varied, but taken together, they were among the most radical responses to the injustices that, in their view, were rending the social fabric of American life.

ABOLITION

The anti-slavery crusade was the first of these defining issues, and the Transcendentalists were at its most militant center. Thoreau famously spent a night in jail protesting the U.S. invasion of Mexico, which served to expand slavery into Texas. His act became a model for practitioners of civil disobedience ever since. Emerson championed the cause of abolitionist and martyr John Brown, which set the stage for the election of President Abraham Lincoln. Parker, the most outspoken minister in Boston, railed against slavery and the complicity of northern manufacturers in support of Slave Power, the political influence held by slaveholders in the South. Higginson led an assault on the federal courthouse in Boston in 1854 in an attempt to free Anthony Burns, a fugitive slave, and went on to become the first to command a free black regiment in the Civil War.

Today it's hard to imagine how any moral, religious, or liberal-minded person, even 150 to 200 years ago, could have failed to demand that slavery be abolished, immediately. Yet in the 1830s most Unitarian ministers were devoted to maintaining the social and religious status quo for their wealthy parishioners. The northern economy was intricately tied up with the South's, and both depended on slavery for the textile industry and the sugar trade. A small number of Unitarian ministers were actively involved in the early anti-slavery movement, but the climate of Unitarian opinion was decidedly against them. Even those, such as William Ellery Channing, who opposed slavery, offered no plan for abolishing it, leaving that to slave owners to decide. Ministers who were more radical, such as Higginson, one of the younger Transcendentalists, were ousted from their pulpits.

At that time Harvard taught its ministers that reform came out of moral suasion and individual change of heart, not coercive legislation or force. That was the view the Transcendentalist ministers had been educated in as well—a view they eventually rejected after the passage of such appalling legislation as the Fugitive Slave Law in 1850 and the Kansas-Nebraska Act of 1854. Most Unitarians, like many others both in the North and South, believed that the rule of law—the Constitution, with its enshrinement of slavery, as well as the new legislation—should above all be followed. They were also fearful that forcing the issue of abolition might dissolve the Union. Brought up in a deeply embedded racist culture, many recoiled at the idea of racial equality, regardless of what they thought about slavery.

Massachusetts abolitionist William Lloyd Garrison spoke out early on in the fight against slavery, through speeches and published writings. In 1831 he founded a magazine called *The Liberator,* attracting a sizeable following. Most Transcendentalists, though sympathetic to the cause, were ambivalent about Garrison's platform. He advocated "immediatism," "disunion," non-resistance, and withdrawal from the political process, which many found problematic. In the early years of the abolition movement numerous proposals were put forth: sending freed slaves back to Africa, establishing a colony for black Americans in the United States, and purchasing their freedom. It took almost twenty years for the anti-slavery movement to gather momentum and sharpen its focus.

Although the passage of the Fugitive Slave Law did much to galvanize them into action, many of the Transcendentalists were involved in earlier stages of the movement. In 1930 Bronson and Abigail May Alcott publicly sided with Garrison. Abigail went on to help found the American Anti-Slavery Society in Philadelphia in 1834. By 1835 members of Ralph Waldo Emerson's family were won over to the cause, including his older brother, Charles, his aunt Mary, and his wife, Lidian. The Thoreau boarding house in Concord became an anti-slavery hangout as the entire family joined in the rising tide of abolitionist sentiment.

One of Garrison's strategies was to recruit women, who were quicker to recognize the barbarity of slavery and less persuaded by arguments of political and economic expediency. They joined the movement in large numbers, forming female anti-slavery societies, including one in Concord in 1837. In the process many women found strength in the fight for social justice and later turned their voices and organizational skills to the struggle for women's rights.

At the request of the Concord Female Anti-Slavery Society, Emerson agreed to deliver an address in 1844 on the tenth anniversary of emancipation in the British West Indies. Although he had spoken against slavery several times before, this was the first of his efforts to go deeply into the subject. He prepared a two-and-a-half-hour discourse, which almost didn't come off. The address was originally planned for the lawn at Emerson's Manse in Concord, but rain precluded an outdoor event. Local churches denied permission to use their buildings. Henry Thoreau rang the bell at the First Parish Church, in defiance of their refusal to allow it. The courthouse was chosen instead. The address marked Emerson's transition from philo-sophical opposition to slavery to active abolitionism. Aligning himself more fully with the abolitionist movement, he began to speak out more frequently and urgently.

Two years later, Thoreau made a point of refusing to pay a local poll tax in protest of the U.S. invasion of Mexico, where slavery was illegal. For that act of civil disobedience, he spent a night in jail in 1846. (Bronson Alcott had made a similar decision three years earlier, though he was not jailed on that account.) Cotton farmers seeking more land to establish plantations couldn't bring their slaves with them across the border into Mexico. By attacking

Mexico and annexing Texas, the United States was able to expand slavery. Thoreau wrote about his arrest and incarceration in a lecture on the individual's relation to the state, delivered at the Concord Lyceum in 1848 and later published by Elizabeth Peabody as "Resistance to Civil Government."

Thoreau called on self-reliant individuals to resist the law on the basis of conscience, which was a central Transcendentalist principle. The Constitution protected slavery. The Transcendentalists appealed to a "higher law," as expressed in the Declaration of Independence: that all people are created equal and possess inalienable rights. "Action from principle," Thoreau said, "is essentially revolutionary."[1] If the law requires us to be agents of injustice, then we must break it, or at any rate refuse to comply with it. The method he called for in this address is passive resistance, which shouldn't be confused with pacifism. He did not advocate violence, but he did not rule it out either. As the abolition cause heated up, Thoreau, like Emerson, became increasingly militant.

Through their assertive words and actions, both men may have played a key role in the 1860 election of Lincoln, and in doing so may have altered the course of American history. Following the abortive raid on Harpers Ferry, Brown was branded a lunatic in the North as well as the South. Starting in 1856, Emerson had helped raise funds to arm Brown, a radical abolitionist, and the Free Soil activists who were fighting against extending slavery into Kansas. As Brown became more desperate, he hatched a plan to precipitate a slave rebellion by raiding the federal arsenal at Harpers Ferry, West Virginia. He was arrested, tried, and executed for the offense. Many called him insane. Few came to his defense.

Among those who did, however, were the Transcendentalists. "It was the Transcendentalists alone who rescued him from infamy and possible oblivion," states American studies scholar David S. Reynolds in *John Brown, Abolitionist: The Man Who Killed Slavery, Sparked the Civil War, and Seeded Civil Rights*.[2] Thoreau delivered "A Plea for John Brown" and, following Brown's execution, another speech on "The Last Days of John Brown." In these speeches Thoreau controversially linked John Brown to Jesus Christ, "the two ends of a chain."[3] Emerson echoed that comparison in a lecture on "Courage" before a large crowd at the Music Hall in Boston in 1859, calling John Brown "that new saint, than whom none purer or braver was ever led by love of men into conflict and death,—the new saint awaiting his martyrdom, and who, if he shall suffer, will make the gallows glorious as the cross."[4] In Reynolds's view, "Emerson was as well positioned as anyone in America to accomplish such a rescue. Thoreau was eloquent about Brown, but he didn't come close to having Emerson's cultural clout."[5]

Commenting on the impact of this speech, Reynolds writes, "When aired publicly by Emerson, the 'gallows glorious' phrase sped through newspapers North and South like a ricocheting bullet. It outraged Brown's opponents and inspired his supporters. It was the most polarizing statement made about John Brown. It added fuel to the already inflamed sectional divisions that led to civil war."[6] Emerson made similar remarks later that month at a fundraising rally for Brown's family. So great was the outcry resulting from these speeches, especially in the South, that it caused a split in the Democratic Party. As a result, the party ran two slates of candidates in the presidential election, thus permitting Lincoln a victory he almost surely would not have won otherwise.[7]

"No one advanced [Brown's] cause more than Emerson," Reynolds writes.[8] He had come a long way. Emerson went on to give fourteen antislavery addresses, some several times. He campaigned for both John Palfrey, a Massachusetts Free Soil candidate for Congress, and for Lincoln's reelection. He became an ardent advocate of war to end slavery. He also argued for the equality of blacks and their right to vote, as well as monetary reparations—not to slave owners, as some proposed, but to the freed slaves: "Pay ransom to the owner / And fill the bag to the brim. / Who is the owner? The slave is owner, / And ever was. Pay *him*."[9] In Reynolds's opinion, Emerson's radicalism exceeded that of many others devoted to the anti-slavery cause.[10]

Even surpassing Emerson in his zeal for the abolition of slavery was Thomas Wentworth Higginson. Drawn to the spiritual vision and social activism of the Transcendentalist movement, he trained for the liberal ministry at Harvard Divinity School. He had agitated against the 1846 U.S. war of aggression against Mexico, before taking his first position as minister in Newburyport, Massachusetts, in 1847. In a Thanksgiving sermon, Higginson reproached church members for their materialism, their tolerance of slavery, and for having helped elect James K. Polk, a Tennessee slave-owner, as president. Rumblings of opposition toward his views began to grow in the congregation, and, as we have noted, he was forced to resign.

Higginson had first declared himself a disunion abolitionist, convinced that the Constitution could never be amended to abolish slavery as long as

the slave states remained in the Union. But with the passage of the Fugitive
Slave Act in 1850—which required northern officials to return suspected run-
away slaves and punished anyone who aided them with food or shelter—he
moved toward a more radical position. Citing "the higher law," he helped
establish the Boston Vigilance Committee, which resisted the new legislation
and helped protect fugitive slaves. In 1851 he participated in the failed attempt
to rescue Thomas Simms, a fugitive slave from Georgia, from a Boston courthouse. Then in 1854 he stormed the federal courthouse with a small group of
men, breaking down the door with a battering ram to free another fugitive
slave, Anthony Burns, who had escaped from Virginia. As Higginson rushed
inside, shots rang out and fighting ensued, leaving one deputy mortally
wounded. Higginson was indicted but never arrested or brought to trial.

The passage of the Kansas-Nebraska Act in 1854 further galvanized abolitionists like Higginson. That law allowed settlers to determine whether
slavery would be permitted in the new territories, nullifying the Missouri
Compromise that had forbidden slavery north of the 36°30' parallel and had
served to hold the Union together. Some New Englanders even moved to
Kansas in order to vote against slavery. Pro-slavery activists from Missouri,
called Border Ruffians, led an attack to try to drive the settlers out. In 1856
a mob of 800 sacked the new town of Lawrence, pillaging and burning the
newspaper office, hotel, and houses. In response, Higginson, acting as an
agent of the Massachusetts State Kansas Aid Committee, purchased guns
and ammunition and delivered them to the Kansas settlers. "I enjoy danger," he wrote in his journal, "while I know that I have incurred the death
penalty for treason under U.S. laws and for arming fugitives to Kansas."[11]

Like Emerson and Thoreau, Higginson also became a champion of John
Brown. He joined with fellow Transcendentalist Theodore Parker and four
others to form the "Secret Six" to raise money for Brown and support his
strategy of inciting a slave insurrection in the South. When Brown was
jailed for the failed raid at Harpers Ferry in 1859, Higginson hatched a plot
to free him, though Brown preferred a martyr's death instead.

Higginson wanted the South to secede. But when Congress, in 1861,
passed the Confiscation Act, emancipating all slaves held by Confederate
forces, he decided to join the Civil War effort on the side of the Union,
saying that as "no prominent anti-slavery man has yet taken a marked share
in the war, . . . I have made up my mind to take part in the affair, hoping
to aid in settling it the quicker."[12] In November 1862 he accepted an offer to

command the first black regiment of the Civil War, the 1st South Carolina Volunteers. The regiment was recruited, trained, and stationed at Beaufort, South Carolina. Many doubted the bravery and fighting ability of freed slaves, but Higginson had confidence in his troops. "Till the blacks were armed, there was no guaranty of their freedom," he wrote in his account called *Army Life in a Black Regiment.* "It was their demeanor under arms that shamed the nation into recognizing them as men."[13]

After Lincoln's assassination, President Andrew Johnson instituted a Reconstruction plan that allowed southern states to elect many of their old leaders and pass Black Codes to deprive the freedmen of many civil liberties. Higginson denounced the plan, saying it legitimized the continued oppression of black people in the South. "It is simply that we are forgiving our enemies," he wrote, "and torturing only our friends."[14]

WOMEN'S RIGHTS

Caroline Healey Dall, who died in 1912, outliving Higginson by a year and a half, was perhaps the last of the Transcendentalists. In an 1895 lecture, Dall argued that the movement began and ended with two women: Anne Hutchison and Margaret Fuller. "The characteristics of the Transcendental movement were shown in the temper of its agitation for the rights of women and the enlargement of her duties." She went on to say, "Every Transcendentalist was ready, and indeed had good reason to assert that there was 'no sex in souls.'"[15] What is good for men is good for women as well:

> Men and women are healthier in their bodies, happier in their domestic and social relations, more ambitious to enlarge their opportunities, more kind and humane in sympathy, as well as more reasonable in expectation, than they would have been if Margaret and Emerson had never lived. Under the influence of transcendental thought and hope, the mind of universal man leaped forward with a bound.[16]

Dall "understood reform of *self* as the key to the reform of *society,* and feminism—grounded in the belief that there was 'no sex in souls'—as the key to unlocking the potential of women's selves," Tiffany K. Wayne writes.[17] Essential to the transformation of both self and society was the notion of self-culture. It provided not only the message of self-reliance but also the means or method of achieving it. For women chafing under male dominance, self-culture gave them female selfhood and empowerment.

Transcendentalism attracted numerous accomplished women in addition to Dall: Margaret Fuller, Elizabeth Palmer Peabody, Julia Ward Howe, Sophia Ripley, Lydia Maria Child, Edna Dow Cheney, as well as Emerson's remarkable aunt, Mary Moody Emerson. These women were among the originators of feminism in America.

Margaret Fuller linked the struggle for women's rights to the abolition movement. Women, too, were held in a form of slavery and lacked fundamental rights, she said. Writing of the nation's march toward freedom and equality, she noted:

> Of all its banners, none has been more steadily upheld, and under none has more valor and willingness for real sacrifices been shown, than that of the champions of the enslaved African. And this band it is, which, partly in consequence of following out of principles, partly because many women have been prominent in that cause, makes, just now, the warmest appeal in behalf of woman.

She recognized, however, that the country as a whole was no more ready to liberate women than enslaved Africans. "'It is not enough,' cries the sorrowful trader, 'that you have done all you could to break up the national Union,'" she wrote, "'but now you must be trying to break up family union, to take my wife away from the cradle, and the kitchen hearth, to vote at polls, and preach from a pulpit?'"[18] In an 1843 essay for the *Dial*, called "The Great Lawsuit," Fuller pleaded the case for American women. She later expanded on the essay in her book *Woman in the Nineteenth Century*, her most significant work as a writer and the first manifesto of its kind produced in America.

Fuller embodied the gospel of self-culture. As we have seen, her motto in life was "extraordinary generous seeking," taken from Goethe, her literary hero. Her close friend James Freeman Clarke wrote that her great "aim, from first to last, was SELF-CULTURE." She said it best herself:

> Very early I knew that the only object in life was to grow. I was often false to this knowledge, in idolatries of particular objects, or impatient longings for happiness, but I have never lost sight of it, have always been controlled by it, and this first gift of thought has never been superseded by a later love.[19]

In "The Great Lawsuit," she applied the notion of self-culture to the empowerment of women. In her view society impeded women in their ability to develop fully as human beings. They were restricted to home, church, and their role as helpmates to men and their ambitions. They had no agency of their own. Even if they were unmarried, as Fuller was, they could not control their own finances, own property, or vote.

As mentioned in the previous chapter, some critics have viewed self-culture as a hindrance to social change. But I believe it had a political dimension as well as a spiritual one. In fact it had a political dimension precisely *because* it had a spiritual one. In discussing the influence of Fuller, David Robinson writes, "The very individualism that self-culture fostered in her took on an inescapably political aspect when she applied it to the condition of women in America. What had been denied women was the opportunity for development; to pursue that opportunity now meant to eliminate the social sources of the denial."[20] In Fuller's words, "We would have every arbitrary barrier thrown down. We would have every path laid open to woman as freely as to man. . . . What woman needs now is not as a woman to act or rule, but as a nature to grow, as an intellect to discern, as a soul to live freely, and unimpeded to unfold such powers as were give her when we left our common home."[21]

To accomplish this result women need to rely on themselves to assert their freedom, not on men to grant it. "Miranda," Fuller's imagined ideal of a liberated woman, tells Fuller, "The position I early was enabled to take, was one of self-reliance. And were all women as sure of their wants as I was, the result would be the same. The difficulty is to get them to the point where they shall naturally develop self-respect, the question is how it is to be done. Once I thought that men would help on this state of things more than I do now." Men, she said, wish "to be lord over a little world, to be superior at least over one." Not only is "man vain and fond of power, but the same want of development, which thus affects him morally in the intellect, prevents him from discerning the destiny of woman." If man is lacking in faith and love, it is "because he is not yet himself an elevated being."[22] Self-culture is the solution to the problem of women's rights on both sides of the equation.

The patriarchy Fuller found in society she saw in the church as well. The churches, dominated by male ministers, were defenders of the status quo, and Fuller found little in Christian scripture that was a useful model for women. She turned to mythology and ancient history to find examples of women's empowerment. In particular, she urged women to embrace the image of Minerva, the Roman goddess of wisdom and war (called Athena by the Greeks), in their struggle for selfhood. Minerva was an emblem of female agency and self-reliance, a virgin goddess beyond male control. Fuller believed women had another side also, represented by the Muse, or female creativity and intuitive power. She envisioned a balance between these two aspects of women's nature, but because the creative powers of the Muse were suppressed by male dominance, women needed to summon Minerva, the warrior within, to throw off their subjugation.

Men, too, are enslaved and impeded in their own self-fulfillment by habit and social customs. Notably, Fuller argued that men and women both possessed masculine and feminine traits. "Male and female represent the two sides of the great radical dualism," she wrote. "But, in fact, they are perpetually passing into one another. Fluid hardens to solid, solid rushes to fluid. There is no wholly masculine man, no purely feminine woman."[23] The self-fulfillment of women *and* men depend on achieving a balance in each between the qualities of both. In seeking self-fulfillment, they should look to their own resources. Relationships are precious, "but only to the soul which is poised upon itself." If people live too much in their relations, they are cut off from "the renovating fountains" of their own inner nature. "Union is only possible to those who are units," she insisted. "To be fit for relations in time, souls, whether of man or woman, must be able to do without them in the spirit." Thus women should resist the idea of being taught or led by men so that they might enter into relations with them "from the fullness, not the poverty of being."[24]

Fuller's book *Woman in the Nineteenth Century* appeared three years before the 1848 Women's Convention in Seneca Falls, New York. It significantly influenced her feminist contemporaries, many of whom went on to lead the fight for women's suffrage. Elizabeth Cady Stanton and Susan B. Anthony said of Fuller that she "possessed more influence upon the thought of American women than any woman previous to her time."[25] Nevertheless, the role of Margaret Fuller and other Transcendentalist women in the struggle for women's rights has only recently received much attention. "Political division between suffrage organizations in New York and Boston had resulted in Stanton and Anthony's substantial effacement of the Boston record," according to women's studies scholar Phyllis Cole.[26] Although Fuller died almost twenty years prior to the formation of the Boston-based American Woman Suffrage Association, its leaders, including

Transcendentalists Dall, Howe, and Peabody, continued to promote Fuller's vision of female self-culture.

Several Transcendentalist men—Parker, William Henry Channing, and Higginson in particular—were strong allies in support of women's rights and suffrage. Higginson, who championed the full empowerment of women in all areas of life, stands out. He signed the call for the first national women's rights convention in 1850 and frequently spoke at women's rights meetings. He advocated equal pay for women, female representation on committees and boards, college education for young women, equality of men and women in marriage, as well as suffrage. "The protest of women," he said in an 1853 address called "Woman and Her Wishes" before the Massachusetts Constitutional Convention, "is not against a special abuse, but against a whole system of injustice; and the peculiar importance of political suffrage to woman is only because it seems to be the most available point to begin with. Once recognize the political equality of the sexes, and all the questions of legal, social, educational and professional equality will soon settle themselves."[27] A close friend of Lucy Stone and Julia Ward Howe, he was a supporter of the American Woman Suffrage Association and for fourteen years served as co-editor and frequent contributor to its publication, *Woman's Journal.*

Despite the activism of Dall, Howe, and Peabody (continuing, in the cases of Dall and Howe, into the early years of the twentieth century), the Transcendentalist strain of feminist thought and action, which they represented, largely disappeared from view as time went on. That obscurity might seem to imply that their strategy of changing society's treatment of women through the education of women themselves, that is, through self-culture, was ineffective. Yet Fuller's words seem as relevant today as they did when she first wrote them:

> Give the soul free course, let the organization be freely developed, and the being will be fit for any and every relation to which it may be called. The intellect, no more than the sense of hearing, is to be cultivated, not that she may be a more valuable companion to man, but because the Power who gave a power by its mere existence signifies that it must be brought out towards perfection.[28]

11

EDUCATION,
ENVIRONMENTALISM,
AND SUSTAINABILITY

In addition to their active involvement in abolition and the promotion of women's rights, some of the Transcendentalists were engaged in other reforms as well. Theodore Parker and William Henry Channing advocated for the working classes. George Ripley and Bronson Alcott conducted experiments in collective living. Margaret Fuller investigated the conditions of the poor and women prisoners in New York and wrote of the woeful treatment of Native Americans. Beyond his strong support of abolition and women's rights, Thomas Wentworth Higginson was committed to rooting out corruption in government, ending American imperialism abroad, and introducing physical education in public schools. Many of these reforms were far-reaching. Three in particular, involving education, the environment, and sustainability, have been especially influential.

EDUCATIONAL REFORM

For all the varied kinds of work and activism their lives led them to, many of the Transcendentalists shared a common start to their careers. They were teachers first: Emerson for five years, Thoreau for four, and Fuller for two (five more if one counts her famous Conversations). Bronson Alcott and Elizabeth Peabody found their vocations as educators, writing treatises on teaching methods and advocating educational reforms. Education, whether implicitly or explicitly, was at the heart of most everything they did: writing, lecturing, or leading conversations. They identified it with self-culture, defined as the education, or as Emerson put it, the "drawing out" of the soul.[1] Though they were all exceedingly well educated, they complained of traditional aims and methods of education, both as students and teachers. "What does education often do?" Thoreau wrote in his journal. "It makes a straight-cut ditch of a free, meandering brook."[2]

In 1837, Emerson was invited to give an address dedicating the Greene Street School in Providence, Rhode Island, where Margaret Fuller was teaching. The school was an experiment in progressive education, founded on the pedagogical principles that guided Bronson Alcott's School for Human Culture—better known as the Temple School—in Boston. Alcott was scheduled to speak until the controversy surrounding his latest book, *Conversations with Children on the Gospels,* caused him to withdraw in favor of Emerson. As the title suggests, Alcott's book consisted of transcriptions of dialogues with children on biblical topics. In one of these conversations, Alcott used the story of the Virgin Mary to introduce the children to the mysteries of birth. When the book appeared, its author was accused of blasphemy and the school lost students, forcing it to close.

In his address, Emerson faulted the education system as serving the needs of a growing capitalist economy more than developing young minds. (He repeated his criticism two months later in his more famous "American Scholar" address at Harvard.) Students' "higher faculties" have been sacrificed to instrumental goods, he charged. Education is focused too much on getting a living rather than making a life. It should develop the whole person and cultivate curiosity, character, and self-confidence. Instead, education "has truckled" to the materialistic spirit of "the times":

> We do not teach [young students] to aspire to be all they can. We do not give them a training as if we believed in their noble nature. We scarce educate their bodies. We do not train the eye and the hand. We exercise their understandings to the apprehension and comparison of some facts, to a skill in numbers, in words; we aim to make them accountants, attorneys, engineers; but not to make able, earnest, great-hearted men. . . .

The great object of Education should be commensurate with the object of life. It should be a moral one; to teach self-trust: to inspire the youthful man with an interest in himself; with a curiosity touching his own nature; to acquaint him with the resources of his mind, and to teach him that there is all his strength, and inflame him with a piety towards the Great Mind in which he lives.[3]

The goal of education should be aligned with the ends of human life—not to make a fortune, but to explore oneself. "If it falls short of this," Emerson said, "if it becomes mere routine, if it teach a little grammar and arithmetic, a little geography and logic, and there stop, it is false to its trust; it then makes no resistance to the torrent that is drowning the intellect and the soul; it then only arms the senses with a little more cunning to pursue their low ends; it makes only more skilful servants of mammon and puffs them up with a seeming wisdom."[4] If his audience expected a few platitudes on the subject, they got a jeremiad instead.

At the Temple School, the model for the Greene Street School and others like it, Alcott introduced reforms in teaching that are taken for granted today. At the time rote learning was the standard method of instruction. Alcott took an inductive approach, using Socratic questioning and inquiry-based investigation. Students sat in a semi-circle so that they and the teacher could all see one another as they spoke. Alcott viewed the teacher as a guide, whose duty was not to drill or threaten students, but to accompany them in their learning. Journals and autobiographies enabled students to develop introspection and writing skills.

Fuller taught briefly at Alcott's Temple School before taking a position at the Greene Street School. But her primary contribution to education was the series of Conversations, primarily with women, which she led over a five-year period at Peabody's West Street salon in Boston. Like Alcott, Fuller believed in using conversation to promote self-culture. And both used Socratic dialogue as their primary teaching method. Fuller felt that she was not "to *teach* any thing," but rather to "call . . . out the thought of others," to facilitate the discussion, not to dominate it.[5]

Henry David Thoreau taught briefly at the public school in Concord after his graduation from Harvard College, but resigned over a disagreement concerning the use of corporeal punishment in the classroom. Shortly after he began teaching, a member of the school committee visited his classroom. Taking Thoreau aside, he demanded that he flog his students lest he spoil them. He handed in his resignation the next day. In 1838 he opened his own school, the Concord Academy, and was soon joined by his brother, John. The two brothers stressed the notion of learning by doing. The students went on field trips to study nature, raised food on plots of land, and learned surveying to develop their mathematics skills. "Knowledge is to be acquired only by a corresponding experience," he wrote. "How can we *know* what we are *told* merely?"[6] When his brother became seriously ill in 1841, Thoreau decided he couldn't carry on by himself and closed the school. But he was long remembered, in the words of one of his students, for having "taught us to admire and appreciate all that was impressive and beautiful in the natural world around us."[7]

Peabody taught at schools in Maine, New Jersey, and Massachusetts, and also with Alcott at the Temple School. Her *Record of a School* describes Temple's pioneering efforts in holistic, progressive education. Peabody had some criticisms of Alcott's methods, believing he was at times too autocratic, but they agreed that child development should unfold naturally, with the guidance of the teacher. In a treatise titled *Theory of Teaching*, she stated, "I will not control, and tutor, and dictate, but . . . supply ample nutriment to heart, intellect and the organs, and let them unfold in their own lovely proportions. I do not expect, by doing so much for them to obviate the necessity of self-education. I mean only to carry them as far as another can; and from this vantage-ground must begin self-education; which alone secures peace and strength."[8] She went on to open the first English-language kindergarten in the United States in 1860, the accomplishment she is most remembered for. Her kindergarten curriculum emphasized physical activity, play, and social interaction.

Brook Farm, the experiment in communal living started by George and Sophia Ripley, also contributed to educational innovations of the time. One of the farm's goals was "to secure to our children and those who may be entrusted to our care the benefits of the highest physical, intellectual and moral education, which in the process of knowledge the resources at our command will permit," according to its constitution.[9] Education was, in the Ripleys' view, the community's leading purpose. Brook Farm offered programs from preschool to college preparation, as well as evening classes for adults, all taught on the basis of Transcendentalist educational principles. The school attracted children and youth of all classes from surrounding towns and integrated them into its community life. It was widely considered to be the most successful of Brook Farm's many undertakings and its chief means of financial support.

In an article written for the *Dial* magazine in 1844, Charles Lane, an English reformer and friend of Bronson Alcott, commented on the school at Brook Farm. "It is time that the imitative and book learned systems of [the New England schools] should be superseded or liberalized, by some plan better calculated to excite originality of thought and the native energies of the mind," he wrote. "Brook Farm, with its spontaneous teachers, presents the unusual and cheering condition of a really 'free school.'"[10]

There was a nursery school for children under six, a primary school for those under ten, and a preparatory school that fitted students for college. The curriculum consisted of languages, literature, music, art, dancing, mathematics, and science. Many of the courses were electives, since the school encouraged students to follow their own course of study. It was also expected that students would work in the shops, the farm, the garden, or the household, selecting their own tasks. John Van Der Zee Sears, a former student, described his own experience in the school at Brook Farm. "School work was done as far as practicable, out of doors," he wrote. "Botany, geology, natural history and what was then called natural philosophy were taught among the rocks, in the woods and in the fields with illustrations from nature."[11]

Because self-culture was viewed as a life-long process, the Transcendentalists did not confine their innovations in education to teaching the young. Like Fuller and Alcott, Thoreau envisioned a similar but more expansive effort in *Walden:*

> We boast that we belong to the Nineteenth Century and are making the most rapid strides of any nation. But consider how little this village does for its own culture. . . . We have a comparatively decent system of common schools, schools for infants only; but excepting the half-starved Lyceum in the winter, and latterly the puny beginning of a library suggested by the state, no school for ourselves. . . . It is time that we had uncommon schools, that we did not leave off our education when we begin to be men and women. It is time that villages were universities, and their elder inhabitants the fellows of universities, with leisure—if they are indeed so well off—to pursue liberal studies the rest of their lives.[12]

Thoreau did little to advance this concept other than to announce it. But Alcott did. Together with educators from Concord and the Midwest, Alcott established in 1879 the Concord School of Philosophy, a "university" for adult education embodying his educational precepts. The school was open to all at nominal cost, and attracted as many as one hundred participants annually from as far away as Michigan and Missouri to attend lectures and conversations on Transcendentalist topics. Although it lasted only nine years, until Alcott's death in 1888, it extended the influence of Transcendentalism well into the late nineteenth century, with growing success each year. The first session was held at Orchard House, once the Alcott family residence. The session continued for five weeks, with daily lectures and conversations Monday through Friday, and special presentations on Saturday. As many as sixty attendees gathered in the Alcotts' parlor or sat on the grass outside. The following year a wooden building, Hillside Chapel, was constructed to the rear of the house, paid for by a wealthy philanthropist from New York. The new Gothic-style building, adorned with busts of Emerson and Alcott by Daniel Chester French, could hold as many as 150 people. Transcendentalist stalwarts such as Peabody, Alcott, Emerson, Howe, Cheney, and numerous other scholars served as faculty. Guest lecturers came from Harvard, Yale, and Cornell, and several midwestern colleges.

As the roster of distinguished speakers grew, Alcott began to worry that the school's offerings had become too academic, to the "suppression even, of the spiritual and the ideal."[13] It was mysticism and the cultivation of the soul that mattered to Alcott, not the recondite philosophies of Kant and Hegel. After the school's last regular session in 1887, the local newspaper praised its successes:

> From nearly, or quite half, the States of the Union, and from many a great city and small hamlet, from seashore and valley and prairie, from the ranks of all professions and from the throngs of common work-a-day life, men and women, young and old, have come here this summer to listen to the most abstruse discussions and participate in the "plain living and high thinking" which are afforded and illustrated here.[14]

A graceful if weathered monument to the enduring allure of "plain living and high thinking," the Hillside Chapel still stands today. It offers summer sessions open to teachers, students, and members of the Thoreau Society who come to Concord each year.

The pedagogical principles the Transcendentalists upheld included the following: educating the whole person, experiential learning, using all the senses, nourishing the inner life and the imagination, and balancing the curriculum between academic subjects and character development. These principles comprise what modern educators call holistic education. Central to this view is the thesis that nurturing the soul is vital to human development, in sharp contrast to modern educational trends that stress a common core curriculum and testing. As in Emerson's day, however, this debate begs the broader questions of the purpose of education and the best methods of achieving it. If we believe that the aims of education should be commensurate with the ends of human life, then their principles are still relevant today.

While some of the principles of holistic education have been adopted in public schools, they are more likely to be implemented in alternative schools, such as Montessori and Waldorf schools. In recent years, programs have been established to educate children in ways that are even more in keeping with Transcendentalist methods. One example, IslandWood, is located where I live: on Bainbridge Island in Washington State. A 255-acre learning center founded in 1999, IslandWood offers students from urban environments the opportunity to explore the natural world, experience the joy of learning outdoors, and discover their own capacity to change the world around them. Each year more than 12,000 students from 160 schools in the Puget Sound area explore their connection to the natural world through week-long immersion programs at the center. Similarly, the Walden Woods Project, located at the Thoreau Institute near Walden Pond, offers classroom activities and field trips designed to bring children and youth into closer contact with the natural world. A quotation from Thoreau's journal on the institute's website captures its educational philosophy: "We are all schoolmasters, and our schoolhouse is the universe. To attend chiefly to the desk or schoolhouse while we neglect the scenery in which it is placed is absurd."[15]

ENVIRONMENTALISM AND SUSTAINABILITY

Literary historian Lawrence Buell has called Thoreau "the patron saint of American environmental writing."[16] Nearly every book about ecology or the environment has at least a few pages, if not a whole chapter, devoted to Thoreau's influence. Roderick Nash, whose *Wilderness and the American Mind* is a classic text on American attitudes toward the wilderness, credits Thoreau, in calling for the preservation of nature, for being the first truly ecocentric voice in America.[17] In his essay "Down the River with Henry Thoreau," environmentalist Edward Abbey likens him to a suburban coyote yipping at the domesticated dogs, "taunting them, enticing them with the old-time call of the wild."[18] In a more reflective mood a few pages later, Abbey writes, "I look for his name in the water, his face in the airy foam. He must be there. Wherever there are deer and hawks, wherever there is liberty and danger, wherever there is wilderness, wherever there is a living river, Henry Thoreau will find his eternal home."[19] Scholar of religion and nature Bron Taylor calls Thoreau America's first prophet of "dark green religion," which he defines as "religion that considers nature to be sacred, imbued with intrinsic value, and worthy of reverent care."[20]

Emerson, like Thoreau, was a major influence on American nature writers, such as John Muir and John Burroughs. As a Romantic, Emerson expressed a mystical, almost pantheistic sense of oneness with nature. "In the woods, we return to reason and faith," he wrote. "There I feel that nothing can befal me in life . . . which nature cannot repair. Standing on the bare ground,—my head bathed by the blithe air, and uplifted into infinite space,—all mean egotism vanishes. I become a transparent eye-ball. I am nothing; I see all. The currents of the Universal Being circulate through me; I am part or particle of God."[21]

Christian scripture had influenced European settlers in America to consider nature—its plants, animals, water soil, and minerals—ripe for the taking, and not as something sacred and worthy of reverence. Nature was a resource to be exploited for human benefit, not something sacred in itself. With the rise of Romanticism, many thinkers began to find a deeper meaning in nature. It became a source of revelation and an object of reverence. The importance of Emerson's anonymously published, slender volume *Nature* cannot be overstated. Emerson articulated an epistemology and a metaphysics that established the basis for a religio-aesthetic appreciation of nature. This validation of natural piety gave credence to the argument that nature is sacred. However, Emerson's Platonic idealism viewed nature as an abstraction. Thoreau was more interested in nature itself—as were Muir and Burroughs—and this quality in his writing has made Thoreau a more lasting influence.

Thoreau was essentially a pastoral writer, idealizing "a less urbanized, more 'natural' state of existence," in Buell's words.[22] Though famous for his remark "In wildness is the preservation of the world," there was little of the wild in his native Concord. The parcels of land surrounding Walden Pond were mostly woodlots, harvested for fuel in home fireplaces. Timber was also logged off for the railroads. Visitors to the site of Thoreau's cabin at Walden Pond today get the impression that it was comfortably nestled in a wooded grove, but in his day Walden Woods was sparser. Thoreau would have had an almost unobstructed view of the pond from his cabin, located a hundred yards or so from the shore. When he did meet the wild face-to-face, as he did on a visit to Mt. Ktaadn in Maine (he preferred the native spelling for the place now commonly known as Katahdin), Thoreau found the experience rather unnerving. As he neared the summit of the mountain, he panicked: "What is this Titan that has possession of me? Talk of mysteries!—Think of our life in nature,—daily to be shown matter, to come in contact with it,—rocks, trees, wind on our cheeks! the *solid* earth! the *actual* world! the *common sense! Contact! Contact! Who* are we? *where* are we?"[23] Still, his alarm at the devastation of the landscape, his identification with nature in its raw or wild state, and his nonconformist lifestyle have endeared Thoreau to preservationists and nature lovers ever since.

Thoreau was equally famous for his voluntary simplicity. Reducing material wants, practicing self-sustainability, and cultivating the soul in leisure and solitude were as important to him as preserving the environment. This process of relinquishment, or purgation, was necessary prior to establishing a better relationship with nature, Buell says. That explains why "Economy" is both the first and the longest chapter of *Walden.* To be initiated, one must first be cleansed. *Walden,* and Thoreau's thinking generally, progresses from an egocentric to an ecocentric ethic. A preoccupation with the self and the accumulation of material goods grows out of the utilitarian view of the world as a resource for human uses. In an ecocentric worldview, everything is related and interdependent. Buell shows that in the book itself there is an inverse ratio between the use of the word "*I*" and references to "*nature,*" reflecting the progression from egoism to ecocentrism.[24] Voluntary poverty functions as a form of *kenosis,* or detachment. By living simply and giving up material possessions, one can shift from the utilitarian perspective of the Understanding to the holistic vantage point of the Reason. This is why voluntary poverty is necessarily related to environmental activism.

The publication of Emerson's *Nature* and Thoreau's *Walden* was the inception of the movement for eco-justice and global sustainability, the largest social movement in human history, according to environmentalist and entrepreneur Paul Hawken in his 2007 book, *Blessed Unrest.* Hawken tells the story of Emerson's visit to the botanical museum in Paris on his first trip to Europe in 1833. There, he experienced an epiphany. Intuitively he realized the interconnectedness of all living things, and "an occult relation" that existed between man and nature. On his return Emerson gave a series of lectures on natural history from an ecocentric perspective at the Boston Society of Natural History. Hawken writes of this discovery:

> Almost as a testament to his discovery of mutual interdependence, Emerson planted seeds that would develop into what were and continue to be, two disparate concepts that animate our daily existence: how we treat nature and how we treat one another—the foundations of environmental and social justice. . . . The morality he proposed came from perceiving and receiving nature, not from established codes or judgments: "I have confidence in laws of morals as of botany. I have planted maize in my field every June for seventeen years and I never knew it come up strychnine. My parsley, beet, turnip, carrot, buckthorn, chestnut, acorn, are as sure. I believe that justice produces justice, and injustice injustice."[25]

Hawken goes on to credit Thoreau's application of Emerson's "moral botany" to the problems of war and slavery. Thoreau noticed that human society is interrelated just as nature is. When one person disrupts the social order by acting from principle—as Thoreau did by protesting the U.S. invasion of Mexico—that small action can have far-reaching consequences "How do we sow our seeds when large, well-intentioned institutions and intolerant ideologies that purport to be our salvation cause so much damage?" Hawken asks. "One sure way is through smallness, grace, and locality. . . . Thoreau insisted in *Civil Disobedience* that if only one man withdrew his support for an unjust government, it would begin a cycle that would reverberate and grow. . . . 'For it matters not how small the beginning may seem to be: what is once well done is done forever.'"[26]

The same is true of Transcendentalism's influence on the eco-justice movement. The thoughts and actions of a small group of individuals have had far-ranging consequences. Literary scholar Robert E. Burkholder writes:

> [The Transcendentalists'] emphasis on the spiritual aspects of nature made it possible to think of it as something more than an object to be exploited for profit, and they made revelation in and wonder of nature a continuing possibility, even in times of cynicism. In sum, their concept

of the potential intimacy of people and nature gave arguments for the preservation of wild land and wildlife a plausibility and power that they would not otherwise have had.[27]

Sustainability and simple living are of a piece with the preservation of wild nature. The Transcendentalists have inspired countless individuals to heed their call, generating such movements as back-to-the-land and, more recently, tiny houses.

Progress has been made in wilderness preservation and environmental protection, thanks to the early advocacy of writers such as Emerson, Thoreau, and all those they inspired. Though a conservationist rather than a preservationist, President Theodore Roosevelt was a fan of Emerson and Thoreau, a friend of Muir and Burroughs, and an avid outdoorsman himself. During his administration, Roosevelt established the United States Forest Service and signed into law the creation of 150 National Forests, 51 Federal Bird Reservations, 4 National Game Preserves, 6 National Parks, and 18 National Monuments. The area of the United States that he placed under public protection totals approximately 230,000,000 acres.[28] The Sierra Club, founded in 1892 by John Muir, and similar organizations have been influential in promoting the creation and preservation of wilderness areas in the years since then. Since the passage of the Wilderness Act in 1964, 750 wilderness areas, including almost 110 million acres of land, have been created.

Gains in living more simply and sustainably have also been achieved. As David E. Shi, author of *The Simple Life: Plain Living and High Thinking in American Culture,* observes, simple living has exercised a powerful influence in American society. "It has, in a sense, served as the nation's conscience," Shi writes, "providing a vivifying counterpoint to the excesses of materialist individualism." Proponents of simple living, such as Emerson, Thoreau, Muir, and Burroughs, have "proved that simplicity could be more than a hollow sentiment or a temporary expedient; it could be a living creed."[29]

Examples of simple living and sustainability since the time of the Transcendentalists are so numerous that it is impossible to name them all. Inspired by the writings of Emerson and Thoreau, naturalist John Burroughs in 1895 created Slabsides, a nine-acre farm and cabin in New York, where he wrote many of his books and raised his own food. Similarly motivated, Helen and Scott Nearing established a homestead in Maine in 1952 where they practiced rural self-sufficiency. They described their nineteen-year back-to-the-land experiment in *Living the Good Life: How to Live Simply and Sanely in a Troubled World.*[30] Their experience has encouraged many others to follow their example.[31] Beginning in the 1980s, the tiny house movement, advocating living simply in very small homes, has gained in popularity. For a number of years, Diana and Michael Lorence lived in a small cabin in the California woods, which they called Innermost House. Diana Lorence describes her experience in words that remind us of Thoreau's life at Walden Pond:

> Innermost House is my home in the woods, where my husband and I have lived for many years. The house is about twelve feet square, and there is no electricity or hot water. Yet we live a life of luxury. The greatest luxury in life is to live with what you truly love.
>
> So many people wish to simplify their lives today. People I meet want to know how I made my way to what I call an Innermost Life. The great question is how—how to make a new beginning at a truly simple life.[32]

Finally, I call attention to the work of *Yes! Magazine,* a quarterly publication promoting ideas for achieving peace and justice, environmental preservation, and simple living and sustainability. The magazine has 150,000 readers and more than 140,000 visits to its website every week. In these and many other ways the Transcendentalist vision of "high thinking and simple living" is alive and well and making a difference in the lives of many people.

12

CHURCH REFORM AND THE FREE RELIGIOUS ASSOCIATION

As we have seen, most of the Transcendentalists were or had been ministers. Those who chose to remain in the ministry introduced reforms in worship and congregational life, visible even today in Unitarian Universalist churches. Yet the breach between the Transcendentalists and the more conservative Unitarians continued to widen as the Unitarian Association, founded in 1825, sought to achieve consensus around a statement of liberal Christian views. Many of the Transcendentalists considered themselves nonsectarian and resisted the attempt to draft a creed, no matter how liberal, on the grounds of religious freedom. This conflict led to the formation of the Free Religious Association in 1867. The first to join was Ralph Waldo Emerson.

CHURCH REFORM

Parishioners at Boston's Second Church liked the preaching of their young minister, Ralph Waldo Emerson, even though his sermon style was unconventional for the early 1830s. He always opened with a brief Bible reading, as was customary, but he seldom referred to the Bible in his sermons, an omission that did not go unnoticed. While his own preaching received favorable reviews, Emerson found most Unitarian preaching, with its heavy reliance on high-sounding words and formal oratorical style, dull and uninspired. "It comes out of the memory, and not out of the soul," he said in his 1938 "Divinity School Address." It was driving people away from church. "I think no man can go with his thoughts about him into one of our own churches, without feeling that what hold the public worship had on men is gone, or going," he observed. "I have heard a devout person, who prized the Sabbath, say in bitterness of heart, 'On Sundays, it seems wicked to go to church.'" Emerson's remedy was to preach from the soul and to breathe new life into "the forms already existing."[1]

Emerson was also moving away from supernaturalism and toward a natural religion. As a result, his views on Christian ritual also changed. When he told his congregation in 1832 that he no longer wished to serve the Lord's Supper, that announcement created an uproar. He didn't find the ritual personally fulfilling nor did he believe that Jesus had sanctioned the practice. Church leaders tried to persuade him otherwise, but he could not agree and voluntarily left the pulpit. From that time on, Transcendentalism was engaged in church reform that altered the course of Unitarianism as well as liberal Christianity as a whole.

The Transcendentalists agreed that what was lacking in worship was spirituality, or soul. They looked to the Romantic writers, to the mystics, and to their own experiences in nature for inspiration. Some left the ministry; those who remained drew on these resources in their preaching and looked for ways to enhance the entire worship experience, with hymns, readings, and rituals that opened the hearts of their congregations, not just spoke to their heads.[2] The "new Church," or the "Church of the Future," and its organization, doctrine and, and rites were frequent topics of discussion at the meetings of the Transcendental Club between 1836 and 1840.[3]

Among the first to experiment with new forms of worship and church organization was Orestes Brownson. In 1836 he organized the Society for Christian Union and Progress. By coincidence, the group met in that hothouse of Transcendentalist activity, the Masonic Temple in Boston, downstairs from Bronson Alcott's Temple School. Few records were kept about the society, which was loosely organized, so details are scarce. Membership was open to anyone who held to Christian morality and free inquiry, and who desired to promote social progress. Brownson dispensed with the custom of pew holding—paying a fee to reserve the same pew to sit in at each meeting—hoping to attract poor and working-class members. In 1844, however, he converted to Catholicism and his services as a Unitarian minister ceased.

Another Transcendentalist, James Freeman Clarke, in forming the Church of the Disciples in 1841, established a set of three principles: the voluntary principle, the social principle, and the principle of congregational worship.[4] Clarke did away with both pew renting and mandatory contributions—the voluntary principle. The social principle involved the creation of discussion groups, prayer meetings, and community service. The principle of congregational worship allowed lay persons to take part in the Sunday service, reading scripture, offering prayers, and singing hymns. Membership was open to those professing Christian belief, but that was liberally interpreted, allowing for seekers and doubters, as well as those settled in their beliefs. An indication of the church's eclectic spirit was the modernization of traditional Christian Feast Days to commemorate such events as the birth of Emanuel Swedenborg, the seventeenth-century Swedish mystic; the death of abolitionist martyr John Brown; and the laying of the Transatlantic telegraph cable.[5] Clarke served as minister to the Church of the Disciples until his retirement in 1887. This was one of the few independent Unitarian congregations to survive the end of the minister's career.

In the early 1840s, Theodore Parker, yet another influential Transcendentalist reformer, was serving a small Unitarian congregation in West Roxbury. He had been shut out of preaching exchanges with other Boston churches due to his controversial views. The 28th Congregational Society was formed in 1845 to provide a Boston pulpit for him. This congregation, too, was established on the voluntary principle. Parker's preaching drew large audiences, but few supported the church financially. Services were held in large auditoriums, first the Melodeon Theater and later the Boston Music Hall. On the stage was a plain wooden desk, with a Bible, a hymnal, and a vase of flowers—Parker was the first minister in Boston to display flowers on his pulpit. The pages of the sermon rested on a red velvet cushion. Readings were from poetry as well as the Bible. Like Emerson, Parker read a biblical text at the beginning of his sermon but omitted any exposition of it in the sermon itself. Membership was open to all, though most attendees elected not to join and few records were kept. Unlike other churches, only one service was offered on Sunday, and Parker often held receptions at his home following the services for discussions.[6]

William Henry Channing, nephew of the more famous William Ellery Channing, gathered a small working-class congregation in Brooklyn in 1842, moving it to New York City the following year. In addition to Sunday services, his Christian Union met for "testimonies" on Sunday afternoons and "conversations" on weekday evenings. In 1846, inspired by his frequent visits to Brook Farm, the younger Channing established the Religious Union of Associationists, organized on Fourierist principles, in Boston. This interfaith religious community had an original take on several rituals. Behind the altar was an empty chair, signifying "the unseen Presence." For Communion, fruit was served, along with bread and water. As the sacraments were distributed, participants were encouraged to converse on topics of a religious nature.[7] Channing later served more conventional Unitarian congregations in Washington, D.C., Rochester, New York, and England.

The hymns and readings in services led by Transcendentalist ministers reflected the spirituality and religious cosmopolitanism of the movement. Parishioners in congregations served by Transcendentalist ministers were likely to sing hymns written by "the two Sams": Samuel Johnson and Samuel Longfellow, younger brother of the poet Henry Wadsworth Longfellow. The two hymnals they produced—*A Book of Hymns for Public and Private Devotion* in 1846, and *Hymns of the Spirit* in 1864—were used widely. Readings were chosen from anthologies of world religious scriptures, such as W. R. Alger's *Poetry of the East,* Moncure Conway's *Sacred Anthology,* and Lydia Maria Child's *Aspirations of the World.* [8]

These independent Unitarian congregations started by the Transcendentalists, sometimes called Free Churches, were open to all who wished to join and were organized on a voluntary principle in hopes of attracting all classes of people. Members came together for worship, conversation, and social reform. The voluntary principle had its drawbacks, however, as the churches suffered for lack of financial support. Nevertheless, they left a lasting legacy, and many liberal religious congregations still practice these innovations in worship and church organization today.

THE FREE RELIGIOUS ASSOCIATION

In April 1865, during the same week that Confederate general Robert E. Lee surrendered to Union general Ulysses S. Grant at Appomattox, representatives of Unitarian congregations throughout the country met at All Soul's Church in New York City for a National Convention of Unitarian Churches. Most who gathered there, both ministers and laity, were avowed Christians. They were still recovering from the theological challenges to their faith that the Transcendentalists had raised before the war, and were alarmed that the virus of independent judgment in religious matters was threatening to break out again. They sought to establish a limit beyond which one could not go and still be considered a Unitarian. "To crush the radicals and secure denominational unity seemed nearly as important as the final defeat of the Confederacy," historian Stow Persons in *Free Religion: An American Faith* writes of this conflict.[9] By tightening theological agreement, traditional Unitarians hoped to strengthen ties among their churches.

In many ways the new threat they perceived was simply a continuation of Transcendentalism. The younger generation of Transcendentalists—or "radicals," as they called themselves—were prepared to go beyond Emerson and Parker in their commitment to religious freedom, even if it meant disloyalty to the traditional Unitarian version of Christianity. Like the first-generation Transcendentalists, they were largely Unitarian clergy, many of whom had been inspired by their theological predecessors.

Henry Whitney Bellows was a Unitarian minister in New York. During the Civil War, he had planned and presided over the United States Sanitary Commission, providing needed aid to sick and wounded soldiers of the U.S. Army. He was also widely recognized as a denominational leader. In 1859, he delivered an address on "The Suspense of Faith, A Discourse on the State of the Church," in which he called out "Emerson and the transcendental school" for being egoistic, self-asserting, and self-justifying at the expense of the vitality of the Unitarian church.[10] In convening the National Convention he hoped to strengthen the denomination by committing the Unitarians to a theological position satisfactory to both the conservatives and the radicals. Though judged a conservative by most historians, Bellows considered himself a moderate, and joined with the "Broad Church men," including Transcendentalist ministers Frederic Henry Hedge and James Freeman Clarke, to forge a consensus.[11] They submitted a constitution stating that members of the conference were "disciples of the Lord Jesus Christ," dedicated to "the advancement of His kingdom."[12] This was unacceptable to the radicals, who did not believe in the supernatural authority of Jesus but rather in a universal form of religious faith. For them that language was too exclusive. They were looking for a wider fellowship and voiced their objections. The conservatives, led by Bellows, brushed their concerns aside. The constitution passed. At the second annual meeting in Syracuse the following year, radical theologian Francis Ellingwood Abbot proposed an amendment, but it was voted down.

Thwarted at the denominational conventions, the radicals decided to form the Free Religious Association (FRA), which became the most significant example of church reform during that time and was the culmination of the Transcendentalist movement in American religious life. The first public meeting of the association was in May 1867, in Boston. The purposes of the organization were to encourage the scientific study of religion, to advocate freedom of religious thought, and to increase fellowship in the spirit. The association was not a break with Unitarianism—most members remained active Unitarians—but a platform for the dissemination of free religious ideas.

The first person to pay his one-dollar dues to join the new organization was Ralph Waldo Emerson, who also spoke on that occasion. A number of other prominent Transcendentalists were on hand also: Bronson Alcott, Cyrus Bartol, and William Furness representing the older group, and Thomas Wentworth Higginson, John Weiss, Samuel Johnson, and Octavius Brooks Frothingham among the younger generation. The younger Transcendentalists shared with their older contemporaries a commitment to social activism, including women's rights and the organization of labor. The conservatives opposed them as much for that activism as they did on theological grounds.

The FRA also continued the Transcendentalists' interest in the comparative study of religions. Johnson wrote his three-volume work on *Oriental Religions and Their Relation to Universal Religion*. Higginson wrote the most popular FRA tract, "The Sympathy of Religions." Believing that "the religious sentiment," as Emerson had termed it, was innate in the human species, Higginson looked for common ground in all the world's religions. "Once these provincial assumptions of unique inspiration were surmounted it would become apparent that the religion of the ages was natural religion, a universal expression of the human soul," Persons writes of these arguments.[13]

For the radicals, another term for natural religion was "free religion"—free in the sense of being universal and rational. In their view, Christianity was neither. That is why they felt the newly adopted Christian confession in the Constitution of the Unitarian Conference was too provincial and constraining. They especially took exception to the term "lordship," which for them signified spiritual slavery, contrary to a universal, democratic faith. They were uncompromising on the principle of absolute freedom of belief. They believed it was the one thread that unified a theologically diverse movement.

"Calvinism rushes to be Unitarianism as Unitarianism rushes to be Naturalism," wrote Emerson in his journal.[14] In many respects, Transcendentalism was a way station between Unitarianism and religious naturalism. Even at the time of its establishment, the FRA included many who considered themselves post-Transcendentalists, such as cofounder Francis Ellingwood Abbot, who also edited *The Index,* one of the two main periodicals of the organization. Abbot, who had served congregations in Dover, New Hampshire, and Toledo, Ohio, was one of the most prominent theologians of the movement and perhaps its most prolific writer. He described himself as a scientific theist, basing his beliefs on rigorous logic and science, rather than revelation or innate religious feeling. He believed that the universe is an infinitely intelligible and intelligent organism in which each part, including the human species, participates in a process of self-realization.[15] In many ways Abbot's views presaged twentieth-century process theology.

Octavius Brooks Frothingham, the FRA's first president, represented on the other hand the mystical wing. For Frothingham, who served churches in Salem and New York City, God was not a person but a force in nature, an unconscious power pervading the universe. In a departure from Emersonian individualism, he believed that God worked through the species collectively, and that individual progress was possible only within the larger context of the human race in general. *The Radical,* a journal published by Sidney Morse, expressed the Transcendentalist viewpoint.

With the rise of the sciences following the Civil War, the Transcendentalists lost influence as their philosophical idealism was met with skepticism or indifference. Empiricism replaced intuition as the epistemology of choice. The scientific theists believed that scientific investigation would reveal ultimate answers and that no aspect of human experience was outside the bounds of scientific inquiry. The Transcendentalists, in fact, had never been opposed to science. Of all the religious groups in America, only they had embraced scientific methods—accepting evolutionary thinking, for example, even before Charles Darwin published *The Origin of Species* in 1859. Conservative Unitarians "remained hostile for some years," in Persons's words, to Darwin's ideas.[16] The theory of evolution left no room for a cosmogony based on scripture. Free Religion believed in an immanent deity working itself out in the universe through the evolutionary process, which allowed acceptance of knowledge gained from both science and religion.

As Darwin's ideas earned greater acceptance and eventually were applied to social theory, two schools of thought developed: the "survival-of-the-fittest" brand of social Darwinism we all know, and a second that combined Emersonian individualism with the progressive implications of evolutionary thought. The first reinforced the rugged individualism that resulted in the laissez-faire minimal-government philosophy that has come to characterize the modern Republican Party. In contrast, the humanitarian individualism of the FRA—based on the principle that the welfare of each was the concern of all—advocated the use of the state to preserve a healthy social and economic environment for individuals. Humanitarian individualism, with its ethic of service, was the philosophical underpinning of the progressive movement of the early twentieth century.

The radical clergy associated with the FRA advocated numerous social reforms during America's late-nineteenth-century "Gilded Age," including socialism, anti-imperialism, cooperative living, and universal suffrage. Its members chided their conservative Unitarian colleagues for supporting the status quo. Abbot characterized reform this way: "the intelligent direction of individual and social energies to the development of a higher civilization, stimulated by undoubting confidence in the capacity of [human beings] to improve their own condition indefinitely through a more complete obedience to the laws of nature."[17] Unfortunately, the FRA's commitment to freedom of conscience limited what it could accomplish as an organization. While the association sought to empower individuals to act for social change, it did not engage in reforms as a body. Many of its own members criticized the FRA for its failure to take stands on the pressing issues of the day.

Over the years, members of the FRA and the Unitarian Conference of Churches attempted reconciliation. Unitarian Christianity was increasingly supplanted by religious naturalism from within its own ranks. In 1882 the Unitarian minister Minot Savage introduced a successful amendment to the denomination's constitution, guaranteeing individual freedom of thought. With that move, most of the Free Religionists rejoined the Unitarian fold. The FRA continued on into the twentieth century, but its force was pretty well spent by the late 1880s.

The Free Religious Association had led the way in attacking denominational and creedal exclusiveness and advocating the universality of the religious sentiment, in Persons's view. It had pioneered the field of comparative religion, helped organize the World Parliament of Religions in 1893, and laid the conceptual groundwork for the International Association for Religious Freedom, whose work continues today. It made a unique contribution to religious discourse through *The Index,* "easily the finest liberal religious journal in America," Persons says.[18] It hastened the transformation of Unitarianism from a Christocentric faith to a pragmatic, humanistic theism. By aggressively attacking social problems it enhanced the influence of liberal religion in American life beyond that attained by the Unitarian denomination.

The Transcendentalists, especially the later radicals, were never destined to create lasting institutions, given their antipathy toward organized activity. Yet they influenced modern Unitarian Universalism far more than their conservative opponents. Much of what Unitarian Universalists take for granted today comes directly from the Transcendentalists and the radicals of the Spiritual Left: their emphasis on social action, their styles of worship and patterns of lay involvement, and their uniquely Unitarian spiritual inheritance.

More broadly, the Transcendentalists and their successors in the FRA contributed to the spreading influence of liberal religion in America. This can be seen in a number of ways. The first of these, which we have already examined, is religious cosmopolitanism. Since the early efforts of the Transcendentalists to explore the wisdom of other religious traditions, and the later attempts of Free Religionists to discern a "sympathy" of religions, succeeding generations of spiritual seekers have embraced many teachings and practices of the world's religions. Another example of their liberalizing influence is the way they embraced a nonsectarian view of religious experience. As Schmidt demonstrates in *Restless Souls,* the Transcendentalists freed the notion of mysticism from its sectarian roots and made it central to their understanding of spirituality.

As time went on, Transcendentalism and Free Religion became both more diffused and widely disseminated in American religious life. Their influence is seen in the development of Ethical Culture and the New Thought Movement. Felix Adler, who founded the first Society for Ethical Culture in New York in 1876, was active in the FRA and served as its president from 1878 to 1882. Ethical Culture promoted an ethical mysticism, the essence of which Adler described in *The Reconstruction of the Spiritual Ideal:*

> Seek to educe in the other the consciousness of his indispensableness, that is, of his membership in the infinite spiritual commonwealth, and in so doing you will gain the conviction of your own membership therein. You will not *save* your soul, but achieve the unshakeable conviction that you are soul, or spirit.[19]

The founder of the New Thought, or Mind Cure, movement, Phineas P. Quimby, was a near contemporary of Emerson but apparently was little influenced by the sage of Concord. Quimby promoted the notion of physical healing through the mind's ability to affect the body. His followers, including Warren Felt Evans and, later on, Horatio Dresser, were well acquainted with the writings of Swedenborg and Emerson, and harnessed Quimby's discoveries to Transcendentalist metaphysics. As a consequence, William James, in his classic study *The Varieties of Religious Experience,* was led to include New Thought, along with Transcendentalism, Vedanta, and Whitmanism, as an example of "the Religion of Healthy-Mindedness."[20]

In yet another example, the influence of Transcendentalism and the FRA can be seen in the development of religious humanism. In a play on Emerson's words, we might say that Transcendentalism rushes to be Free Religion just as Free Religion rushes to be Humanism. Theologian Gary Dorrien notes in his book *The Making of American Liberal Theology* that "the spiritual descendants of Free Religion joined John Dewey and others in issuing 'A Humanist Manifesto'" in 1932.[21] In these and many other ways, the ideas of Transcendentalism and Free Religion have permeated American religious life.

13

THE LEGACY OF
TRANSCENDENTALISM

On June 12, 1872, Bronson Alcott stopped by the Emerson home in Concord and invited the family's houseguest, Mary Adams of Dubuque, Iowa, for a walk to a Unitarian picnic at Walden Pond. There they saw "several of the young preachers, who express[ed] sympathy with the growing Idealism, and the hope of a spiritual Church," he wrote in his journal.[1] He pointed out to Adams the cabin site of Henry David Thoreau. The celebrated author had died ten years before at age forty-four after suffering from chronic tuberculosis.

Over the years, other pilgrims and curiosity seekers had come looking for the site but could no longer determine the exact location. Adams suggested to Alcott that visitors to Walden should bring a stone for building a monument to Thoreau. She started the monument by laying the first stones on the site. Some picnickers added stones as well. Thanks to this chance meeting between a midwestern spiritual seeker and a local sage who knew the cabin's spot and its significance, a cairn was born. "The rude stones were a monument more fitting than the costliest carving of the artist," Alcott noted. "Henry's fame is surely to brighten with years, and this spot be visited by admiring readers of his works."[2]

Alcott was more prescient than he probably realized. The Walden Pond Reservation today logs in 600,000 visitors each year, from around the world. It has become a major pilgrimage site, in recognition of Thoreau's importance as a writer and thinker. Many visitors bring stones with them to add to the cairn. As a frequent visitor to the cairn myself, I have seen pieces of the Berlin Wall, stones inscribed with names of deceased loved ones, and rocks colorfully decorated by youthful admirers deposited in homage to Thoreau's memory.

The cairn is just one visible sign of the ongoing impact of Transcendentalism on American intellectual and spiritual life. There are many others. Not far from Walden Pond is the Thoreau Institute, a research library dedicated to preserving Walden Woods and promoting the writings and legacy of Thoreau. The Thoreau Society, whose members include scholars, activists, and earnest Thoreauvians from as far away as Russia and Japan, is the largest society devoted to an American author. Princeton University Press has been issuing scholarly editions of his works, fifteen volumes thus far. Literary critics and environmentalists have canonized Thoreau in their own writings, and generations of seekers consider him a spiritual guide. His influence has never been stronger than it is today.

Thoreau may be the best-known Transcendentalist, but many others in the movement have also received increasing attention in recent years. Scholarly biographies and critical works about the movement and its major figures have emerged steadily. Four biographies of Margaret Fuller have been published since the 1990s, and others are on the way. Hardly a week goes by without a column, review, or article in the print media or on the web referring to the Transcendentalists or one of their circle. Even more widespread has been their influence on American spirituality. Sociological studies—such as *A Generation of Seekers, Spiritual but Not Religious,* and *The Transformation of American Religion*—have traced current recent religious trends to New England Transcendentalism and the rise of liberal spirituality in nineteenth-century America.[3]

The activist movements of the 1960s rediscovered the Transcendentalists' message and brought them back into public attention. A new generation took up the strategy of civil disobedience and protested environmental destruction, just as Thoreau did. At the same time, similar to the Transcendentalists, many young people were seeking out broader spiritual experiences than they were finding in traditional churches. However, along with the new interest came misunderstandings about what the movement stood for. Some in both liberal and conservative religious circles construed key Transcendentalist ideas, such as self-culture and self-reliance, as narcissism and a consumer-oriented approach to faith. I couldn't disagree more. In fact, I find these dismissals of spiritual seeking that is not rooted in a specific religious tradition condescending and elitist.

The spiritual and religious lives of Americans today are more complex than a simple sectarian categorization. In leaving behind traditional religious rites and scriptures, the Transcendentalists and the spiritual seekers that followed them were free to examine their inner selves, the world of nature, and multiple sources of wisdom for moral and spiritual guidance. Free inquiry has resulted in the diversity of religious viewpoints we see today, which may feel perplexing and unnerving to those in more traditional faiths. Whether they initiated this trend or merely accelerated it, the Transcendentalists played a prominent role in validating it, exploring its implications for their own spiritual practice, and providing inspiration for succeeding generations of religious wayfarers.

People who claim no particular religious affiliation (sometimes called "nones") numbered 23 percent in the 2015 Pew Research Center's Religious Landscape Study.[4] The term, however, includes those with varying theological points of view. Some have no interest in religion or spirituality (the secular nones) and some say they are spiritual but reject religious labels and churches (often referred to as "spiritual but not religious"). The rise of the nones has caught the attention both of denominational leaders and of sociologists. It is often said to account for the declining membership of Catholic, Protestant, and even Unitarian Universalist churches.

A number of critics have viewed the rise of the "spiritual but not religious" with dismay, as further evidence of an individualistic, consumer-oriented approach to religion that can be traced back to the Transcendentalists. One of these critics, Robert Bellah, says that individualism has eroded the sense of religious community and social solidarity. Bellah singles out Emerson for promoting the view that "the self is the only real thing in the world," which Bellah calls "ontological individualism."[5] Emerson leaves himself open to this criticism through his comments concerning institutions and philanthropies.[6] Coming as they do in the essay on "Self-Reliance," such remarks give the impression that Emerson is promoting autonomy and self-sufficiency, whereas what he really means by self-reliance is self-trust. For

Emerson, the self is trustworthy because the Universal Soul dwells within the soul of each individual person, providing the basis for compassion, justice, and social solidarity.

In Bellah's view, Emerson's religious individualism "is linked to an economic individualism which, though it makes no distinctions between persons except monetary ones, ultimately knows nothing of the sacredness of the individual."[7] For some critics it is an article of faith that Emersonian self-reliance is individually isolating and socially destructive. A closer reading, however, shows that the true meaning of the term "self-reliance" is not autonomy, but authenticity.

In *The Ethics of Authenticity*, philosopher Charles Taylor claims that the idea of authenticity arose in the Western intellectual tradition largely in reaction to other forms of individualism. Human beings possess an innate moral sense and an ability to discern right from wrong intuitively. Morality was once grounded in external sources—scriptures, religious traditions, moral codes—but now the source of morality is deep within. Taylor's insights on the ethic of authenticity can help us see the connection with Emerson's understanding of self-reliance:

> This is the powerful moral ideal that has come down to us. It accords crucial moral importance to a kind of contact with myself, with my own inner nature, which it sees as in danger of being lost, partly through the pressures towards outward conformity, but also because in taking an instrumental stance to myself, I may have lost the capacity to listen to this inner voice. . . . Being true to myself means being true to my own originality, and that is something only I can articulate and discover. . . . This is the background understanding to the modern ideal of authenticity, and to the goals of self-fulfillment or self-realization in which it is usually couched. This is the background that gives moral force to the culture of authenticity, including its most degraded, absurd, or trivialized forms.[8]

The moral ideal of authenticity, though not without its problems, defines modern consciousness and should be taken seriously, in Taylor's view. "Critics of contemporary culture tend to disparage it as an ideal, even to confound it with a non-moral desire to do what one wants without interference," he tells us. "Many of the things critics of contemporary culture attack are debased and deviant forms of this ideal." He goes so far as to say that the ideal is not only "very worthwhile in itself," but "unrepudiable by moderns." What we need, he says is a "work of retrieval, through which this ideal can help us restore our practice."[9] The same can be said of self-reliance. It is as much a mistake, I believe, to condemn self-reliance as it is to excuse its distortions. Self-reliance "was not narcissism, monomania, or isolation," according to Emerson scholar Wesley Mott. "Indeed, it was the *answer* to these diseases of the self, as well as the remedy for the 'existing evils' of institutional and social life."[10] The proper response to these criticisms of Emerson, I believe, is not to dispense with his ideas, but to reclaim and interpret them for contemporary audiences.

The situation Emerson addressed in his later essay on "Worship" is not very different from the one we face today. "The stern old faiths have all pulverized. 'T is a whole population of gentlemen and ladies out in search of religion," he observed. "We live in a transition period, when the old faiths that have comforted nations, and not only so, but have made nations, seem to have spent their force." Yet in the face of skepticism and religious decline Emerson continued to believe that the religious sentiment was an essential aspect of human nature and that the answer to bad religion is a better one through the cultivation of the soul. "There is always some religion," he said, "some hope and fear extended into the invisible,—from the blind boding which nails a horseshoe to the mast or the threshold, up to the song of the Elders in the Apocalypse. But the religion cannot rise above the state of the votary."[11] The important question is, What are the means by which the votary, or would-be follower, is elevated?

Transcendentalism offers today's religious seekers a rich spiritual tradition that is uniquely American, intellectually credible, and committed to human rights, environmentalism, and social justice. Many are already following a path that was laid down by the "restless souls" of the Transcendentalist movement almost two hundred years ago, often with little awareness of those who blazed the trail. What makes Transcendentalist spirituality unique is its combination of mysticism, reverence for nature, religious cosmopolitanism, and "action from principle." To study Transcendentalism as a literary movement confines it to the middle nineteenth century. But, as a spiritual practice, it is as timeless as the perennial philosophy the Transcendentalists themselves sought to embody.

The Transcendentalists sought to "elevate the votary" by means of a discipline that included solitude, contemplation, walks in nature, simplicity, reading, conversation and journal-keeping. They pursued these practices not for health or financial reward, but for self-culture, or the cultivation of the soul. Self-culture is as important today as ever and is as authentic and rewarding as any other form of spiritual practice. Many of the restless souls who have attended my classes over the years have been surprised to discover that the spiritual practices they were looking for were ones that they already were following, albeit in an informal way.

We often think of spiritual disciplines as requiring devoted practice— daily prayer, meditation, yoga, and the like. Many of these ancient religious practices were developed to focus the mind, purify the body, and transcend the ego with the goal of achieving enlightenment and peace of mind. In comparison, the Transcendentalists' spiritual practices might seem quite tame. They weren't monks, yogis, or ascetics. They probably did not even view their practices as an explicitly spiritual regimen. Yet self-culture, I believe, was indeed a religious practice that required dedication and resulted in transcendence, much like any other.

The exercises the Transcendentalists engaged in are simple and common—walking, reading, musing, conversing—and they are mostly free and can be performed at any time. But, as a spiritual practice, they are not necessarily easy. As Frederic Hedge wrote in his essay on "The Art of Life":

> The work is hard and the wages are low. . . . The only motive to engage in this work is its own inherent worth. . . . Much, that other men esteem as highest and follow after as the grand reality, he will have to forego. No emoluments must seduce him from the rigor of his devotion. No engagements beyond the merest necessities of life must interfere with his pursuit. A meagre economy must be his income.[12]

Self-culture is, above all, a way of life that is both attained and main-tained by means of these spiritual exercises. Pierre Hadot, a French historian of philosophy, defines spiritual exercises as "voluntary, personal practices meant to bring about a transformation of the individual, a transformation of the self."[13] Collectively, the Transcendentalists' spiritual exercises are a form of *askesis* or discipline by which we can, in William Ellery Channing's terms, on the one hand, enter into and search ourselves and, on the other hand, determine and form ourselves.[14]

Emerson said that none of the Transcendentalists lived "a purely spiritual life," but they were "harbingers and forerunners."[15] They were ministers and morally instructive writers, calling their audiences to embrace a new and different way of life. Though I can't claim to have lived a purely spiritual life myself, I continue to find insight and inspiration in their example and their teachings. They have guided my ministry, my writing, and my outlook on life. In this book I have sought to retrieve their message and reclaim its value for spiritual seekers today. There is some irony in doing this. As Thoreau said, "I would not have anyone adopt *my* mode of living on any account; for, beside that before he has barely learned it I may have found out another for myself, I desire that there may be as many different persons in the world as possible; but I would have each one be very careful to find out and pursue his *own way*, and not his father's or his mother's or his neighbor's instead."[16]

Since the founding of the Concord School of Philosophy in 1879, numerous institutes and spiritual centers have sprung up, offering workshops on mysticism, healing, creativity, mindfulness, drumming, and stress relief. Since Thoreau's early experiments with yoga, Americans have taken up a panoply of spiritual practices, such as Zen, Insight Meditation, Tai Chi, and Sufi dancing. Elizabeth Lesser, cofounder of the Omega Institute in Rhinebeck, New York, has catalogued the practices in a wonderful compendium called *The New American Spirituality: A Seeker's Guide*. She states that "we are witnessing the birth of a wisdom tradition that is uniquely American."[17]

Uniquely American, yes; but not totally new. This new spirituality might have been taken directly from the Transcendentalists: self-reliance, religious cosmopolitanism, simple living, the sacredness of nature, and an open-ended quest for wholeness and religious truth. The roots of the new spirituality lie in the Transcendentalists' notion of self-culture. While the term "self-culture" may sound quaint to the modern ear, it means nothing other than the cultivation of the soul. I would not for a moment disparage other forms of spiritual practice, but I have found the teachings of the Transcendentalists to be most congenial to the cultivation of my own soul. And, judging from the shock of recognition that I have seen in those who have taken my classes over the years as they come to understand the nature of Transcendentalist spirituality, others have too.

NOTES

INTRODUCTION

1. See Lawrence Buell, *Literary Transcendentalism: Style and Vision in the American Renaissance* (Ithaca: Cornell University Press, 1973), 135.
2. Ralph Waldo Emerson, *The Collected Works of Ralph Waldo Emerson,* vol. 2, ed. Alfred R. Ferguson et al. (Cambridge: Harvard University Press, 1971–2013), 27.
3. Leigh Eric Schmidt, *Restless Souls: The Making of American Spirituality* (San Francisco: HarperSanFrancisco, 2005), xii.
4. David M. Robinson, "Unitarian History and the Transcendentalist Literary Consciousness," Henry Whitney Bellows Lecture, Unitarian Church of All Souls, New York, 1989. Unpublished transcript in author's collection.
5. See, for example, Elizabeth Lesser, *The New American Spirituality: A Seeker's Guide* (New York: Random House, 1999); Amanda Porterfield, *The Transformation of American Religion: The Story of a Late Twentieth-Century Awakening* (New York: Oxford University Press, 2000); and Robert Wuthnow, *After Heaven: Spirituality in American since the 1950s* (Berkeley: University of California Press, 1998).
6. Emerson, *Collected Works,* vol. 6, 108, 110, 114.
7. Ibid., vol. 1, 92.
8. Ibid., 145.
9. On this issue I am in some disagreement with Arthur Versluis, author of *American Gurus: From Transcendentalism to New Age Religion.* He characterizes Transcendentalist spirituality as a form of "immediatism," by which he means to suggest that one "can achieve enlightenment or spiritual illumination spontaneously, without any particular means, often without meditation or years of guided praxis" (2). While it is true that ecstasies may occur spontaneously, they are generally of such significance that efforts are made to cultivate awareness to the extent that they might recur. This is certainly true in the case of the Transcendentalists. Self-culture, as I aim to show in the course of this book, was a spiritual practice consisting of contemplation, reading, solitude, walks in nature, simple living, conversation, and so on, which was intended to provide favorable conditions for the reception of "divine illumination," in Emerson's phrase. See Arthur Versluis, *American Gurus:*

From Transcendentalism to New Age Religion (New York: Oxford University Press, 2015), 1–14.

10. Robert D. Richardson, "The Social Imperatives of Transcendentalism," *Religious Humanism* 22 (1988): 87–88.

11. Quoted in James Elliot Cabot, *A Memoir of Ralph Waldo Emerson* (Boston: Houghton Mifflin, 1887), vol. 1, 249.

1

"THE SOUL OF THE AGE"

1. Emerson, *Collected Works,* vol. 5, 7, 12, 9.

2. Emerson, *The Early Lectures of Ralph Waldo Emerson,* ed. Stephen E. Whicher et al. (Cambridge: Harvard University Press, 1961–1972), vol. 2, 187.

3. Isaiah Berlin, *The Roots of Romanticism* (Princeton: Princeton University Press, 1999), 1.

4. Quoted in Cabot, *Memoir,* vol. 2, 245.

5. Quoted in James Freeman Clarke, *Autobiography, Diary and Correspondence* (New York: Negro Universities Press, 1968), 86.

6. Emerson, *The Complete Works of Ralph Waldo Emerson* (Boston: Houghton Mifflin, 1904), vol. 10, 325.

7. Emerson, *Journals and Miscellaneous Notebooks of Ralph Waldo Emerson,* ed. William H. Gillman et al. (Cambridge: Harvard University Press, 1960–1982), vol. 3, 70.

8. Emerson, *Collected Works,* vol. 10, 108, 110.

9. Emerson, *Early Lectures,* vol. 3, 188.

10. William Wordsworth, *William Wordsworth,* ed. Stephen Gill (New York: Oxford University Press, 1984), 134.

11. Emerson, *Collected Works,* vol. 1, 37.

12. Quoted in M. H. Abrams, *Natural Supernaturalism: Tradition and Revolution in Romantic Literature* (New York: W. W. Norton, 1971), 67–68.

13. Ibid., 68.

14. William Wordsworth, *The Poetical Works of William Wordsworth* (London: Edward Moxon, 1840), vol. 6, xiii.

15. Emerson, *Collected Works,* vol. 1, 43–44.

16. Perry Miller, *The Transcendentalists: An Anthology* (Cambridge: Harvard University Press, 1960), 34.

17. Quoted in ibid., 35.

18. Clarke, *Autobiography,* 39.

19. Emerson, *Journals,* vol. 5, 270–72.

20. Ibid., 274.

21. Emerson, *Collected Works,* vol. 2, 160.

22. It is well known that meditation can activate the operations of the right brain. This can also occur as a result of a stroke affecting the left side of the brain, as in Jill Bolte Taylor's account of her own experience: "My left hemisphere had been trained to perceive myself as a solid, separate from others. Now, released from that restrictive circuitry, my right hemisphere relished in its attachment to the eternal

flow. I was no longer isolated and alone. My soul was as big as the universe and frolicked with glee in a boundless sea." Jill Bolte Taylor, *My Stroke of Insight: A Brain Scientist's Personal Journey* (New York: Plume, 2009), 71.

23. Emerson, *Collected Works*, vol. 1, 201.

24. Wordsworth, *William Wordsworth*, 301.

25. Leon Chai, *The Romantic Foundations of the American Renaissance* (Ithaca: Cornell University Press, 1987), 10.

26. Wordsworth, *Poetical Works*, vol. 6, 120.

27. Wordsworth, *William Wordsworth*, 302.

28. Emerson, *The Later Lectures of Ralph Waldo Emerson, 1843–1871*, ed. Ronald A. Bosco and Joel Myerson (Athens: University of Georgia Press, 2001), vol. 2, 355.

29. Emerson, *Journals*, vol. 5, 275–76.

2
THE TRANSCENDENTALIST CRISIS OF FAITH

1. Ronald A. Bosco and Joel Myerson, eds., *The Emerson Brothers: A Fraternal Biography in Letters* (New York: Oxford University Press, 2006), 97.

2. William Ellery Channing, *William Ellery Channing: Selected Writings*, ed. David Robinson (New York: Paulist Press, 1985), 72.

3. Emerson, *Complete Works*, vol. 4, 367–68.

4. Andrews Norton, "The Latest Form of Infidelity," in *A Documentary History of Unitarian Universalism*, ed. Dan McKanan (Boston: Skinner House Books, 2017), vol. 1, 281.

5. Emerson, *Collected Works*, vol. 1, 85.

6. Norton, "The New School in Literature and Religion," in *The American Transcendentalists*, ed. Lawrence Buell (New York: Modern Library, 2006), 149.

7. Theodore Parker, *Autobiography, Poems and Prayers* (Boston: American Unitarian Association, 1907), 355.

8. Anne C. Rose, *Transcendentalism as a Social Movement, 1830–1850* (New Haven: Yale University Press, 1981), 17.

9. Parker, *Autobiography*, 299.

10. Ibid., 300.

11. Ibid., 300, 302.

12. Emerson, *Collected Works*, vol. 1, 85.

13. Kneeland adopted free-thinking religious views and published scathing critiques of biblical Christianity. These led to a trial for blasphemy in which both prosecutor and judge were Unitarians. Kneeland was convicted and served sixty days in prison.

14. Quoted in Rose, *Transcendentalism*, 45.

15. Channing, *Selected Writings*, 148.

16. Schmidt, *Restless Souls*, 11–12.

17. Channing, *Selected Writings*, 197, 207.

3
Transcendentalist Spirituality

1. Emerson, *Journals,* vol. 5, 218.
2. *Christian Register and Boston Observer,* Aug. 21, 1841, 134.
3. Emerson, *Collected Works,* vol. 1, 201.
4. Ibid., 205–6.
5. Ibid., 213.
6. Ibid., 213–14.
7. Ibid., 216.
8. Robert N. Bellah, *Religion in Human Evolution: From the Paleolithic to the Axial Age* (Cambridge: Harvard University Press, 2011), 11.
9. Ibid., 1–4.
10. Abraham H. Maslow, *Toward a Psychology of Being* (Princeton: D. Van Nostrand, 1968), 73–83.
11. Clarke, *Events and Epochs in Religious History* (Boston: James R. Osgood, 1881), 293.
12. William James, *The Varieties of Religious Experience* (New York: Longmans, Green, 1925), 379. First published 1902.
13. Emerson, *Collected Works,* vol. 2, 159.
14. Ibid., 160
15. Ibid., 161.
16. Ibid., 175.
17. Ibid., vol. 1, 43.
18. Ibid., 145.
19. Abraham Maslow, "The 'Core-Religious' or 'Transcendent' Experience," in *The Highest State of Consciousness,* ed. John White (New York: Doubleday Anchor Books, 1972), 357.
20. Emerson, *Collected Works,* vol. 3, 153.
21. Ibid., vol. 2, 93.
22. Quoted in John Weiss, *Life and Correspondence of Theodore Parker* (Freeport, NY: Books for Libraries Press, 1969), vol. 1, 55. First published 1864 (New York: D. Appleton and Company).
23. Jeffrey Steele, ed., *The Essential Margaret Fuller* (New Brunswick, NJ: Rutgers University Press, 1992), 10–11.
24. Thoreau, *The Journal of Henry David Thoreau* (Boston: Houghton Mifflin, 1949), vol. 2, 306–7.
25. Wordsworth, *William Wordsworth,* 301.
26. Thoreau, *Journal,* vol. 2, 468–69.
27. Thoreau, *The Writings of Henry David Thoreau* (Boston: Houghton Mifflin Company, 1906), vol. 5, 151.
28. Margaret Fuller, *The Letters of Margaret Fuller,* ed. Robert N. Hudspeth (Ithaca: Cornell University Press, 1983–1994), vol. 2, 110.
29. Thoreau, *Walden: An Annotated Edition,* ed. Walter Harding (Boston: Houghton Mifflin Company, 1995), 86. First published 1854 as *Walden; or, Life in the Woods* (Boston: Ticknor and Fields).
30. Ibid., 92.

4
The Art of Life

1. Mark G. Vasquez, *Authority and Reform: Religious and Educational Discourses in Nineteenth Century New England Literature* (Knoxville: University of Tennessee Press, 2003), 30.

2. For Wilhelm von Humboldt, elevation of the soul was the final aim of self-cultivation:

   "I use this expression intentionally in order not to exclude any means that a man may choose for his spiritual improvement. For he can raise himself to a higher stage of spirituality by a continually fuller and purer development of his ideas, by more and more vigorous efforts to improve his character." Quoted in W. H. Bruford, *The German Tradition of Self-Cultivation: "Bildung" from Humboldt to Thomas Mann* (Cambridge, UK: Cambridge University Press, 2010), 27.

3. M. Le Baron Degerando, *Self-Education; or the Means and Art of Moral Progress*, trans. Elizabeth Palmer Peabody (Boston: Carter and Hendee, 1830), iv.

4. Arminianism, attributed to the influence of Dutch theologian Jacobus Arminius (1560–1609), held that human beings possessed the capacity for goodness as well as evil and that by developing the capacity for goodness they might overcome the temptation to sin. In adopting this view, the liberal Christians abandoned the Calvinist doctrines of innate depravity and divine predestination. See Conrad Wright, *The Beginnings of Unitarianism in America* (Boston: Starr King Press, 1955), 3–6.

5. Robinson, *Apostle of Culture: Emerson as Preacher and Lecturer* (Philadelphia: University of Pennsylvania Press, 1982), 12.

6. Channing, *Selected Writings*, 226.

7. Ibid., 228.

8. Ibid., 231.

9. Ibid., 232.

10. Ibid., 235–36.

11. Ibid., 259.

12. Emerson preached the sermon a total of nine times between 1830 and 1839.

13. Emerson, *Early Lectures*, vol. 2, 215–21.

14. Ibid., 250–51.

15. Ibid., 252–57.

16. Ibid., 261.

17. Ibid., 275.

18. Ibid., 345–46.

19. Frederic Henry Hedge, "The Art of Life, The Scholar's Calling," *The Dial* 1, no. 2 (Oct. 1840): 176.

20. Thoreau, *Walden*, 6.

21. Thoreau, *Early Essays and Miscellanies* (Princeton: Princeton University Press, 1975), 117.

22. Thoreau, *Walden*, 87.

23. Thoreau, *Reform Papers* (Princeton: Princeton University Press, 1973), 3, 16–17.

24. Tiffany K. Wayne, *Woman Thinking: Feminism and Transcendentalism in Nineteenth-Century America*, (Lanham, MD: Lexington Books, 2005), 29.

25. Fuller, *Memoirs of Margaret Fuller Ossoli* (Boston: Phillips, Sampson, 1851), vol. 1, 133.

26. Ibid., 132.
27. Ibid., 98–99.
28. Ibid., 197.
29. James Freeman Clarke, *Self-Culture, Physical, Intellectual, Moral and Spiritual* (Boston: Houghton Mifflin, 1889), 48. First published 1880.
30. Orestes A. Brownson, "Brook Farm," *The United States Magazine, and Democratic Review,* Nov. 1842, 484.
31. See, for example, Philip F. Gura, *American Transcendentalism: A History* (New York: Hill and Wang, 2007), 208, 240–41.
32. Robinson, "Margaret Fuller and the Transcendentalist Ethos: *Woman in the Nineteenth Century,*" *PMLA* 97, no. 1 (1982): 96.
33. Clarke, *Self-Culture,* 31.
34. Ibid., 36.
35. M. Scott Peck, *The Road Less Traveled and Beyond: Spiritual Growth in an Age of Anxiety* (New York: Simon and Schuster, 1997), 116.
36. John T. Lysaker, *Emerson and Self-Culture* (Bloomington: Indiana University Press, 2008), 5.

5
Three Prerequisites of the Spiritual Life

1. Thoreau, *Journal,* vol. 2, 469.
2. Wordsworth, *William Wordsworth,* 134.
3. Emerson, *Collected Writings,* vol. 1, 7.
4. Ibid., 7, 9, 10.
5. Ibid., 12–13.
6. Ibid., 18, 19, 23.
7. Ibid., 26, 27.
8. Ibid., 37, 39.
9. Ibid., 43.
10. Ibid., 27–28.
11. Ibid., 38.
12. "Deep ecology" is a term coined by Norwegian philosopher Arne Naess. This viewpoint holds that the well-being and flourishing of human and nonhuman life on Earth have intrinsic value, independent of the usefulness of the nonhuman world for human purposes.
13. Thoreau, *Walden,* 119.
14. Richard Louv, *The Nature Principle: Reconnecting with Life in a Virtual Age* (Chapel Hill, NC: Algonquin Books, 2012), 62–64.
15. Emerson, *Early Lectures,* vol. 2, 273.
16. Thoreau, *Walden,* 135.
17. Thoreau, *Walden,* 108–9.
18. From which we get the word "school." Josef Pieper explains, "The name for institutions of education and learning mean *leisure.*" Pieper, *Leisure: The Basis of Culture* (South Bend: St. Augustine's Press, 1998), 4.

19. Seneca, *The Stoic Philosophy of Seneca,* trans. Moses Hadas (New York: W. W. Norton, 1958), 105.

20. Thoreau, *Walden,* 7.

21. Channing, *Selected Writings,* 259–60.

22. Thoreau, *Journal,* vol. 4, 433.

23. Critics of the so-called "Me" generation have been quick to trace its origins to Emerson's "Self-Reliance." See especially Robert N. Bellah et al., *Habits of the Heart: Individualism and Commitment in American Life* (New York: Harper and Row, 1985). For a more contextualized view see Wesley T. Mott, "'The Age of the First Person Singular': Emerson and Individualism," in *A Historical Guide to Ralph Waldo Emerson,* ed. Joel Myerson (New York: Oxford University Press, 2000), 61–100.

24. Emerson, *Collected Works,* vol. 2, 37.

25. Ibid., 27–28.

26. Ibid., 31–33.

27. Ibid., 34, 37.

28. Ibid., 40–42.

29. Ibid., 43, 47, 51.

30. Emerson, *Collected Works,* vol. 2, 84; vol. 3, 40.

31. In 1854 members of the society asked Emerson to address the anti-slavery issue on the occasion of the tenth anniversary of the emancipation of slaves in the British West Indies. According to Sandra Harbert Petrulionis, the speech "is generally heralded as his first major antislavery address, marking a decided swing toward abolitionism." Petrulionis, *To Set This World Right: The Anti-Slavery Movement in Thoreau's Concord* (Ithaca: Cornell University Press, 2006), 45.

32. Parker J. Palmer, *Let Your Life Speak: Listening for the Voice of Vocation* (San Francisco: Jossey-Bass Publishers, 2000), 12.

33. Thomas Moore, *Original Self: Living with Paradox and Originality* (New York: HarperCollins, 2000), v.

34. Steele, *Essential Margaret Fuller,* 10–11.

35. Thoreau, *Walden,* 211.

6

SOLITUDE, CONTEMPLATION, SAUNTERING, AND SIMPLE LIVING

1. Arnold I. Davidson, "Introduction," in Pierre Hadot, *Philosophy as a Way of Life* (Malden, MA: Blackwell Publishing, 1995), 21.

2. For instance, Kathryn Schulz, in "Pond Scum," a caustic take-down of Thoreau written for the October 19, 2015, issue of the *New Yorker* magazine, argues that *Walden* is "a fantasy about escaping the entanglements and responsibilities of living among other people." In my view, Thoreau didn't go to the woods to escape people, but to find himself. Even while he lived at the pond he was not a recluse, and in any event he was there for only twenty-six months. More important, as he said himself, living at Walden Pond was an "experiment" in learning to live deliberately. Solitude and simplicity were essential elements of his experiment. To find fault with

these values is to condemn Jesus, the Buddha, and countless others who sought to turn inward on occasion as relief from the superficiality and frenetic pace of everyday life. For Schulz's article see "Pond Scum: Henry David Thoreau's Myopia," http://www.newyorker.com/magazine/2015/10/19/pond-scum, October 19, 2015.

3. Thoreau, *Journal,* vol. 1, 244.
4. Ibid., 299.
5. W. Barksdale Maynard, *Walden Pond: A History* (New York: Oxford University Press, 2004), 83–84.
6. Johann G. Zimmermann, *An Examination of the Advantages of Solitude; and of its Operations on the Heart and Mind,* trans. "F. S." (London: Vernor and Hood, 1804), vol. 1, 134.
7. Thoreau, *Walden,* 320, 6, 126, 127.
8. Ibid., 128, 130.
9. Schulz, for instance, considers Thoreau hypocritical for aspiring "to solitude and self-sufficiency" while "going home for cookies and company." See Schulz, "Pond Scum."
10. Zimmerman, *Solitude,* vol. 1, p. 5.
11. Ibid., vol. 2, 402–3.
12. Emerson, *Journals,* vol. 2, 329.
13. Ibid., vol. 7, 14.
14. Anne Morrow Lindbergh, *Gift from the Sea* (New York: Pantheon Books, 1955), 49–50.
15. Ester Schaler Buchholz, *The Call of Solitude: Alonetime in a World of Attachment* (New York: Simon and Schuster, 1997), 16.
16. Thoreau, *Writings,* vol. 4, 471.
17. Wordsworth, *The Prelude,* quoted in Raymond Dexter Havens, *The Mind of a Poet: A Study of Wordsworth's Thought* (Baltimore: The Johns Hopkins Press, 1941), vol. 1, 65.
18. Blaise Pascal, *Thoughts on Religion, and Other Subjects,* trans. Edward Craig (Edinburgh: H. S. Baynes and Son, 1825), 30. First published 1670 as *Pensees.*
19. Thoreau, *Journal,* vol. 9, 246.
20. Emerson, *Early Essays,* vol. 2, 261.
21. Thoreau, *Writings,* vol. 1, 128.
22. Thoreau, *Journal,* vol. 4, 351.
23. Wordsworth, *William Wordsworth,* 130.
24. Emerson, *Collected Works,* vol. 1, 90.
25. Thomas Merton, *The Inner Experience: Notes on Contemplation* (San Francisco: HarperSanFrancisco, 2003), 58.
26. Thoreau, *Writings,* vol. 1, 111.
27. Jon Kabat-Zinn, *Wherever You Go, There You are: Mindfulness Meditation in Everyday Life* (New York: Hyperion, 1994), xvii.
28. Emerson, *Complete Works,* vol. 12, 217.
29. Parker J. Palmer, *The Active Life* (New York: Harper Collins, 1991), 17, 26, 29.
30. A. Bronson Alcott, "The Forester," in *Pertaining to Thoreau,* ed. Samuel Arthur Jones (Detroit: Edwin B. Hill, 1901), 109.
31. Jean-Jacques Rousseau, *Reveries of the Solitary Walker,* trans. Peter France (New

York: Penguin Books, 2004), 35. First published 1782 as *Les Rêveries du promeneur solitaire.*

32. Perhaps as much as 180,000 miles, according to Thomas De Quincey. See Rebecca Solnit, *Wanderlust: A History of Walking* (New York: Viking, 2000), 114.

33. Thoreau, *Writings,* vol. 5, 207.

34. Ibid., 210–11.

35. Ibid., 209.

36. Thoreau, *Journals,* vol. 9, 208.

37. Thoreau, *Writings,* vol. 5, 207.

38. Emerson, *Journals,* vol. 3, 136–37.

39. Emerson, *Complete Works,* vol. 12, 158–59.

40. Solnit, *Wanderlust,* 253.

41. Thoreau, *Writings,* vol. 5, 209.

42. Wordsworth, *William Wordsworth,* 285.

43. Octavius Brooks Frothingham, *Memoir of William Henry Channing* (Boston: Houghton Mifflin Company, 1886), 166.

44. Thoreau, *Walden,* 2, 6.

45. Ibid., 13.

46. Ibid., 314–15.

47. George Ripley, "Ripley to Emerson, 9 November 1840," in Buell, ed., *American Transcendentalists,* 202.

48. Elizabeth Peabody, "Plan of the West Roxbury Community," in Buell, ed., *American Transcendentalists,* 233.

49. Thoreau, *Journal,* vol. 2, 164.

50. Thoreau, *Writings,* vol. 6, 294.

7

Reading, Conversation, and Journal Writing

1. Henry Steele Commager, *Theodore Parker: Yankee Crusader* (Boston: Little Brown, 1936), 122.

2. Ibid.

3. Emerson, *Journals,* vol. 5, 72.

4. Richardson, *First We Read, Then We Write: Emerson on the Creative Process* (Iowa City: University of Iowa Press, 2009), 8.

5. Emerson, *Collected Works,* vol. 7, 97, 96, 110, 111.

6. Emerson, *Journals,* vol. 4, 360.

7. Richardson, *First We Read,* 9.

8. Emerson, *Collected Works,* vol. 7, 150.

9. Ibid., vol. 1, 56–57.

10. Thoreau, *Walden,* 97–98, 100–101.

11. Ibid., 105–7.

12. Emerson, *The Letters of Ralph Waldo Emerson,* ed. Eleanor M. Tilton (New York: Columbia University Press, 1990), vol. 7, 393.

13. Michel de Montaigne, *The Essays of Montaigne*, trans. E. J. Trenchman (New York: Oxford University Press, 1927), vol. 2, 384.

14. See Joel Myerson, "A Calendar of Transcendental Club Meetings," *American Literature* 44 (May 1972): 197–207.

15. Emerson, *Collected Works*, vol. 7, 55.

16. Ibid., vol. 2, 184.

17. Ibid., 164–65.

18. Emerson, *Later Lectures*, vol. 2, 364–65.

19. Fuller sometimes refers to Athena as "Minerva," the Roman name for the Greek goddess.

20. Fuller, *Letters*, vol. 2, 86–87.

21. Alcott, *The Journals of Bronson Alcott*, ed. Odell Shepherd (Boston: Little, Brown, 1938), 103–4.

22. Thoreau, *Walden*, 136.

23. Sherry Turkle, *Reclaiming Conversation: The Power of Talk in a Digital Age* (New York: Penguin Press, 2015), 3.

24. Emerson, *Collected Works*, vol. 3, 109.

25. Emerson, *Early Lectures*, vol. 2, 261.

26. Thoreau, *Journal*, vol. 4, 223.

27. Thoreau, *Journal*, vol. 1, 206–7.

28. Pierre Hadot, *The Inner Citadel*, trans. Michael Chase (Cambridge: Harvard University Press, 1998), 51.

29. Alcott, *Journals*, xiv.

30. Julia Cameron, *The Artist's Way: A Spiritual Path to Higher Creativity* (New York: G. P. Putnam's Sons, 1992), 14–15.

31. Janet Conner, *Writing Down Your Soul: How to Activate and Listen to the Extraordinary Voice Within* (Berkeley: Conari Press, 2008), 9.

8

RELIGIOUS COSMOPOLITANISM

1. W. T. Harris, "Emerson's Orientalism," in *The Genius and Character of Emerson*, ed. Franklin Sanborn (Port Washington, NY: Kennikat Press, 1971), 376. First published 1885.

2. Emerson, *Collected Works*, vol. 9, 365.

3. The Bhagavad Gita, trans. Barbara Stoller Miller (New York: Columbia University Press, 1986), 32.

4. Emerson, *Collected Works*, vol. 4, 30.

5. Ibid., 28, 31.

6. Thoreau, *Journal*, vol. 1, 261.

7. Thoreau, *Writings*, vol. 6, 175.

8. *Bhagavad Gita*, 64.

9. Thoreau, *Walden*, 78.

10. Ibid., 82–83.

11. Thoreau, *Journal*, vol. 1, 299.

12. Paul Friedrich, *The Gita within Walden* (Albany: SUNY Press, 2009), 33.

13. Thoreau, *Walden,* 317–18.

14. Mircea Eliade, *Patterns in Comparative Religion,* trans. Rosemary Sheed (London: Sheed and Ward, 1958), 100.

15. Thoreau, *Writings,* vol. 1, 141.

16. Ibid., 146.

17. Ibid., 155.

18. Lydia Maria Child, *The Aspirations of the World: A Chain of Opals,* (New York: Roberts Brothers, 1878), 46–49.

19. Samuel Johnson, *Oriental Religions and Their Relation to Universal Religion: India.* (Boston: James R. Osgood, 1872), vol. 1, 32, 6.

20. Thomas Wentworth Higginson, "The Sympathy of Religions," in Buell, ed., *American Transcendentalists,* 183–84.

21. Emerson, *Later Lectures,* vol. 2, 273.

22. Thoreau, *Writings,* vol. 1, 150.

9

SELF-CULTURE AND SOCIAL CHANGE

1. Quoted in *Emerson's Antislavery Writings,* ed. Len Gougeon and Joel Myerson (New Haven: Yale University Press, 1995), liv.

2. John Carlos Rowe, *At Emerson's Tomb: The Politics of Classic American Literature* (New York: Columbia University Press, 1997), 21.

3. See Rose, *Transcendentalism,* chap. 6.

4. See, for example, Robert C. Albrecht, "The Theological Response of the Transcendentalists to the Civil War," *New England Quarterly* 38 (1965): 21–34.

5. Robert Bellah, "Individualism and Commitment in American Life," a speech given at the University of California, Santa Barbara, February 20, 1986, www.robertbellah.com/lectures_4.htm.

6. See, for example, Gura, *American Transcendentalism,* 136–37.

7. C. S. Griffin, *The Ferment of Reform, 1830–1860* (Wheeling, IL: Harlan Davidson, 1967), 22.

8. Richardson, *Henry David Thoreau: A Life of the Mind* (Berkeley: University of California Press, 1986), 73–74.

9. Emerson, *Collected Writings,* vol. 1, 59.

10. Quoted in Octavius Brooks Frothingham, *George Ripley* (Boston: Houghton Mifflin, 1882), 307–8.

11. Emerson, *Collected Works,* vol. 10, 180.

12. Ibid., vol. 1, 147, 152, 153–55.

13. Ibid., 155–56.

14. Ibid., 158–59.

15. Ibid., 159–60, 145.

16. Robinson, *Emerson and the Conduct of Life* (New York: Cambridge University Press, 1993), 40–41.

17. Ibid.

18. Emerson, *Collected Works,* vol. 1, 173.

19. Robinson, *Emerson,* 41–42.

20. Brownson, "The Laboring Classes," in Buell, ed., *American Transcendentalists*, 197, 200.

21. Margaret Fuller, *Woman in the Nineteenth Century* (Chapel Hill: University of South Carolina Press, 1980), 89. Originally published 1845 (New York: Greeley and McElrath).

10
ABOLITION AND WOMEN'S RIGHTS

1. Thoreau, *Reform Papers*, 72.

2. David S. Reynolds, *John Brown, Abolitionist: The Man Who Killed Slavery, Sparked the Civil War, and Seeded Civil Rights* (New York: Alfred A. Knopf, 2005), 426.

3. Thoreau, *Reform Papers*, 137.

4. Emerson, *Complete Works*, vol. 2, 427.

5. Reynolds, *John Brown*, 363–64.

6. Ibid., 367.

7. See ibid., 402–37.

8. Ibid., 365.

9. Emerson, *Collected Works*, vol. 9, 383.

10. Reynolds, *John Brown*, 484.

11. Quoted in Tilden G. Edelstein, *Strange Enthusiasm: A Life of Thomas Wentworth Higginson* (New Haven: Yale University Press, 1968), 190.

12. Quoted in ibid., 248.

13. Higginson, *Army Life in a Black Regiment* (Boston: Fields, Osgood, 1870), 267.

14. Quoted in Edelstein, *Strange Enthusiasm*, 304.

15. Caroline Healey Dall, *Transcendentalism in New England: A Lecture* (New York: Roberts Brothers, 1897), 24.

16. Ibid., 25.

17. Wayne, *Woman Thinking*, 2.

18. Fuller, "The Great Lawsuit," in Buell, ed., *American Transcendentalists*, 303.

19. Fuller, *Memoirs*, vol. 1, 133.

20. Robinson, "Margaret Fuller," 86.

21. Fuller, "The Great Lawsuit," 307.

22. Ibid., 309–10.

23. Ibid., 319.

24. Ibid., 320.

25. Quoted in Joan Von Mehren, *Minerva and the Muse: A Life of Margaret Fuller* (Amherst: University of Massachusetts Press, 1994), 2.

26. Phyllis Cole, "Woman's Rights and Feminism," in *The Oxford Handbook of Transcendentalism*, ed. Joel Myerson, Sandra Harbert Petrulionis, and Laura Dassow Walls (New York: Oxford University Press, 2010), 222.

27. Higginson, *Woman and Her Wishes* (Boston: Robert F. Wallcut, 1853), 17.

28. Fuller, "The Great Lawsuit," 317.

11
EDUCATION, ENVIRONMENTALISM,
AND SUSTAINABILITY

1. Emerson, *Journals,* vol. 3, 282. Immediately preceding these words is this comment: "The things which are taught children are not an education but the means of education. The grammar & geography & writing do not train up the child in the way that it should go but may be used in the service of the devil."

2. Thoreau, *Journal,* vol. 2, 83.

3. Emerson, *Early Lectures,* vol. 2, 199.

4. Ibid., 203.

5. Quoted in Charles Capper, *Margaret Fuller: An American Romantic Life, The Private Years* (New York: Oxford University Press, 1992), 296.

6. Thoreau, *Writings,* vol. 1, 389.

7. Quoted in John P. Miller, *Transcendental Learning: The Educational Legacy of Alcott, Emerson, Fuller, Peabody and Thoreau* (Charlotte, NC: Information Age Publishing, 2011), 67.

8. Elizabeth Peabody, *Theory of Teaching, with a Few Practical Illustrations* (Boston: E. P. Peabody, 1841), 8.

9. George Ripley, "Ripley to Emerson," in Buell, ed., *American Transcendentalists,* 239.

10. Quoted in John Thomas Codman, *Brook Farm: Historical and Personal Memoirs* (Boston: Arena Publishing Company, 1894), 303. Lane is best remembered as cofounder, with Alcott, of Fruitlands, a utopian community located in Harvard, Massachusetts.

11. John Van Der Zee Sears, *My Friends at Brook Farm* (New York: Desmond FitzGerald, 1912), 121–22.

12. Thoreau, *Walden,* 105.

13. Alcott, *Journals,* 518.

14. Quoted in Austin Warren, "The Concord School of Philosophy," *The New England Quarterly* 2, no. 2, (April 1929): 226–27.

15. Thoreau, *Journal,* vol. 12, 387.

16. Lawrence Buell, *The Environmental Imagination: Thoreau, Nature Writing, and the Formation of American Culture* (Cambridge: Harvard University Press, 1995), 115.

17. Roderick Nash, *Wilderness and the American Mind* (New Haven: Yale University Press, 1982), 84.

18. Edward Abbey, "Down the River with Henry Thoreau," *Down the River* (New York: Penguin Books, 1982), 39.

19. Ibid., 48.

20. Bron Taylor, *Dark Green Religion: Nature, Spirituality, and the Planetary Future* (Berkeley: University of California Press, 2010), ix, 56.

21. Emerson, *Collected Works,* vol. 1, 10.

22. Buell, *Environmental Imagination,* 31.

23. Thoreau, *The Maine Woods* (Princeton: Princeton University Press, 1972), 71.

24. According to Buell's calculations, the letter "I" is used in *Walden* an average of 6.6 times per page through the first two chapters, decreasing to 3.6 times per page in

the last five. References to nature occur once every 1.8 pages in the first two chapters and 2.3 times per page in the final chapters. Buell, *Environmental Imagination,* 122.

25. Paul Hawken, *Blessed Unrest: How the Largest Social Movement in History is Restoring Grace, Justice, and Beauty to the World* (New York: Penguin Books, 2007), 73–74.

26. Ibid., 85.

27. Robert E. Burkholder, "Nature Writing and Environmental Activism," in *Oxford Encyclopedia of Transcendentalism,* ed. Joel Myerson, Sandra Harbert Petrulionis, and Laura Dassow Walls (New York: Oxford University Press, 2010), 657.

28. See Douglas Brinkley, *The Wilderness Warrior: Theodore Roosevelt and the Crusade for America* (New York: HarperCollins, 2009), 825–30.

29. David E. Shi, *The Simple Life: Plain Living and High Thinking in American Culture* (New York: Oxford University Press, 1985), 278.

30. Scott Nearing, *Living the Good Life: How to Live Simply and Sanely in a Troubled World* (New York: Schocken Books, 1970).

31. For a description of these and other examples of modern homesteading, see Rebecca Kneale Gould, *At Home in Nature: Modern Homesteading and Spiritual Practice in America* (Berkeley: University of California Press, 2005). In her survey Gould finds that homesteading narratives "often model themselves on Thoreau's example and on *Walden* as an ideal text" (38).

32. Diana Lorence, "Words from the Woods," www.innermosthouse.com/#/words-from -the-woods/the-art-of-love.

12
CHURCH REFORM AND THE FREE RELIGIOUS ASSOCIATION

1. Emerson, *Collected Works,* vol. 1, 88, 92.

2. Of seventeen Unitarian ministers originally identified with the Transcendentalist movement, eleven remained as ministers. This is not counting an additional number of second-generation Transcendentalists who were active in the ministry for the Unitarian and Free Churches.

3. Myerson, "Calendar," 205–6.

4. Clarke, *Autobiography,* 158.

5. William R. Hutchison, *The Transcendentalist Ministers: Church Reform in the New England Renaissance* (Boston: Beacon Press, 1965), 150.

6. Dean Grodzins, "Theodore Parker and the 28th Congregational Society: The Reform Church and the Spirituality of Reformers in Boston, 1845–1859," in *Transient and Permanent: The Transcendentalist Movement and Its Contexts,* ed. Charles Capper and Conrad Edick Wright (Boston: Massachusetts Historical Society, 1999), 73–91.

7. Hutchison, *Transcendentalist Ministers,* 176.

8. William Rounseville Alger, *The Poetry of the East* (Boston: Roberts, 1856); Moncure Conway, *The Sacred Anthology* (New York: Holt, 1874); Child, *Aspirations.*

9. Stow Persons, *Free Religion: An American Faith* (New Haven: Yale University Press, 1947), 2.

10. Henry Whitney Bellows, "The Suspense of Faith, a Discourse on the State of the Church," in *American Reformation: A Documentary History of Unitarian Christianity*, ed. Sydney E. Ahlstrom and Jonathan S. Carey (Middletown, CT: Wesleyan University Press, 1985), 385. Originally published 1859.

11. See Conrad Wright, *The Liberal Christians: Essays on American Unitarian History* (Boston: Beacon Press, 1970), 84.

12. Ibid., 15.

13. Persons, 24.

14. Emerson, *Journals*, vol. 15, 228.

15. Persons, 35.

16. Ibid., 111.

17. Ibid., 139.

18. Ibid., 90.

19. Felix Adler, *The Reconstruction of the Spiritual Ideal* (New York: D. Appleton and Company, 1924), 56–57.

20. James, *Varieties of Religious Experience*, 94.

21. Gary Dorrien, *The Making of American Liberal Theology: Imagining Progressive Religion, 1805–1900* (Louisville, KY: Westminster John Knox Press, 2001), 109.

13

The Legacy of Transcendentalism

1. Alcott, *Journals*, 425

2. Ibid., 426.

3. See Wade Clark Roof, *A Generation of Seekers: The Spiritual Journeys of the Baby Boom Generation* (San Francisco: HarperSanFrancisco, 1993); Robert C. Fuller, *Spiritual but Not Religious: Understanding Unchurched America* (New York: Oxford University Press, 2001); and Amanda Porterfield, *The Transformation of American Religion*.

4. Pew Research Center, www.pewresearch.org/fact-tank/2015/11/11/religious-nones-are-not-only-growing-theyre-becoming-more-secular, November 11, 2015.

5. Bellah, "Individualism and Commitment in American Life."

6. See Emerson, *Collected Writings*, vol. 2, 30–31.

7. Bellah, "Unitarian Universalism in Societal Perspective," a speech given at the UUA General Assembly, Rochester, NY, 1998, www.robertbellah.com/lectures_7.htm.

8. Charles Taylor, *The Ethics of Authenticity* (Cambridge, MA: Harvard University Press, 1991), 28–29.

9. Ibid., 21, 23.

10. Mott, "'Age of the First Person Singular,'" 91.

11. Emerson, *Collected Writings*, vol. 6, 108–9, 110.

12. Hedge, "The Art of Life," 177.

13. Pierre Hadot, *The Present Alone Is Our Happiness* (Palo Alto: Stanford University Press, 2009), 87.

14. See Channing, *Selected Writings*, 227.

15. Emerson, *Collected Writings*, vol. 1, 205–6.

16. Thoreau, *Walden*, 68.

17. Lesser, *New American Spirituality*, 51–53.

Further Reading

Romanticism

Abrams, M. H. *Natural Supernaturalism: Tradition and Revolution in Romantic Literature.* New York: W. W. Norton, 1971.

Chai, Leon. *The Romantic Foundations of the American Renaissance.* Ithaca: Cornell University Press, 1985.

Keane, Patrick J. *Emerson, Romanticism, and Intuitive Reason.* Columbia: University of Missouri Press, 2005.

Unitarianism

Howe, Daniel Walker. *The Unitarian Conscience: Harvard Moral Philosophy, 1805–1861.* Cambridge: Harvard University Press, 1970.

Robinson, David. *The Unitarians and the Universalists.* Westport, CT.: Greenwood Press, 1985.

Wright, Conrad. *The Beginnings of Unitarianism in America.* Boston: Starr King Press, 1955.

Transcendentalism

Boller, Paul F., Jr., *American Transcendentalism, 1830–1860: An Intellectual Inquiry.* New York: Putnam, 1974.

Frothingham, Octavius Brooks. *Transcendentalism in New England: A History.* Gloucester, MA: Peter Smith, 1965. First published 1876 by G.P. Putnam's Sons.

Gura, Phillip F. *American Transcendentalism: A History.* New York: Hill and Wang, 2007.

TRANSCENDENTALIST SPIRITUALITY

Andrews, Barry M. *Emerson as Spiritual Guide.* Boston: Skinner House Books, 2003.

———. *Thoreau as Spiritual Guide.* Boston: Skinner House Books, 2000.

James, William. *The Varieties of Religious Experience.* New York: Longmans, Green, 1925. First published 1902.

SELF-CULTURE

Lysaker, John T. *Emerson and Self-Culture.* Bloomington: Indiana University Press, 2008.

Moore, Thomas. *Care of the Soul.* New York: Harper Collins, 1992.

Robinson, David. *Apostle of Culture: Emerson as Preacher and Lecturer.* Philadelphia: University of Pennsylvania Press, 1982.

NATURE

Albanese, Catherine L. *Nature Religion in America: From the Algonkian Indians to the New Age.* Chicago: University of Chicago Press, 1990.

Gatta, John. *Making Nature Sacred: Literature, Religion, and Environment in America from the Puritans to the Present.* New York: Oxford University Press, 2004.

Louv, Richard. *The Nature Principle: Reconnecting with Life in a Virtual Age.* Chapel Hill, NC: Algonquin Books, 2012.

LEISURE

De Grazia, Sebastian. *Of Time, Work and Leisure.* New York: Vintage Books, 1994.

Kleiber, Douglas. *Leisure Experience and Human Development.* New York: Basic Books, 1999.

Pieper, Josef. *Leisure, the Basis of Culture.* South Bend: St. Augustine's Press, 1998.

SELF-RELIANCE

Kateb, George. *Emerson and Self-Reliance.* Walnut Creek, CA: AltaMira Press, 2000.

Moore, Thomas. *Original Self: Living with Paradox and Originality.* New York: HarperCollins, 2000.

Palmer, Parker J. *A Hidden Wholeness: The Journey toward an Undivided Life.* San Francisco: Jossey-Bass, 2004.

SOLITUDE

Buchholz, Ester Schaler. *The Call of Solitude: Alonetime in a World of Attachment*. New York: Simon and Schuster, 1997.

Koch, Philip. *Solitude: A Philosophical Encounter*. Chicago: Open Court, 1994.

Lindbergh, Anne Morrow. *Gift from the Sea*. New York: Pantheon Books, 1955.

CONTEMPLATION

Kabat-Zinn, Jon. *Wherever You Go, There You Are: Mindfulness Meditation in Everyday Life*. New York: Hyperion, 1994.

McCowan, Donald, and Marc S. Micozzi. *New World Mindfulness: From the Founding Fathers, Emerson, and Thoreau to Your Personal Practice*. Rochester, VT: Healing Arts Press, 2012.

Merton, Thomas. *The Inner Experience: Notes on Contemplation*. New York: Harper Collins, 2003.

WALKING

Gros, Frederic. *A Philosophy of Walking*. New York: Verso, 2015.

Smith, David C. *The Transcendental Saunterer: Thoreau and the Search for Self*. Savannah, GA: Frederic C. Beil, 1997.

Solnit, Rebecca. *Wanderlust: A History of Walking*. New York: Viking, 2000.

SIMPLE LIVING

Andrews, Cecil. *The Circle of Simplicity: Return to the God Life*. New York: Harper Perennial, 1998.

Segal, Jerome M. *Graceful Simplicity: Toward a Politics and Philosophy of Simple Living*. New York: Henry Holt, 1999.

Shi, David E. *The Simple Life: Plain Living and High Thinking in American Culture*. New York: Oxford University Press, 1985.

READING

Dreyfus, Hubert, and Sean Dorrance Kelly. *All Things Shining: Reading the Western Classics to Find Meaning in a Secular Age*. New York: Free Press, 2011.

Richardson, Robert D. *First We Read, Then We Write: Emerson on the Creative Process*. Iowa City: University of Iowa Press, 2009.

CONVERSATION

Gibian, Peter. *Oliver Wendell Holmes and the Culture of Conversation*. Cambridge: Cambridge University Press, 2001.

Miller, Stephen. *Conversation: A History of a Declining Art*. New Haven: Yale University Press, 2006.

Sandra, Jaida n'ha. *The Joy of Conversation: The Complete Guide to Salons*. Minneapolis: Utne Reader Books, 1997.

JOURNAL WRITING

Conner, Janet. *Writing Down Your Soul: How to Activate and Listen to the Extraordinary Voice Within*. Berkeley: Conari Press, 2008.

Rosenwald, Lawrence. *Emerson and the Art of the Diary*. New York: Oxford University Press, 1988.

Young, Malcolm Clemens. *The Spiritual Journal of Henry David Thoreau*. Macon, GA: Mercer University Press, 2009.

RELIGIOUS COSMOPOLITANISM

Christy, Arthur. *The Orient in American Transcendentalism*. New York: Octagon Books, 1969. First published 1932 by Columbia University Press.

Schmidt, Leigh Eric. *Restless Souls: The Making of American Spirituality*. San Francisco: HarperSanFrancisco, 2005.

Versluis, Arthur. *American Transcendentalism and Asian Religions*. New York: Oxford University Press, 1993.

REFORM

Delano, Sterling F. *Brook Farm: The Dark Side of Utopia*. Cambridge, MA: Harvard University Press, 2004.

Ghose, Sisirkumar. *Mystics as a Force for Change*. Wheaton, IL: Theosophical Publishing House, 1981.

Stoehr, Taylor. *Nay-Saying in Concord: Emerson, Alcott and Thoreau*. Hamden, CT: Archon Books, 1979.

ANTI-SLAVERY

Gougeon, Len. *Virtue's Hero: Emerson, Antislavery, and Reform*. Athens: University of Georgia Press, 1990.

Petrulionis, Sandra Harbert. *To Set This World Right: The Antislavery Movement in Thoreau's Concord*. Ithaca: Cornell University Press, 2006.

FEMINISM AND WOMEN'S RIGHTS

Argersinger, Jana L., and Phyllis Cole, eds. *Toward a Female Genealogy of Transcendentalism.* Athens: University of Georgia Press, 2014.

Wayne, Tiffany K. *Woman Thinking: Feminism and Transcendentalism in Nineteenth-Century America.* Lanham, MD: Lexington Books, 2008.

EDUCATION

Haefner, George E. *A Critical Estimate of the Educational Theories of A. Bronson Alcott.* Westport, CT: Greenwood Press, 1970.

Miller, John P. *Transcendental Learning: The Educational Legacy of Alcott, Emerson, Fuller, Peabody and Thoreau.* Charlotte, NC: Information Age Publishing, 2011.

ENVIRONMENTALISM AND SUSTAINABILITY

Buell, Lawrence. *The Environmental Imagination: Thoreau, Nature Writing, and the Formation of American Culture.* Cambridge, MA: Harvard University Press, 1995.

Gould, Rebecca Kneale. *At Home in Nature: Modern Homesteading and Spiritual Practice in America.* Berkeley: University of California Press, 2005.

Hawken, Paul. *Blessed Unrest: How the Largest Social Movement in History is Restoring Grace, Justice, and Beauty to the World.* New York: Penguin Books, 2007.

Taylor, Bron. *Dark Green Religion: Nature Spirituality and the Planetary Future.* Berkeley: University of California Press, 2010.

CHURCH REFORM AND FREE RELIGION

Hutchison, William R. *The Transcendentalist Ministers: Church Reform in the New England Renaissance.* Boston: Beacon Press, 1965.

Persons, Stow. *Free Religion: An American Faith.* New Haven: Yale University Press, 1947.

THE LEGACY OF TRANSCENDENTALISM

Lesser, Elizabeth. *The New American Spirituality: A Seeker's Guide.* New York: Random House, 1999.

Taylor, Charles. *The Ethics of Authenticity.* Cambridge: Harvard University Press, 1991.

Teasdale, Wayne. *The Mystic Heart: Discovering a Universal Spirituality in the World's Religions.* Novato, CA: New World Library, 1999.

INDEX

Abbey, Edward, 127

Abbot, Francis Ellingwood, 137–39

abolition, 107–15, 155n31; and disunion, 113–14. *See also under names of individuals*

Abrams, M. H., 11

The Active Life (Palmer), 72–73

Adams, Mary, 142

Adler, Felix, 141

Aids to Reflection (Coleridge), 12–13

Alcott, Abigail May, 111

Alcott, Bronson, 26, 28, 31, 73; and abolition, 111; and conversation, 84, 86–87, 122; and education, 47, 121–25; and FRA, 137; and Fruitlands, 120; and HDT, 142–43; and journal writing, 88, 90. *See also individual works by*

Alger, William Rounseville, 98–99, 135

All Soul's Church, New York City, 136

American Anti-Slavery Society, 111

American Gurus: From Transcendentalism to New Age Religion (Versluis), 149n9

"The American Scholar" (Emerson), 25, 71–72, 82, 121–22

American Unitarian Association, 132

American Woman Suffrage Association, 118–19

Anthony, Susan B., 118

antinomianism, 61

Aristotle, 56

Arjuna, 96

Arminianism, 40–41, 153n4

Army Life in a Black Regiment (Higginson), 115

"The Art of Life" (Hedge), 147

The Artist's Way (Cameron), 90

Aspirations of the World (Child), 135

At Emerson's Tomb (Rowe), 101

Athena, 118

attachment, 68–69

Aurelius, Marcus, 90

authenticity, 145–46

Autobiography (Clarke), 12

Bartol, Cyrus, 137

beauty, and nature, 52

Being cognition (B-cognition), 31–32, 34–35

Bellah, Robert, 31–32, 101, 144–45

Bellows, Henry Whitney, 136–37

Berlin, Isaiah, 8

Bhagavad Gita, 45, 93–96

Bible, and historical context, 18–20, 23

Blessed Unrest (Hawken), 129

A Book of Hymns for Public and Private Devotion (S. Johnson and S. Longfellow), 135

Border Ruffians, 114

Boston Daily Advertiser, 22

Boston Music Hall, 134

Boston Public Library, 81

Boston Quarterly Review, 107

"Brahma" (Emerson), 93–94

brain, left and right, 14, 150–51n22

Brook Farm, 28, 47, 78–79, 103–4; school at, 123–24
Brown, John, 112–13, 134
Brownson, Orestes, 26, 103; and church reform, 133–34; and self-culture, 47–48, 101, 107
Buchholz, Ester Schaler, 68–69
Buddhism, 92, 99
Buell, Lawrence, 126–28, 161n24
Burkholder, Robert E., 129–30
Burns, Anthony, 114
Burroughs, John, 130

The Call of Solitude (Buchholz), 68–69
Calvinism, 40–41
Cameron, Julia, *The Artist's Way,* 90
Carlyle, Jane Welsh, 7–8
Carlyle, Thomas, 7–8, 11, 51–52
Chai, Leon, 15
Channing, William Ellery, 18–19, 21, 26–27; and abolition, 110; and ecstasy, 147; and leisure, 57; and self-culture, 40–42, 47, 57; and solitude, 65
Channing, William Henry: and church reform, 135; and simple living, 76, 79; and women's rights, 119
Chardon Street Chapel, Boston, 104
Cheney, Edna Dow, 116, 125
Child, Lydia Maria, 97, 116, 135
Christian Examiner, 8–9
Christian Register, 29, 93
Christianity: and rationalism, 21; secularization of, 10; vs. Universal Religion, 138
church membership, 133–35
Church of the Disciples, 134
"Circles" (Emerson), 85
"Civil Disobedience" (Thoreau), 3, 129
Civil War, U.S., 114–15, 136
Clarke, James Freeman, 9; and church reform, 134; on Coleridge, 12; on MF, 46, 116; and religious cosmopolitanism, 92; on RWE, 33; and self-culture, 47–49; on Transcendental Club, 5
Cole, Phyllis, 118
Coleridge, Samuel Taylor, 7–8, 12–13, 82
Commager, Henry Steele, 80
Concord, Massachusetts: ecology of, 127–28; and Romanticism, 8
Concord Academy, 123
Concord Female Anti-Slavery Society, 111
Concord School of Philosophy, 87, 125

Confiscation Act, 114
conformity, 62
Conner, Janet, 90
consumerism, 56
contemplation, 56, 70–73
conversation, 84–88. *See also* Conversations series; *under names of individuals*
Conversations series, 84, 86–87
Conversations with Children on the Gospels (B. Alcott), 121
Conway, Moncure, 98–99, 135
corporeal punishment, 122–23
"Courage" (Emerson), 112–13

Dall, Caroline Healey, 88, 115
Darwin, Charles, 139
Davidson, Arnold, 64
deep ecology, 154n12
Deficiency cognition (D-cognition), 31–32, 34–35
Dewey, John, 141
Dial (magazine), 9, 78, 92, 104, 124
discipline, and nature, 52
"Divinity School Address" (Emerson): A. Norton on, 22; H. Ware on, 41; and Unitarian preaching, 21–22, 133
Dorrien, Gary, 141
double consciousness, 30
"Down the River with Henry Thoreau" (Abbey), 127

ecstasy, 4, 33–37, 149n9; integration of, 38–39. *See also under names of individuals*
education: adult, 124–25; classical, 63–64; HDT on, 83; reform of, 120–26; Transcendentalist principles of, 125–26. *See also under names of individuals*
egotism, 10, 49, 61, 136
Eichorn, Johann Gottfried, 18–19
Emerson, Edward, 19
Emerson, Mary Moody, 116
Emerson, Ralph Waldo (RWE): and abolition, 107–8, 111–13, 155n31; and church reform, 132–33, 138; and contemplation, 70–72; and conversation, 85–86; and ecstasy, 4, 16, 30, 34–36; and education, 121–22, 161n1; and environmentalism, 127; European travel of, 7–8, 129; "First Philosophy" of, 13–14; and FRA, 137; and fragmentation of society, 25; and genius, 2, 59; journal of, 9–14; and

journal writing, 88–89; legacy of, 144–47; on miracles, 21; on property laws, 106; and reading, 81, 83; and religious cosmopolitanism, 92–94, 98; and reform, 61, 103–7; and Romanticism, 9, 15–16; and self-culture, 42–44; and self-reliance, 58–61, 144–45; and simple living, 105; and solitude, 67–68; on spiritual hunger, 3–4; on Transcendentalism, 29–31; and walking, 75. *See also individual works by*
Emerson, William, 18–30
Emerson and Self-Culture (Lysaker), 49
empiricism, 13, 138–39
England, 7
environmentalism, 126–31
"Essential Principles of Religion" (Emerson), 98
Ethical Culture Movement, 141
Ethics of Authenticity (C. Taylor), 145–46
evolution, 139
Experience as a Minister (Parker), 24
Ezekiel, 52

Feast Days, 134
feminism, 116. *See also* women's rights
The Ferment of Reform: 1830–1860 (Griffin), 102
First Church, Boston, 22
First Parish Church, Concord, Massachusetts, 111
1st South Carolina Volunteers, 115
Flint's Pond, 65
Formation of Christian Character (Ware), 41
Franklin Institute, Boston, 41
Free Religion, 138–41. *See also* Free Religious Association
Free Religion: An American Faith (Persons), 136
Free Religious Association (FRA), 132, 137–41; and nonsectarianism, 140–41; and reform, 139; and religious cosmopolitanism, 137–38, 140; and Unitarianism, 139–40. *See also* Free Religion
French, Daniel Chester, 125
Friedrich, Paul, 95–96
Friends of Universal Reform, 104
Frothingham, Octavius Brooks, 137–38
Fruitlands, 104, 120, 161n10
Fugitive Slave Act, 114
Fuller, Margaret (MF): on Coleridge, 12; and Conversations, 28, 84, 86–87; and

ecstasy, 36–38; and reading, 81; and self-culture, 17, 45–48; and self-reliance, 62; and women's rights, 26, 116–19

Garrison, William Lloyd, 110–11
gender, 118
genius, 2, 59, 62
Gérando, Joseph Marie, baron de, 40
Germany, philosophy of, 8–9
Gift from the Sea (Lindbergh), 68
The Gita within Walden (Friedrich), 95–96
God, 60; and human consciousness, 26–27; personality of, 35. *See also* Over-soul
Goethe, Johann Wolfgang von, 19, 45–46, 81, 116
Göttingen, University of, 18
"The Great Lawsuit" (Fuller), 116
Greene Street School, Providence, 121
Griffin, C. S., 102

Hadot, Pierre, 90, 147
Hale, Edward Everett, 9
Harpers Ferry, 112, 114
Harvard Divinity School, 22; B. Alcott and, 87; curriculum of, 9, 28; H. Ware and, 41; J. F. Clarke and, 92; and reform, 110; RWE and, 19; T. W. Higginson and, 113. *See also* "Divinity School Address"
Hawken, Paul, 129
Hedge, Frederic Henry, 8–9, 17, 44, 136, 147
Henry Thoreau: A Life of the Mind (Richardson), 102–3
Higginson, Thomas Wentworth, 97–99, 110, 113–15, 119–20, 137–38
Hillside Chapel, 126
Hinduism, 39, 92–97
homesteading, 162n31
Howe, Julia Ward, 116, 119
"Human Culture" (Emerson), 42, 54, 89
"A Humanist Manifesto" (Dewey et al.), 141
"Humanity's Likeness to God" (W. E. Channing), 26–27
Humboldt, Wilhelm von, 40, 153n2
Hume, David, 12
Hymns of the Spirit (S. Johnson and S. Longfellow), 135

idealism, 14, 29, 31
The Index, 138, 140
industrialization, 24–25
Innermost House, 131

IslandWood, 126
Italy, 47

James, William, 33, 141
Jesus: and conversation, 85, 86–87; and
    deliberate living, 156; J. Brown and,
    112; and Lord's Supper, 133; miracles of,
    20–21, 51; and supernatural authority, 137
*John Brown, Abolitionist: The Man Who
    Killed Slavery, Sparked the Civil War, and
    Seeded Civil Rights* (Reynolds), 112–13
Johnson, Andrew, 114
Johnson, Samuel, 92, 97, 137
journal writing, 88–90
journalism, 46–47

Kabat-Zinn, Jon, 72
Kant, Immanuel, 13, 125
kindergarten, 123
Kneeland, Abner, 25, 151n13
Krishna, 94

"The Laboring Classes" (Brownson), 107
Lane, Charles, 124, 161n10
language, and nature, 52
Lawrence, Kansas, 114
leisure, 55–58
Lesser, Elizabeth, 148
Let Your Life Speak (Palmer), 61
liberalism, religious, 3, 27
The Liberator, 110
Life of Solitude (Petrarch), 65
"Life without Principle" (Thoreau), 69
Lincoln, Abraham: election of, 109, 112; and
    RWE, 113
Lindbergh, Anne Morrow, 68
*Living the Good Life: How to Live Simply
    and Sanely in a Troubled World* (Nearing),
    130–31
Locke, John, 12, 20–21
loneliness, 66–67
Lorence, Diana, 131
Lorence, Michael, 131
Louv, Richard, 54
Lysaker, John, 49

The Making of American Liberal Theology
    (Dorrien), 141
"Man the Reformer" (Emerson), 35, 104–7
Maslow, Abraham, 31–32, 35
Masonic Temple, Boston, 133

Massachusetts Constitutional Convention,
    119
Massachusetts State Kansas Aid Commit-
    tee, 114
materialism, 13, 25, 29
Mechanics' Apprentices' Library Associa-
    tion, 104
Mediations (Aurelius), 90
Melodeon Theater, Boston, 134
Merton, Thomas, 72
Mexico, U.S. invasion of, 111–12
millennialism, 103
Miller, Perry, 12
mindfulness, 43, 70
Minerva, 118
miracles, 11–12, 20–21, 51
Missouri Compromise, 114
"Modern Literature" (Emerson), 9
Montaigne, Michel de, 84
Moore, Thomas, 61–62
Morse, Sidney, 138
Mott, Wesley, 146
Mt. Ktaadn (Katahdin), 128
Muir, John, 130
Muse, 118
"The Mystics in All Religions" (Clarke), 33
mythology, women in, 117–18

Naess, Arne, 154n12
Nash, Roderick, 126–27
National Convention of Unitarian
    Churches, 136
nature: as commodity, 52; estrangement
    from, 53–55; as manifestation of divine,
    10–11; and revelation, 51, 53–54; and
    Romanticism, 50–51, 127
Nature (Emerson), 11, 51–53; and environ-
    mentalism, 127; and miracles, 11–12
The Nature Principle (Louv), 54
nature writing, American, 54
Nearing, Helen, 130–31
Nearing, Scott, 130–31
*The New American Spirituality: A Seeker's
    Guide* (Lesser), 148
New Thought Movement, 141
*New Views of Christianity, Society, and the
    Church* (Brownson), 103
New-York Tribune, 37, 46, 81
1960s activism, 143–44
nones, 144
Norton, Andrews, 20, 22

Orchard House, Concord, Massachusetts, 125
Oriental Religions and Their Relation to Universal Religion (S. Johnson), 97, 137
Ossoli, Margaret. *See* Fuller, Margaret
Over-soul, 34, 60, 93, 145
"The Over-Soul" (Emerson), 33–35, 85

Palfrey, John, 113
Palmer, Parker, 61, 72–73
Parker, Theodore, 9; and abolition, 109–10, 114; on Bible, 23; and church reform, 134–35; and ecstasy, 36; on Jesus's teachings, 21; preaching of, 134–35; and reading, 80–81; on religion and human consciousness, 24, 35; and religious cosmopolitanism, 23, 91; on Unitarian clergy, 22; and women's rights, 119
Pascal, Blaise, 69
patriarchy, 117–18
Peabody, Elizabeth, 28, 116; and American Woman Suffrage Association, 118–19; bookstore of, 84, 86; on Brook Farm, 78; and education, 121, 123, 125; and journal writing, 88; as publisher, 112; and religious cosmopolitanism, 92; and self-culture, 40–41, 49
Peck, M. Scott, 48–49
Persons, Stow, 136–38
Petrarch, 65
philosophy: German, 8–9; and spirituality, 64
Plato, 84
"Plato; or, the Philosopher" (Emerson), 94
poetry, RWE on, 9–10
Poetry of the East (Alger), 135
"Pond Scum" (Schulz), 155–56n2, 156n9
"The Present Age" (Emerson), 9–10
Princeton University Press, 143
Progress of Religious Ideas through Successive Ages (Child), 97
property laws, 106

Quimby, Phineas P., 141

The Radical, 138
reading, 80–84. *See also under names of individuals*
"Reading" (Emerson), 81
Reason, 12–14, 33–35; and contemplation, 71–72; and nature, 52–53; and revelation, 51

Reclaiming Conversation: The Power of Talk in a Digital Age (Turkle), 87–88
Reconstruction, 115
The Reconstruction of the Spiritual Ideal (Adler), 141
Record of a School (Peabody), 123
Record of Conversations on the Gospels (B. Alcott), 47
reform, church, 132–35. *See also* Free Religious Association
reform, social, 26, 100–108; and the individual, 61, 107; RWE on, 61; and self-culture, 4–5, 47–48, 103; Transcendentalists criticized regarding, 100–101. *See also* abolition; education; environmentalism; reform, church; sustainability; women's rights
religion: Eastern, 14, 92–99; experiential, 31; and human consciousness, 24, 26–27; natural vs. revealed, 51. *See also* Universal Religion; *names of individual religions and concepts*
Religion in Human Evolution (Bellah), 31
religious cosmopolitanism, 3–5, 91–99; and FRA, 137–38, 140
Religious Union of Associationists, 135
reparations, 113
Representative Men (Emerson), 35, 94
"Resistance to Civil Government" (Thoreau), 112
Restless Souls (Schmidt), 3, 99, 140–41
revelation: and nature, 51, 53–54. *See also* ecstasy
Reveries of the Solitary Walker (Rousseau), 73
Reynolds, David S., 112–13
Richardson, Robert D., 4, 6, 81, 102–3
Ripley, George, 78, 103–4, 123
Ripley, Sophia, 78, 123
The Road Less Traveled (Peck), 48
Robinson, David, 3, 6, 40–41, 48, 106–7, 117
Romantic Foundations of the American Renaissance (Chai), 15
Romanticism, 8; and nature, 12; RWE on, 9
Roosevelt, Theodore, 130
Rose, Anne C., 101
Rousseau, Jean-Jacques, 73
Rowe, John Carlos, 101
Roy, Ram Mohan, 93

Sabbath day, 55
Sacred Anthology (Conway), 135
sacred writings: HDT on, 83; RWE on, 81–82. *See also* Bhagavad Gita; Bible
salons, literary, 84
Sartor Resartus (Carlyle), 11
sauntering. *See* walking in nature
Schmidt, Leigh Eric, 2–3, 26–27, 99, 140–41
School for Human Culture. *See* Temple School
Schulz, Kathryn, 155–56n2, 156n9
scientific theism, 138–39
Scotland, 7–8
Sears, John Van Der Zee, 124
Second Church, Boston, 7, 19, 41, 42, 132–33
Secret Six, 114
self. *See* subjectivity
Self-Culture (Clarke), 17, 47–49
self-culture, 4–5, 40, 147–48, 153n2; criticism of, 47–48; and education, 124–26; as end in itself, 42; and inertia, 49; and the masses, 41–42; practice of, 43–45, 47; and women's rights, 116–19
Self-education; or, the Means and Art of Moral Progress (Gérando), 40
self-reliance, 58–62, 144–45
"Self-Reliance" (Emerson), 59, 61, 144–45
Seneca, 56
Seneca Falls, Women's Convention in, 118
Shi, David E., 130
Sierra Club, 130
Simms, Thomas, 114
The Simple Life: Plain Living and High Thinking in American Culture (Shi), 30
simple living, 45, 76–79, 104–5; and sustainability, 128. *See also under names of individuals*
Slabsides, West Park, New York, 130
slavery. *See* abolition
social theory, 139
Society and Solitude (Emerson), 81
Society for Christian Union and Progress, 133–35
solitude, 43; criticism of, 64, 68
Solitude (Zimmerman), 65–66
Solnit, Rebecca, 75
soul, individual, 34
spiritual but not religious, 144
spirituality: freedom of, 27; ecstasy, 16
Stael, Germaine de, 84

Stanton, Elizabeth Cady, 118
Stoicism, 56
subjectivity: RWE on, 9–10
A Summer on the Lakes (Fuller), 46
"Suspense of Faith, A Discourse on the State of the Church" (Bellows), 136
sustainability, 126–31
Swedenborg, Emanuel, 134
"The Sympathy of Religions" (Higginson), 137–38

"Table Talk" (Emerson), 85–86
Taylor, Bron, 127
Taylor, Charles, 145–46
Taylor, Jill Bolte, 150–51n22
Temple School, 90, 108, 121–23
Ten Great Religions (Clarke), 92
theism, scientific. *See* scientific theism
Theory of Teaching (Peabody), 123
Thoreau, Henry David (HDT): and abolition, 111–12, 129; and the Bible, 96; and contemplation, 71; and conversation, 87; criticism of, 67; and ecstasy, 37–38; and ecocentrism, 128; and education, 83, 121–23; and genius, 62; and journal writing, 89; legacy of, 3, 142–43, 148; and leisure, 55, 57–58; and nature, 54–55; and reading, 82–83; and religious cosmopolitanism, 92, 94–98; and self-culture, 44–45, 50; and self-reliance, 62; and simple living, 39, 76–77, 79, 128; and socializing, 67; and solitude, 38–39, 64–67, 69–70; and vocation, 65; and walking, 73–76. *See also individual works by*
Thoreau, John, Jr., 123
Thoreau Institute, 126, 143
Transcendental Club, 5, 44, 46, 84, 133
Transcendentalism: criticism of, 30; legacy of, 1–6, 142–48; misunderstanding of, 143–44; and mysticism, 33; scholarship on, 102–3; as term, 5, 28–29
Transcendentalism as a Social Movement (Rose), 101
"The Transcendentalist" (Emerson), 14
"The Transient and the Permanent in Christianity," 21
"Treatise on the Doctrine and Discipline of Human Culture" (B. Alcott), 17, 47
Turkle, Sherry, 87–88
28th Congregational Society, 134–35

Understanding, 12–14, 33; and nature, 52–53
"Unitarian Christianity" (W. E. Channing), 18–19, 21
Unitarian Conference, Constitution of the, 138
Unitarian Universalism, 132
Unitarianism: and the Bible, 19; and FRA, 137; and rationalism, 20; and reform, 110; and religious feeling, 21–22; and Romanticism, 9; and spiritual freedom, 27; and Transcendentalism, 2–3, 92, 133–35, 162n2; and unity, 136–37
United States Sanitary Commission, 136
Universal Mind, 33
Universal Religion, 91, 97–98, 137–38
Upanishads, 94

The Varieties of Religious Experience (James), 33
Vasquez, Mark G., 40
Vedas, 83
Versluis, Arthur, 149n9
Virgin Mary, 121
vocations, 26, 46–47

Walden (Thoreau), 1, 38–39; and Bhagavad Gita, 95; and conversation, 87; criticism of, 155–56n2, 156n9; "Economy," 77, 128; and education, 124; legacy of, 1; linguistic analysis of, 161–62n24; and self-culture, 44–45; and simple living, 76–77; "Sounds," 55; "Where I Lived, and What I Lived For," 38–39. *See also* Thoreau, Henry David

Walden Pond, 1, 17, 38, 64–67, 142–43; and RWE, 65. *See also Walden* (Thoreau)
Walden Woods Project, 126
"A Walk to Wachusett" (Thoreau), 37–38
"Walking" (Thoreau), 73–75
walking in nature, 43, 73–76
Wanderlust (Solnit), 75
Ware, Henry, Jr., 41
Wayne, Tiffany K., 46, 115
A Week on the Concord and Merrimack Rivers (Thoreau), 71, 95
Weiss, John, 137
Wilderness Act, 130
Wilderness and the American Mind (Nash), 126–27
"Woman and Her Wishes" (Higginson), 119
Woman in the Nineteenth Century (Fuller), 3, 46, 116, 118
Woman Thinking: Feminism and Transcendentalism in Nineteenth-Century America (Wayne), 46
Woman's Journal, 119
women's rights, 115–19; and men, 118–19
Wordsworth, William, 7–8; and ecstasy, 37; *The Excursion,* 15–16; "Ode," 14–15; *The Prelude,* 69; "Prospectus" for *The Recluse,* 11; "Tintern Abbey," 10, 50–51; and walking, 73
World's Parliament of Religions, 99
"Worship" (Emerson), 146
Writing Down Your Soul (Conner), 90

Yes! Magazine, 131

Zimmerman, Johann Georg, 65–67

BARRY M. ANDREWS was born in Seattle. A graduate of Gonzaga University, he also earned a Doctor of Ministry degree from Meadville-Lombard Theological School. He has been a Scholar in Residence at the Thoreau Institute and a Merrill Fellow at Harvard Divinity School. He is author of *Thoreau as Spiritual Guide* and *Emerson as Spiritual Guide* and has edited anthologies of writings by Emerson, Thoreau, and Margaret Fuller. As a Unitarian Universalist minister, he has served congregations in Spokane, Manhattan, San Diego, and Manhasset, NY. He is now an independent scholar, living on Bainbridge Island, WA, with his wife, Linda.